Madonna

Madonna King is one of Queenslar
broadcasting and writing on issues
phenomenon to the future of our cons
and newspaper column are the result of twenty years working as a journalist in Brisbane, Canberra, Sydney and the United States. Her career has taken her from the police rounds desk of the *Courier-Mail* to presenting the morning current affairs program on 612 ABC Brisbane. Along the way, she was a national political correspondent in Canberra for the *Courier-Mail*, Queensland political correspondent for *The Australian*, ran the Sydney office of *The Australian*, set up the Olympics coverage for News Limited papers, and served three years as deputy editor of Sydney's *Daily Telegraph*. She is also a published author — her first book, *Catalyst*, was released in 2005. Madonna is a University of Queensland graduate, a member of the World Press Institute and a former visiting fellow in journalism at Queensland University of Technology. She is also a board member of the Walkley advisory committee, which oversees media industry awards.

Cindy Wockner

Cindy Wockner is one of the leading writers on crime and legal issues in Australia and the Pacific region, and has been recognised with awards for her outstanding reporting. Cindy covered the series of gang rapes of teenage girls in western Sydney in 2000, leading the *Daily Telegraph*'s coverage and penning a book on the crime wave. Sent to Indonesia to cover the 2002 Bali bombings, Cindy subsequently moved there. She is now a recognised international authority on many of the ongoing events that have unfolded in that time in Indonesia. Her access to authorities in both Indonesia and Australia ensures her radio, television and newspaper commentary has led much of the debate about events in the region. She has written and commented widely on issues as diverse as the Australian Embassy bombing, the tsunami in Aceh, the arrest and trial of Schapelle Corby, the arrest of the Bali Nine and the second Bali bombing. Cindy is a Murdoch University graduate, and has also worked as a senior journalist in Brisbane, Sydney and Canberra.

The Untold Story of the **Bali 9**

One-way Ticket

Cindy Wockner &
Madonna King

HarperCollins*Publishers*

HarperCollins*Publishers*

First published in Australia in 2006
by HarperCollins*Publishers* Australia Pty Limited
ABN 36 009 913 517
www.harpercollins.com.au

HarperCollins*Publishers*
25 Ryde Road, Pymble, Sydney, NSW 2073, Australia
31 View Road, Glenfield, Auckland 10, New Zealand
77–85 Fulham Palace Road, London, W6 8JB, United Kingdom
2 Bloor Street East, 20th floor, Toronto, Ontario M4W 1A8, Canada
10 East 53rd Street, New York NY 10022, USA

National Library of Australia Cataloguing-in-Publication data:

Wockner., Cindy.
One-way ticket : the untold story of the Bali 9.
ISBN 0 7322 8346 9.
ISBN 9780 73228 3469.
1. Drug traffic – Indonesia – Bali Island. 2. Prisoners – Indonesia – Bali Island – Biography. 3. Trials (Narcotic laws) – Indonesia – Bali Island. I. King, Madonna, 1965- . II. Title.
365.4

Front and back cover images: Lukman S Bintoro, Getty and Newspix
Front cover (L to R)
Top: Martin Stephens, Michael Czugaj, Renae Lawrence
Middle: Michael Czugaj, Scott Rush, Martin Stephens
Bottom: Scott Rush, Martin Stephens, Michael Czugaj, Renae Lawrence
Back cover (L to R)
Top: Andrew Chan, Matthew Norman, Myuran Sukumaran
Middle: Michael Czugaj, Andrew Chan, Renae Lawrence
Bottom: Tan Duc Thanh Nguyen, Si Yi Chen, Renae Lawrence
Cover design by Geeza Pty Ltd and Katy Wright, HarperCollins Design Studio
Typeset in 10.5/14pt Sabon by Helen Beard, ECJ Australia Pty Limited
Printed and bound in Australia by Griffin Press on 79gsm Bulky Paperback White

5 4 3 2 1 06 07 08 09

To our nieces and nephews: Cody, Ella, Darcy, Emmalee, Charlie, Lauren, Chelsea, Mitch, Nathan and Tanya — and to all your nieces and nephews. May every one of them grow up believing in themselves.

Acknowledgments

No book that aims to trace the lives of nine young Australians over two countries can be written without the generous effort and time of many people. We want to acknowledge and thank all those who helped make that possible.

To the family, friends, classmates and work colleagues in Australia who helped us build a profile of the nine youths, thank you for the generosity of your time and your recollections. Some offered their help publicly, some preferred to remain anonymous, but their overwhelming commitment was to help us create a real picture of the nine young people at the centre of this worldwide story.

To medicos, like Dr Peter Carson; university experts; researchers, and the drug addicts who spoke to us — thank you for helping us to understand the nature of addiction and the scourge of drugs like heroin.

To the many lawyers who helped navigate our understanding of the case, and fellow journalists like Marnie O'Neill, Debbie White, Paul Toohey, Mark Burrows, Tim Palmer, Marian Carroll, Rob Taylor, Sian Powell and Stephen Fitzpatrick who offered insight, and to Rehame, for providing an analysis of talkback callers, thank you.

Komang Suriadi deserves special mention. He was our translator, fixer extraordinaire and driver. So does Lukman S Bintoro, our photographer. Together they, and their families, have become part of our families, providing valuable insight, unwavering loyalty, hard work, dedication and definitely friendship. We couldn't have done this without you.

Thanks also to Erwin Pietersz, Putu Diah Kusumastuti Budhyasa, Sonny Tumbelaka, Made Nagi, Komang Sutrisna, Miftahudin M. Halim, Darma Putra; Warung proprietors Ibu Abas, Ibu Slamet and Pak Firman; staff at the Denpasar District Court, including I Wayan Yasa Abadi and Made Sukarta; police including Antonious Reniban and Bambang Sugiarto; Wayan Ana; Denpasar prosecutors including Olopan Nainggolan, Putu Indriati, David Adji, Wayan Sinayarti, Made Sudarmawan, Suhadi, Wayan Nastra, Ida Bagus Wiswantanu; lawyers Mochamad Rifan, Anggia Browne, Wirawan Adnan, Robert Khuana, Daniar Trisasongko, and Fransiskus Passar and Dr Anak Agung Hartawan.

On a personal level, Jeff Fagan, Rita King, Tony King, Robert King and Wayan Kardani helped ease our workload, as did David Fagan, who offered us both unbridled support. Sue and Thurlow Wockner were always a phone call away.

And, finally, to three people who made it happen. Our agent, Bill Tikos, who suggested we do it; our publisher, Alison Urquhart, who had faith from the start, and our editor, Sophie Hamley, whose good humour, calm manner and sage advice were invaluable. Thank you.

Contents

THE BALI NINE

Andrew Chan (Sydney)
Si Yi Chen (Sydney)
Michael William Czugaj (Brisbane)
Renae Lawrence (Newcastle)
Tan Duc Thanh Nguyen (Brisbane)
Matthew James Norman (Sydney)
Scott Anthony Rush (Brisbane)
Martin Eric Stephens (Illawarra)
Myuran Sukumaran (Sydney)

FAMILIES

Ken and Helen Chan
Edward Chen and Jian Yun Gao
Stephan and Vicki Czugaj
Robyn Davis (mother of Matthew Norman)
Bob and Jenny Lawrence
Michael Norman
Christine and Lee Rush
Bill and Michele Stephens
Sam and Rajini Sukumaran
Bev and Steve Waterman (mother and stepfather of Renae Lawrence)

POLICE/CUSTOMS

Lt-Col Bambang Sugiarto (Police)
Nyoman Gatra
Made Maja
Gede Senopati
Ketut Sumarka

LAWYERS

Mochamad Rifan (Chan, Sukumaran, Norman, Chen and Nguyen)
Yan Apul, Anggia Browne, Haposan Sihombing (Lawrence)
Wirawan Adnan (Stephens)
Robert Khuana and Daniar Trisasongko (Rush)
Fransiskus Passar (Czugaj)

JUDGES

I Gusti Ngurah Astawa, Putu Widnya and Ni Made Sudani (Lawrence and Czugaj trials)
I Gusti Lanang Dauh, Wayan Yasa Abadi and RR Suryowati (Sukumaran)
Made Sudia, I Gusti Ngurah Astawa, Edy P. Siregar (Rush and Stephens)
Arif Supratman, Wayan Suastrawan and Ketut Wiartha (Chan)
Rahayu Istiningsih, Dewa Made Puspa Adnyana and Ni Made Sudani (Norman, Chen and Nguyen)

1

Dressed and Ready

Renae Lawrence and Martin Stephens turned to each other, smiled and shook hands. They'd done it. Or so they thought. It was the performance of their lives and everyone seemed to have fallen for it, right from the moment they climbed out of their taxi in front of Bali's Ngurah Rai international airport. They had looked just like everyone else, holiday-weary and sunburnt, as they grabbed their bags and headed for the queue to check in to their Australian Airlines flight back to Sydney and their homes.

It had been a long eleven days, looking over their shoulders, worried about the moment when they would alight from their taxi and begin an eight-hour act aimed at fooling those trained to see through their disguise. Their clothes had cost just a few dollars at one of the hundreds and hundreds of market stalls lining the busy Kuta streets, the loud shirts, baggy shorts and thongs looking almost like the tourist-issue uniform. That's what people wore every day on their island holiday: in the bars that served cheap beers and exotic cocktails; in the hotels where accommodation costs were half the price they were back home. Lawrence and Stephens hadn't even picked out the clothes they wore now — someone else had done that for them. Just like someone else had dressed them, plastering chunks of heroin onto their thighs and torsos with cheap adhesive tape. But no one else knew that. No one was watching them. They looked just like everyone else, going home tired from the holiday of a lifetime. They were fitting in just fine.

It was just a few minutes past 8 p.m. on Sunday, 17 April 2005. Climbing out of the taxi, Stephens and Lawrence were careful to carry their own bags, politely refusing the offers of the porters who make their living in the airport forecourts. They didn't fidget or look nervous, their self-assurance strong that their secret was safe. After all, Lawrence had done this once before — just six months ago, she told police — and nothing had gone wrong; the $10 000 bonus she received at the other end proof she had survived the few nerves that surfaced every now and again.

Together, the pair of Sydneysiders walked purposefully through the doors of the big international departure terminal, past the colourful Garuda bird carving, the statues of squat little men wearing traditional black-and-white checked sarongs, and the maroon umbrellas. Once inside, they dumped their bags on the big X-ray conveyor belt that scans tourists' luggage, its technology wired up to alert officers to anything suspicious or dangerous.

A dog sat at the other end, where the conveyor belt spat out the checked luggage. Not a fruit-finding beagle, either: a dog trained to sniff out those who broke Indonesia's tough drug laws; a dog that could help assign the guilty to a frightening death by way of a bullet to the heart. Indonesia was tough on drug smugglers; it was an attempt by those in charge to stamp out a ballooning problem that was playing havoc with the republic's young. Lawrence and Stephens knew they had to walk past the dog without it picking up the scent of the wads of heroin strapped to their bodies — the 4.8 kilograms of smack that could fetch between $1.4 million and $2 million on the streets of Sydney. But at that time they didn't know how much was taped to them, or what it was worth. They did, however, know it was a risk; a life-threatening one.

It was just on 8.15 p.m. when they wandered past the canine trained to pick up the scent of law-breakers. If they were nervous they hid it well, their act so polished that it could fool anyone who had not been tipped off to their secret.

Lawrence and Stephens chatted, taking their place at the popular Qantas/Australian Airlines check-in counter, handing over their tickets and waiting to be assigned their seats. And with their luggage on its way to the plane's cargo hold — or so they thought — the pair continued their journey. The canine reappeared, its handlers ensuring that not much space was left between the two Australian travellers and their dog. But still nothing. Not a whiff. The dog, like all the others at the airport, was trained to sit down quickly on its haunches the moment things weren't right. Everything seemed to be okay with these two though, and the dog and its handlers moved on.

Lawrence and Stephens walked towards the escalator. Twice in a matter of minutes, they had evaded the front-line policing at Bali's international airport. Twice they'd been tested, and neither had folded. No alert. No alarm. No suspicion. And that's when they turned and smiled conspiratorially at each other. They had made it, their handshake an intimate sign of victory that their secret was safe. Onwards and upwards from here, across the skies that joined Australia and its back-yard island holiday destination. Without a hitch.

Well, almost. Renae Lawrence could feel one of the packs on her thigh begin to slip and it was working itself loose with each step. Something like this could undo everything; she knew it had to be fixed, properly and quickly. So Lawrence ducked into the ladies' toilet to make sure the pack couldn't fall further, below her shorts and down her leg. She didn't take long, and shortly rejoined Stephens. They strolled by the duty-free shops where throngs of passengers were looking for one last good deal, something for someone back home or even something to help them remember April in Bali.

Neither Stephens nor Lawrence was interested. They wandered on by, the young woman from Wallsend in Newcastle and the 29-year-old born-and-bred Illawarra boy, who shared a workplace in Sydney. This wasn't a holiday, after all — their family and friends were unaware that they had left Australian shores. No need for memories of this trip, either — batik shirts and sarongs were an unnecessary reminder that this 'holiday' was work. Hard work.

Departure gates three and four loomed large in front of them, presenting them with the challenge of one more security check before stepping onto the plane. Most travellers didn't bother with it until the last minute, spending their time looking through the shops and making use of the last cigarette stop in one of the many cafés that allowed it, or savouring the last moments of their holiday. Not Stephens and Lawrence. They marched on, keen to pass through security and board their plane. But it wasn't to be. The flight was not yet open and staff told them to take a seat nearby. They would hear the flight being called.

From the moment Lawrence and Stephens alighted — even before — their every movement was being tracked; surveillance teams who had spent the past four days watching them heralded their arrival. The agents watched as the pair stepped out of their taxi disguised as tourists. Watched as they passed through the first security check, and by the customs dog that guarded it. Watched as they booked into their flight and passed their second brush with the drug-detection dog. And that's when they almost lost one of them.

One officer radioed ahead, warning his colleague that Lawrence and Stephens had separated when Lawrence walked into a toilet on her own. A search couldn't locate their target, and it was only when Lawrence walked back out that, relying on pictures of the surveillance targets, they realised the stockily built twenty-seven year old with short hair and a manly gait was actually a woman.

Back on track, the surveillance team kept up with the pair, determined to do the job assigned to them. They were just part of a larger outfit — others had watched the pair and their friends for days, ever since the tip-off from the Australian Federal Police.

Renae Lawrence. Martin Stephens. They were just two of the bunch. A further three would come later: Michael Czugaj, Scott Rush and Andrew Chan. All of them were involved in smuggling drugs, according to intelligence gathered first in Australia and now here, on Indonesian soil. It was going to be a busy night. Still others in the surveillance team were assigned elsewhere — to Matthew Norman, Tan Duc Thanh Nguyen and Si Yi Chen. And the other one — the black-skinned man who didn't have a name.

Customs officers Gede Senopati and Ketut Sumarka strode towards Renae Lawrence and Martin Stephens. It was time to act.

'I am a Customs officer. Would you follow me. We want to check your luggage, your hand-carry luggage and your body,' they were told.

Stephens's answer hid the panic that was almost certainly gripping his big frame. 'My body — why?' he asked Senopati. He wanted to look innocent in the face of overwhelming guilt.

Senopati was aware of that, and his answer was not 100 per cent truthful. 'This is just a routine check,' he said. 'You are part of a random check. Just follow me.' He guided them to a small Customs room nearby, home to searches night and day.

Senopati knew the drill backwards. He went through the motions of searching the duo's hand luggage, finding nothing except some DVDs, clothes and a few wooden souvenirs. He wasn't surprised at the stash of DVDs — they were all pirated, able to be picked up for just over a dollar in Bali, and most travellers stocked up before leaving the island.

Stephens's and Lawrence's performances, which had been so polished to this point, started to falter. That's what happens when terror grips the body — you can forget your lines. The colour began draining from their faces, leaving both deathly white. But Senopati kept going — his job just started. He called for one of Customs' drug detection dogs, but not the canine that had let the pair slip through the net earlier. This new dog, Maxy, wandered around and around his targets. However, he remained standing — an indicator that the pair was free of drugs.

Not convinced, Senopati ordered Lawrence and Maxy from the room. He told Stephens to unbutton his shirt. He did, with his singlet still hiding his secret. Senopati asked him to take down his shorts. Now Stephens was trapped. But he followed the orders given to him, revealing his tightly bandaged thighs. Still he tried to perform. With every ounce of his being, he tried to stop the inevitable.

'What's this?' the investigator asked.

'Nothing. Just an accident,' Stephens responded.

'What kind of accident?' said Senopati.

'A banana-boat accident. It's a very dangerous game, you know.'

Stephens was filled with panic. Terror. He knew he was moments away from being caught attempting to smuggle drugs out of Indonesia.

Senopati reached for Stephens's thigh, squeezing it to see if

Stephens gulped in pain. But Stephens had obviously forgotten his last line — he didn't even wince.

Both he and Senopati knew the game was up.

Outside, the same fear that was engulfing Stephens was gripping Renae Lawrence's guts. She puffed away on a cigarette, ignoring the no-smoking signs, desperate for the nicotine to help keep her thoughts in check. She didn't know what was happening to Stephens — but she knew her turn was next. She never uttered a word while she waited.

Customs officer Ketut Sumarka, a 25-year veteran of Bali airport, stood next to her. He had seen this performance time and time again and he allowed her to flaunt the no-smoking rules. Worse was to come, he knew. He kept a gentle hold on her arm before leading her into the room. Then he touched her thigh, instinctively identifying her secret.

'There is something here,' he said.

II

The Support Crew

Scott Rush and Michael Czugaj had never heard of Renae Lawrence and Martin Stephens. Nor, at 8.30 p.m. on this night, could they have cared who they were. Their focus was elsewhere. They'd just checked out of the Adhi Dharma Hotel and were about to board their second international flight ever; their first had been only nine days earlier, when they boarded the Australian Airlines flight from Sydney to Denpasar. And now they were returning home. The two Brisbane boys, who first met playing sport at school, checked in before climbing the elevator at Ngurah Rai international airport and paying the airport tax with money handed to them less than an hour earlier. Then they stood at the immigration counter, waiting to have their passports stamped. The whole process was new to them — as was the ordeal they had just gone through.

The pair had stood in a room, taking their turns to have chunks of heroin taped to their thighs and waists. They'd had their eyes shut as they balanced on one leg, the other resting on the bed in room 105. It had taken an hour or so, and then they'd been sent packing with some strict instructions: call Andrew Chan on their way to the airport. Call him again the moment they arrived at the airport. And call the number that had been put into Rush's mobile telephone the instant their Australian Airlines flight landed at Sydney's international airport. Then they'd get paid for the 3.4 kilograms of heroin that now clung to their bodies. Five thousand dollars in cash. Five thousand dollars each.

At that point in time, however, standing in front of the immigration counter, it's unlikely either Rush or Czugaj were thinking of any of that. They were just concentrating on moving on, through immigration, and onto their plane.

It's unclear whether the two mates saw the officer in front of them raise his hand. It wasn't a dramatic signal — just a movement, really. A subtle wave. But it was the look on the officer's face that told his colleagues the second lot of targets had arrived at Bali's international airport. The officer held on to the shiny new passports, delaying the process of stamping them.

Rush and Czugaj waited. Time seemed to stand still. And then — from out of thin air, it seemed — they were surrounded. Customs officers. Police officers. By their side. Talking to them. Telling them to step inside the office nearby. Rush and Czugaj walked with them, first to the small office, and then back down the escalator and into another office. Renae Lawrence and Martin Stephens were there, hunched over in their seats, the air thick with panic.

The colour drained from the faces of the two Brisbane boys as the wads of heroin strapped to their bodies were revealed. The game was up, and each of the young people in that room now knew that this was all part of a bigger picture. It wasn't just two Sydneysiders acting as mules on the order of a co-worker. It wasn't only two young Brisbane teenagers, one awfully good-looking and the other seeming much younger than his nineteen years. Four young Australians with a total heroin haul of 8.2 kilograms, worth up to $4 million on the streets of Sydney, bound to their bodies; and now caught in Indonesia, where drug smugglers are warned off by a penalty of death administered on a lonely beach, or in a park, or on a golf course sometime down the track.

Senopati couldn't help thinking that Rush and Czugaj looked like a couple of schoolboys sent to the headmaster's office for their first caning. He glared at their passports and saw that Rush, the good-looking lad, was only nineteen years of age. *Kasian*, he thought. That's the word Indonesians use for pity. Sumarka couldn't think of another word — *kasian* summed it up. With a quarter of a century in the job, and the high-profile arrests of at least seven foreign drug dealers and couriers to his credit, he had never before felt pity for any of them — he always thought they deserved what they got. But this time it was different. These people were just children, the same age as his own son.

The four young Australians sat in the airless and featureless Customs room, the whirr of Indonesian policing happening around them.

Just outside, someone they all knew was arriving at the same airport, with plans to board the same flight back to Sydney. It was Andrew Chan.

Muhammad Zakaria pulled up his Komotro Taxi No 099 outside the airport. It was just on 8.30 p.m., and Chan looked like any other tourist: baggy blue shorts with yellow floral motifs, a grey T-shirt and his Bali souvenirs — a large wooden fish and a long, bizarre-looking, wooden voodoo stick. He looked almost comical. Having the fish was understandable: they are sold in markets and stalls all over the place. But the voodoo stick, with its hairy top, was not so common. It's impossible to know what would have attracted him to it.

Nonchalantly, Chan strolled through the airport doors, having done this sort of job before, and if he was harbouring any doubts that his operation had worked, they remained deeply hidden. He checked in for the same flight as Martin Stephens and Renae Lawrence — who also worked with him in Sydney — and the two Brisbane boys introduced to him by Tan Duc Thanh Nguyen. With his airport tax paid and his passport stamped, the clock showed that he still had more than an hour before boarding. Chan didn't seem to mind, according to those watching him; the time allowed him to indulge in one of his biggest passions, reading. He sat down and opened a book. But Customs and police arrived quickly, asking for his passport and tickets. He looked at them, warily at first, puzzlement filling his face. They asked him to follow them to an office.

Chan's body might not have been home to chunks of heroin, but there was plenty of intelligence information to justify detaining this twenty-one year old from Sydney.

It was 9 p.m. on Sunday, 17 April. Less than an hour had passed since the first of these five young Australians pulled up in a taxi to catch their flight home to Sydney. Now they were being driven down the road, this time to the main Customs office, where the bigger space allowed for unfinished business. They looked helpless, their future seemed hopeless, and their ordeal was about to make international news that would flood the local and Australian media, call into question the role of the Australian Federal Police and irrevocably change the lives of everyone who knew them.

Michael Czugaj looked like he would burst into tears.

III

A Free Ride

The air inside the car was heavy with desperation. Ketut Sumarka, driving the short distance from the airport to the main Customs office just down the road, couldn't help glancing in the rear-vision mirror. His three passengers appeared to be shell-shocked. Their bodies seemed to have shrunk inside their oversized shirts. There was little sound.

Michael Czugaj began to cry. His face was red; so were his eyes. Tears fell silently. It was a pitiful sight. Touching him gently on the shoulder, Renae Lawrence, eight years his senior, implored him to calm down. Pimples still on his pasty face, he was a picture of dreadful sadness. So too was his mate, Scott Rush, but he was not crying. In the next car, Martin Stephens was wearing a defeated and haunted look. He is a big fellow but he too had shrunk.

The four were taken into the office of the Customs boss, Bernadus, and sat awkwardly on shabby brown lounge chairs. They were the very same brown chairs on which, six months earlier, another Australian had sat. In front of her on the ground had lain a 4.1 kilogram bundle of marijuana found in her luggage. Her name was Schapelle Corby.

Corby's circumstances, however, had been different. Whilst the drugs had been found in her bag, she had vehemently denied that they were hers and had tried to show there was no proof that she had put them there. At the end of the day, it hadn't mattered: she had been convicted.

Now, for these four Australians in the office, there was no doubting the evidence — the heroin was strapped to their bodies. They couldn't argue that they didn't know it was there.

The four sat on the L-shaped lounge, Lawrence and Stephens next to each other on one side, Rush and Czugaj on the other. Thirty minutes later, Andrew Chan was also driven down to the Customs building, but he was in a different office just next door. He also appeared to be in a different frame of mind to the other four: his face didn't bear the same haunted look, and he didn't look like he might burst into tears at any second. He was the antithesis of the other four — his confidence seemed intact, even at this dire and low point in his life. The Customs officers and police thought to themselves that it was probably all a façade, but a good one at that. But as Chan smiled and joked with his captors, acting almost like the class clown, next door, despair was invading every pore of his four colleagues.

'Will I die for this?' one of the four whispered to Gede Senopati; the officer can't remember who actually asked the question.

Senopati was diplomatic in his reply: 'We will see at the trial.' He knew he could not offer any comfort to these four young Australians. They had spectacularly flaunted one of the most unforgiving of Indonesia's laws — the narcotics legislation — and the ultimate sanction was a lonely death by firing squad. While he felt *kasian* for them, he couldn't and wouldn't give them any false hopes. The law was the law and they had done what they had done.

Rush and Czugaj, both the youngest at nineteen, looked like little boys who needed their parents. They hung their heads, trying to shield their faces from the police cameras that were documenting every second of the arrest. Again the officers were struck by their youth as they asked to search the luggage of each person.

There are Customs officers, airport security and police everywhere. Among them, the *bule* — or Western — face of a man called Paul Hunniford stood out. Better known by his nickname, Reg, he wore an Australian Federal Police (AFP) ID tag around his neck. He was the AFP liaison officer based at the Australian Consulate in Bali, and he had intimate knowledge of this operation from the beginning.

Martin Stephens seemed to be about to dissolve in a flood of tears. Next to him, Renae Lawrence tried to control her emotions. All smoked heavily. Senopati gave Stephens a plastic cup full of water, which he gulped down furiously. He asked for another and another until he had drunk about four altogether. Senopati assumed it was because of nerves. The Australians also ran out of cigarettes, and officers obliged by giving them more.

One by one, the four readily answered questions, like the spelling of their names, their ages and professions. The full force of the shock had yet to set in for any of them. Stephens whispered quietly to Rush and Rush shrugged his shoulders; only they know what they were conferring about, and perhaps now they can't remember.

The door to the nearby room, where the jovial Chan was sitting, was ajar, giving the four a reasonable view of him. Stephens whispered to Sumarka that he wanted to tell him something. 'He is very dangerous,' he said, pointing to Chan, before asking Sumarka to close the door.

Lawrence kicked off both the leg strappings and put them on the coffee table in front of her, while Stephens searched in his bag for some paper to fan himself with. It was hot in the office, the temperature elevated by the fear that seemed to have sapped the room of its oxygen. Senior Bali drug squad officer Made Maja, who speaks English, was there. He leant over, deep in conversation with Lawrence and Stephens. What Lawrence heard was not making her happy. Maja was urging her to 'talk the truth' regarding the whole sorry episode, but the look on her face was one of defiance.

Maja and AFP agent Hunniford then moved closer to Stephens, talking furtively with him. It was early on but already the four, and especially Stephens and Lawrence, were considering the consequences of ratting on the leaders of the operation and, unsurprisingly, the police were urging them to do so. Especially since Chan had been caught at the airport with not a gram of heroin on him, while the others were carrying a total of 8.2 kilograms between them. But for Lawrence there were other considerations. Officials' cameras, filming the events of that night, caught her remonstrating privately with Stephens.

'You have gotta dob some other cunt in, I'm not killin' my family,' she said leaning back, looking almost resigned. Stephens's face was completely blank, his eyes empty, as he listened. Within a second she sat forward again with renewed vigour, looking at her colleague. The emotion in her voice was unmistakable. 'And what's the point anyway, because if we dob them in, right — think about it — if we dob them in, they kill our family and then we are dead anyway? Don't tell them and they just kill us instead and leave them alone.' Lawrence let out a breath and then leant back again. Tears were welling in her eyes and she fought desperately to stop them spilling over onto her face, revealing the true depths of her own personal despair. She bit her lip.

Stephens didn't reply, looking lost in his own thoughts. Then, almost as if to divert her own emotions and avert an episode of the sobs building inside, Lawrence reached under her shirt. 'Can I take this off?' she asked officers, referring to the heroin strapped around her waist. Soon enough the ignominy that would result from that request became apparent. Because Lawrence is a woman, she was taken to a separate room, where female officers conducted the official search and the heroin taped to her waist was removed. It was the same procedure for the other three. There were 890.84 grams of heroin taped around Martin Stephens's waist under a back-support strap that felt excruciatingly tight, like a corset pulled too taut, and his skin dimpled accordingly. Even before the arrest he was in pain, wincing internally with every step.

Stephens tried to help the officers pull the offensive package off. It was stuck to him like glue though, so eventually a Stanley knife was produced for the final stages. Then the tape was unravelled from both his thighs. Nearby sat a big set of scales with an electronic display. Stephens was ordered to crouch beside it as the three packages taken off him were dumped on the scales together. The display illuminated with the gross weight of 3.3 kilograms. Flashes go off — police are recording the event. So too are lots of others, some snapping away with in-built mobile phone cameras.

Each parcel was then weighed individually. The weight for each was displayed — more flashes went off. Stephens was a shadow of his former self, deflated and helpless. Strangely, underneath it all he felt a sense of relief at having been caught, despite the harsh drug penalties of Indonesia. Plus, he was in shock, so a state of denial might also exist. Martin Stephens wasn't cut out to be a drug courier and the whole experience had been alien to him. He never truly agreed with what he was doing, but later said he didn't have a choice — after the threats to his life and the lives of his family members were delivered. And if he got back to Australia safely, he had planned to tell Lawrence, his work colleague — whom he had barely known before this, and whom he didn't trust, nor she him — exactly what he thought of her. He intended using the F-word and severing their short friendship.

The drugs were also stripped from Rush and Czugaj, their more hollow chests testament to their tender ages. It was the same procedure, too, for weighing the drugs, and they were forced to crouch by the scales for photos.

Field test kits used by officers confirmed the powder was heroin. And by that time some of the officers were sneezing — pepper had been poured on top of the heroin to throw the drug detection dogs off the scent. This tactic had evidently worked, but the four Australians needed more than pepper to save them from what, that evening, looked like an increasingly uncertain fate.

Czugaj hung his head — he didn't want to pose for the cameras. He looked younger than ever now. Czugaj had said little throughout the evening and had been crying all the while. But it was not so in the next room.

Chan was the image of a man with little to fear. 'One, two, three,' someone said before a flash went off; Chan grinned like a Cheshire cat, joking with officers. The atmosphere was far from tense. Chan even readily obliged when one officer asked to borrow his matches to light up a cigarette. Outwardly, at least, he was a cool customer. When Senopati asked if he could check the contents of Chan's luggage, the twenty-one year old was not the least bit perturbed. 'Yes, please, of course,' he said. There was not much in there except more than 100 DVDs, including some pornographic material.

However, some witnesses say that Chan was not nearly as brave as he was making out and that it was all an act, a bit of false bravado to get him through the night. He might well have not been so flippant and so ready to please had he known what evidence police had already compiled on him. He would find out soon enough.

It was almost 4 a.m. the next day, 18 April, when the group were shown to their cells and temporary new homes in the jail at Polda, the Denpasar police headquarters. They were officially suspects in an international heroin trafficking operation. If the night had gone as originally planned, by this time they would have been preparing to land at Sydney airport.

IV

Bust at the Melasti

Knock, knock, knock.

Police stood outside room 136 of the Melasti Beach Bungalows, waiting for the door to open. It was getting late, and five young Australians were already undergoing questioning less than 5 kilometres away. But the plain-clothes officers assigned to this job were not yet finished. Just two minutes before, the rest of their targets in this operation had pulled up outside the Melasti in a taxi. Now, as the officers stormed into the reception area, they found that their targets had gone.

The officers headed straight for the check-in counter, demanding to know about the 'black man' who had just checked in. For the police who had filled their days following him, Myuran Sukumaran didn't even have a name. He wasn't in the intelligence reports given to them by the Australian Federal Police, and they didn't otherwise know who he was. But he was important — they were sure of that. And they were on orders now: it was time to act.

Ten minutes later, another four police arrived. For 45-year-old Rai Sidan, the chief of security at the hotel for the last five years, it was the most dramatic thing to have happened there so far. He listened to the police and their demands — they wanted to be taken to the room which had just been let to Sukumaran and his friends. These people were drug suspects, he was told. Sidan didn't hesitate, taking the police straight to room 136.

Knock, knock, knock.

Someone opened the door. Sukumaran and his friends were sitting around, smoking. Nothing special.

'We are the police,' one officer said, showing his badge. 'Sit down. We have information you bring heroin.' The word 'police' caught the attention of the young men. The expressions on their faces changed. Slowly at first — and then completely. Everyone was quiet. Silent, in fact. Sidan looked at them: Myuran Sukumaran, the black man whom police still could not identify by name; Matthew Norman, who was on the original list sent over by the Australian Federal Police, as was Tan Duc Thanh Nguyen; and Si Yi Chen, the lad from Doonside in Sydney. But there was no doubt where the terror struck first: Matthew Norman, the eighteen year old, was backed into a corner like a frightened child, cringeing. A little boy trying to play the role of a man.

April 17, 2005 was Myuran Sukumaran's twenty-fourth birthday. Until a few moments before he was preparing to celebrate another year. The four in the room had been planning to head out on the town a little later on to celebrate. At least, that's what they would claim later. But they didn't get that far, so no one really knows.

The quartet had moved out of the Adhi Dharma Hotel soon after the rest of their contingent had headed for Bali's international airport. And some time after 10 p.m. — close to 10.40 p.m., perhaps — they'd checked into a room here, at the Melasti Beach Bungalows in the beating heart of bustling Kuta. They didn't have a booking. They just arrived in a taxi and asked whether a room was available. There was nothing unusual about that; tourists wanting to savour a few more days of their Indonesian holiday did it all the time. And the Melasti's not a bad place to stay — it's close to everything, just a stone's throw from Kuta square and the shops, and right on the main road. Its prices are fairly reasonable too — not that Sukumaran and his friends seemed too worried about that. For US$50 a night they could share a comfortable, air-conditioned room with a television. There was a swimming pool nearby, the ambience of the area obviously Balinese. A small Hindu temple, where staff members routinely place their offerings to the gods, was just outside room 136. What the young men didn't know was that every movement they made had been watched.

Ida Bagus Dalem didn't know that, though he had been working on the front desk when the Australians arrived. He'd noticed nothing out of place, odd or suspicious about the young men opting to rent room 136 on the ground floor, adjacent to the temple. They had arrived in two taxis — three men in one taxi and one in the other. The only unusual aspect — although Dalem barely thought about it at the time — was that they said that not all of them intended sleeping there; they just wanted to keep their bags inside. But tourists had all sorts of requests and this one didn't strike Dalem as being as strange as some he had received.

Sukumaran told Dalem that he would check out again at 6 a.m. the next day. The room was booked in Si Yi Chen's name. Because there were only two beds, they requested a third fold-up bed. Five minutes later, they were registered. They seemed calm, accepting the traditional welcome drink offered at all Balinese hotels upon check-in. They must have felt confident too: despite the incriminating contents of their suitcase, they agreed to the bellboy carrying some of their luggage to their room.

* * *

Police were interested in the contents of the group's suitcases and bags, which were still unopened as they had just arrived in the room. And when police opened them on the Australians' behalf, they felt they had struck gold.

How would four young men explain away this paraphernalia? Inside the blue and black rucksack, wrapped in newspaper, were two plastic bags containing 334.26 grams of heroin and another plastic bag of conventional pepper powder. Its smell was strong; Sidan started sneezing. Black and pink rubber gloves, light brown–coloured Leukoplast adhesive tape, a waist support belt, screwdrivers, seven rolls of yellow adhesive tape, five of white plus three rolls of light brown–coloured cloth adhesive tape, along with seven brown-coloured rolls and one white roll. It was all there. Right in front of them.

Sukumaran quickly denied ownership of the bag. In fact, no one wanted to claim it. 'It's not mine' — the mantra was repeated over and over. And over. Police insisted to Sukumaran that it must be his. He insisted back that he knew nothing about it. Angry and argumentative, Sukumaran sat in a chair, his pose arrogant. He complained about police taking his picture and documenting everything on film. One of the officers felt like punching him, wanting to knock some of the hot air out of him.

Nguyen, Chen and Norman had sweat pouring from their brows. Nguyen and Chen were sitting on a bed; Norman had his legs drawn up to his chest, hoping for comfort. Hours passed. The clock ticked towards 3 a.m. Police searched and re-searched. Checked and re-checked. And then, the four who had arrived in a taxi, wearing façades of holidaymakers about to hit the town for a good time, left in handcuffs. The destination: Polda police jail, where they would soon be joined by five

Australians they thought would now be back in Sydney. Nine young Australians, aged eighteen to twenty-nine, suspected of involvement in an international drug-smuggling racket.

It had been a fruitful week's work for the Indonesian National Police.

V

Friendship in the West

Andrew Chan always walked with the same swagger. It was half boastful, half blustering, but that was enough to scare off some of the students he shared a classroom with at Homebush Boys High School. He was a mischief-maker who could rule his small clique of Asian friends like a mini gang, bullying those less confident than himself and trying to lure into his group others whom he believed might fit the bill. He thought he was a leader, and those who followed him soon treated him that way. And he could stare down anyone.

Like the time someone saw him steal a mobile phone on a boat cruise. Chan was asked, along with all the other youths on board, whether he was responsible for the theft. Others on the cruise were pointing at him, some even gesturing towards his pocket. But Chan turned the tables on everyone. He got angry. 'Go on, check me,' he challenged, the defiance in his eyes matching his stiff body language. 'I've got nothing to hide. I don't have it.' The boy sitting near him, along with many others, had seen the class troublemaker put it in his pocket, but no one was going to check him. Chan walked off the boat with a new mobile phone; the boy watching him wondered whether he would ever be caught out.

When the same lad was told by a friend of Chan's arrest in Bali, he immediately searched for all the details he could find on the internet. He battled with a mix of shock and delight.

'To be honest, I was quite relieved,' he admits. 'I know it's really bad for me to say that, but he did give me a lot of trouble.'

Once, in junior high school, Chan had tried to flog the boy a sports jumper he told him he had stolen from a local store. Other times when Chan was short on cash, he would come up, his friends sometimes looking on, and demand money.

'He'd say, "Give me some fucking money", and I couldn't do anything about it,' he says. But he drew the line when Chan's group of try-hards went on a recruitment drive, imploring other local teenagers to join their group.

'I didn't want to join the gang,' he says. 'I just kept saying "no" and he kept bullying me. One incident — I was at the train station and he came around with his mates and said, "Why the fuck won't you join my gang", and [was] yelling at me. He grabbed my ears and pulled me. I wasn't scared of him; I was more scared of his mates because there were a whole group of them.'

That group of mates, some of whom still wander around the same areas of Sydney, frequenting the shopping areas of Strathfield and the railway platforms of western Sydney, is the reason this former classmate is keen to stay anonymous.

However, that group — despite these stories and others, like Chan's penchant for biting off his fingernails and spitting them at people — has remained steadfastly loyal to Chan. They look at their former friend — none has had contact with him since his arrest — sitting in a jail cell in Bali with an uneasy awe. They tell a different story about Chan, and that's the interesting point about the fourth child and youngest son of Helen and Ken

Chan, born in Sydney on 12 January 1984. Andrew Chan could be as loyal as he was loathed. He could be your best mate, or your worst enemy; it all depended on whether he saw you as being on his side. Some colleagues tell of the love and respect he showed to his parents and his sister, and the friendship he shared with one of his brothers. The same people talk of a teenager trying to find his way in life, going to two different high schools before leaving in 2000, and working at a string of places serving food and washing cars before taking on a casual job at a catering company that serviced the Sydney Cricket Ground. Chan called himself a logistics helper, but the job description was akin to being a food runner.

Chan, if you take it on the say-so of many of those who know him, can be a chameleon. He is either a menace or a clown; a good friend or a dangerous foe. People either like him or loathe him — there aren't many emotions in between. But certainly he was a teenager who seemed to struggle to find his place in the big melting pot of western Sydney. Most of his self-confidence was bluff, but he wielded it effectively, and sometimes with intimidation.

The role Chan seemed to drift towards constantly was that of a small-time brute. He was loud. He could be a bully. And he demanded respect. Indeed, the most important thing to him seemed to be the accolades of others. His friends were almost all Asian, and he wanted them to look up to him. He wanted to be their leader.

'Back in those days it was kind of hard for us,' explains one of his friends who has considered travelling to Bali to see him. The streets of western Sydney were bubbling away with all sorts of gang activity, and Asian boys found themselves easy prey for other groups looking for a quick fight or to mark out their own territory. 'It's just that if we [were] in a group and then another group comes by or something, there was likely to be trouble. He [Chan] wasn't a bad guy at all. To his friends, he was very loyal.

He had respect for a lot of us and we had a lot of respect for him too. He might just look like a bad person but the real Andrew that no one really knows, he's not like that.'

The friend talks about low-level gang activity — like knocking off someone's wallet or handbag, vandalism and the odd fight — as just part of the make-up of the day on some western Sydney streets. And he laughs at the description of Chan as a small-time gangster, the term given to him by some people.

'It was just boys being boys really. He would intimidate a few people here and there. But it wasn't just him. The whole school would tease ... you know how it is, in every school there's always a guy who will get teased no matter what. It's not just Andrew doing it. It's really everyone doing it, but because Andrew is the type of person to joke around more, to other people's eyes it might seem a bit serious, but everyone knew he was just joking around, having a laugh.'

The word 'gang' keeps coming up when Chan's background is discussed, but it's used fairly loosely. To the public, 'gang' usually denotes small and often ethnic groups of male teenagers, prowling western Sydney creating waves of crime with violence and standover tactics. And these groups exist, but gangs of young youths drawn together by boredom just as much as ethnicity also form part of the subculture of many Sydney suburbs.

Of the Lebanese and Middle Eastern gangs in Bankstown and Canterbury or the Asian groups in Cabramatta, some are dangerous and territorial, luring in adolescent boys and spitting out hardened criminals. The gang people talk about when describing Andrew Chan's teenage years was not like that. It was more like a loose group of Asian boys, linked by friendship and background, brought up in similar families in the city's suburban melting pots. There are hundreds of them across

Sydney — teenagers who would meet before and after school, hanging out in shopping malls and public places, going to the movies, sitting in parks, and spending money in loud, dark game parlours. Crimes are committed, but they are hardly ever violent. Bag-snatches, petty theft, the odd brawl with another group of boys — that's the type of gang both Chan's friends and foes describe when talking about the young man Indonesian intelligence officers marked early as a ringleader.

Chan's friend says that the way Chan has been painted, as using his teenage years to build a reputation as a big-time drug warlord or godfather, is preposterous. The fights that Chan usually found himself in were not even started by him or his friends.

'He wasn't the one to go out and start trouble,' says the friend. In fact, more often than not, he was misconstrued as being a big bully when he was just having a bit of a laugh at someone else's expense. 'He was the class clown. He made a lot of people laugh. He mucked around. He was witty. He had all these jokes.' It's just if you weren't on his side, you didn't often find them very funny.

After swapping schools, Chan seemed to knuckle down a bit more — for a little while, at least — and would even acknowledge his old adversaries when he spotted them. He'd nod, and they'd nod too, but neither side seemed keen to stop for a chat. Time had moved on, and the past stayed where it belonged.

It was usually in the Strathfield area, where hordes of youths would sit on seats and just while the world away, that you might run into Chan and his mates. They'd meet before or after work, or even during work hours for those without a job or on casual employment. They'd just hang out, having a laugh and carrying on, much like other youths scattered across the big Sydney area. Chan and his friends would buy food from one of the takeaway joints nearby, wander the shopping centre aimlessly and catch a movie on some days.

Some of those Chan would hang out with were old friends like Myuran Sukumaran and Si Yi Chen, who, Chan told police, had been his mates since school. Sukumaran, who sometimes used the name Mark, was born a few years earlier than Chan, in April 1981, to parents Sam and Rajini in London. He was the eldest of three children, with a younger sister and brother. He didn't have the same profile as Chan in the local area. Sukumaran spent most of his days working, after graduating from Homebush Boys High School. First up he worked for ten months in the passport office in Sydney, before going to a bank and then a finance company during 2003, up until November 2004. He boasted a monthly salary of $2500.

Sukumaran was physically bigger and more imposing than Chan, had a penchant for shaving his head, and had a big scar down the back of his neck. He could appear threatening, scary even, and always looked older than he was. But he kept his own counsel, comfortably sitting in the background, allowing others to do the talking. He'd been like that for years, but it was that personality trait which evaded intelligence detection for a while both in Australia and overseas. Australian officers had never heard his name, despite knowing of and having dossiers on many of his colleagues, and Indonesian surveillance teams invariably called him 'the black-skinned man', 'the negro' and 'the dark man'. No one knew his name for a long time. And that's how Myuran Sukumaran seemed to like it.

Si Yi Chen was a year younger than Chan, born on 19 March 1985 in Guangzhou, China, to parents Edward Chen and Jian Yun Gao, who then settled in Doonside in Sydney. He was an only child; solid, almost pudgy, with a fat, round face. Apart from that, not a lot stood out about the twenty year old who always seemed happier to let the conversation swirl around him. He was there, but never the ringleader; in the background, rarely giving his opinion.

Chen had a regular job, in a mobile phone shop, and was earning about $2000 each month. He spent his spare time hanging out with his friends. One of them worked with Andrew Chan at the catering company at the Sydney Cricket Ground. He was a young man from Quakers Hill called Matthew Norman.

Matthew Norman and Andrew Chan, along with Martin Stephens and Renae Lawrence, were employed casually and worked on and off at one of Eurest's Sydney sites — the Sydney Cricket Ground and Aussie Stadium. Eurest is a big food service company which supplies, prepares and serves food at functions. It has a big workforce across the nation — up to 5000 casual employees in various states, many of them young and fit. Chan, Norman, Lawrence and Stephens were like many others who would be called up to help out at functions.

Jobs for Eurest's big casual workforce are both seasonal and dependent on the size of the functions being staged. Some months are always busier than others, especially when sport is involved. Chan, Norman, Lawrence and Stephens would be called to work in the lead-up to and during events like a cricket game or rugby league match. Sometimes they'd be required to work an eight-hour shift, sometimes even a five-hour shift. On rare occasions they might only be needed for three hours, but it was never less than that. And the boss had a rap on all of them: they were good employees — reliable and punctual, with a strong work ethic. Stephens had not been there long, but even in that short time he had shown that he was like the others. And so they were called back often to work on all the big functions.

By any assessment, the job was pretty mundane, and they all carried the title of food runners. At some events there could be up to 100 food outlets and it was important that stock never ran out. Norman, Chan, Stephens and Lawrence, along with all Eurest's other casually employed food runners, would have to make sure that the food was delivered to the right outlet prior to the game. Get that wrong and the complaints would flow in. On some occasions, outlets would vary their deliveries on the day before the match. Other outlets might stipulate that they needed it one hour before kickoff. And then during the event — as any sports-lover can attest — it's important that food does not run out, and the job of the stadium's food runners was to ensure that it was replaced as quickly as it was purchased. It wasn't brain surgery, but it required robust and reliable young workers, and they all fitted that bill.

At first, none of the four young workers knew each other. They hadn't been to school together, they came from different suburbs, and they were all different ages.

Matthew Norman, whose father and sisters lived in Quakers Hill and whose mother lived at Port Macquarie, was the first to get employment at Eurest. A good worker, he had been employed for more than four years, starting with the company in February 2001. He started as a vendor, before moving into retail, and then finally working as a food runner. His employers knew he had another job as a forklift driver, but as far as Eurest was concerned, it was not possible to fault the nineteen year old's work.

Chan, too, had a good work ethic, and it was quickly apparent that he didn't mind carrying heavy loads. He was always punctual, a stickler for starting work on time. Indeed, no one can remember him ever being late to work since beginning his job with Eurest in November 2002 as a kitchen assistant, and then as a food runner.

Lawrence, whose family lived up in Wallsend in Newcastle, started in September 2003. A no-nonsense worker like her colleagues, she could average $2300 a month.

Stephens was the last to gain employment there, beginning only a few months earlier as a cellar person. The young man who had come from Adelaide, but who had grown up in the Illawarra area south of Sydney, was only just getting into the swing of things; the seasonal rush when he would be rostered regularly was still some time away. But he'd had enough shifts to enable him to meet co-workers Lawrence, Chan and Norman.

VI

Growing up in Wallsend

From an early age, Renae Lawrence was an all-or-nothing type of girl. She tipped the baby scales in October 1977 at a bonny 10-pounds-something, her father says, but the school photographs he shows off are of a wispy-thin adolescent.

Renae lived with her mother as a child, swapping to live with her father during her teenage years. And then, after a fiery clash in the wake of her eighteenth birthday, she snapped off all contact with Bob Lawrence. Father's Day was forgotten, his birthday ignored and Christmases never acknowledged, as her new life revolved around her older and wiser lover. But when that relationship fractured and broke, she reappeared in her father's life, and now, from her cell in a Bali jail, sends cards addressed to 'My dearest Daddy', tears welling in her piercing blue eyes when told he might be unable to make it for her first court appearance.

As far back as memories go, Renae Lawrence searched for a sense of belonging, but when she found it she often thrust it aside in an instant. She had to do things 100 per cent or not at all. Life was black and white; shades of grey were nonexistent. Her highs were dizzy, her lows dismal. School could be such fun, friends filling her home with the contagious giggles of teenage girls, but in the same week she could — and once did — take a handful of muscle relaxant pills her father used for his crook neck, and swallow some of them. That incident, while she was still at school, would be copied again in her young life: when she broke up with her lover, and again when life got too hard living in an Indonesian police holding cell, she would find a way to try to take her life. But the next day, or the day after, the cheeky smile would reappear and Renae would be back on track.

The young woman who was unable to live by half measures had never travelled north of Scotts Head in NSW before adulthood. But in the six months between October 2004 and April 2005, she travelled overseas three times, Bali always the destination. She had known her co-worker Andrew Chan for less than a year before her first flight. But that didn't stop her returning to Australia with him, chunks of heroin strapped firmly to her thighs. After that, he seemed to have a hold on her, the fat envelope containing $10 000 handed to her only hours after that first trip cementing their one-sided relationship.

Two months later and in the lead-up to Christmas, she was back in Kuta again, but this time she returned empty-handed. Then, in April 2005, came her last trip; she teamed up with another of her co-workers, Martin Stephens. She had only met him a couple of months earlier, but, like everything else in her life, Renae didn't need to be acquainted with someone for years before making a judgment on them. She either liked them or despised them — no middle ground there, either.

The young woman who had grown up in a small western suburb of Newcastle, attending the local high school and living in the area until she boarded her flight direct from Sydney to Denpasar, would soon become international news. Again it was all or nothing: Renae Lawrence, who grew up yearning to be a police officer, would end up belonging in the annals of history as a drug smuggler.

Each year in Australia, more than 50 000 divorces are granted, with about half of them involving children. Renae's mother and father joined the queue of parents whose relationships crack and then break early; according to Bob Lawrence, it was around the time their little girl became a toddler. It wasn't a benevolent parting, the way Bob explains it, and the relationship between Renae's parents remains splintered. Renae was too young to understand her parents' fraught relationship, and went to live with her mother, her father counting down the days to every second weekend, when she would come to stay. But that changed, too, when he broke his neck a couple of years later. Bob Lawrence found he couldn't care for his little charge and, without anyone to help, he gave up the precious weekends they had shared.

Almost a year passed without any regular contact between father and daughter. But once Bob had recuperated from the operation on his neck, the little girl began visiting again, every second weekend. And her visits comfortably replaced the weekend fishing and shooting trips he had liked so much.

'One day I smacked her on the back of the hand because she broke the stereo needle,' Bob recalls. 'I said, "You're not supposed to touch that!" and I smacked her ... and she cried and cried and cried. She cuddled up to me and said, "You're not supposed to smack me", and I said, "Why's that?" and she said, "You love me".'

Renae was three at the time but already she ruled the house. It was only a handful more years later when, on the brink of adolescence, Renae moved in with her father. From day one she had him wrapped around her little finger, controlling what, how and when they did things. Bob was strict — really strict — in a protective sort of way, but Renae got what she wanted most times. 'If I had a lady friend and she didn't like her, that was it,' Bob says by way of explanation. Given that, it was just as well that Renae took a shine to Bob's second wife, Jenny, from their first meeting.

All kids have a passion, and Renae's is obvious from the moment you take the lid off the olive green shoe box brimming with photos and memorabilia. 'For the best Fisher Man in the world', the card reads. 'For you dad cause you're the best and only dad anyone would want and have.' You can't miss the big fish that acts as the focus of the card, and it's not the only clue to Renae's first love. Photographs of Renae fishing dominate her teenage years; it seemed to be everything to her. She loved getting dressed to go fishing, carefully packing her rod and tackle, setting out for the adventure, and beating everyone else to the catch of the day. At the annual local junior fishing championships, she would take home the trophy on more than one occasion, even beating the boys. When Renae cast her rod into the water, the whole world stopped. She belonged.

Often Bob and Renae would set off together, rods over the shoulder, to try their luck, leaving Jenny behind. At other times Jenny would tag along. 'We'd go out weekends,' Jenny says. 'I'd go out on the boat but they'd fish all weekend.' Renae's relationship with her stepmother was good right from the time they met. Bob had taken his daughter down to the local club for a cheap dinner. Renae would tease her father about Jenny, who also clicked quickly with the tomboy by her father's side. Soon the three of them got on like wildfire, the two women in the house plotting and planning to get their own way. And they always did.

Renae loved animals, especially dogs. One day she decided she wanted a pet dog, and with Jenny onside Renae fronted her father, who was working in the family garage. He agreed, suggesting that it should be a border collie. Renae knew immediately that she had won and, minutes later, she and Jenny were back, car keys at the ready. They'd found a pedigree border collie advertised in the local newspaper — just the one Bob had wanted, they said — and it was only up the road. Misty joined the family the same afternoon.

It was that love of animals and fishing that served as the bedrock of Renae's adolescence. She spent time with both her families — her father and stepmother, and her mother and stepfather — and the small circle of friends she had made at her local high school. They were friends who understood that her passion for school started and ended with soccer and woodwork. Most of the other classes failed to capture her interest, with some people believing she battled academically along the way.

After school, and on weekends, all that was forgotten and Renae Lawrence would spend most of her time at home, rarely out of her father's sight. And that's the way Bob liked it. Although dollars were stretched and holidays not common, every now and again they would get away, and it was on one of those trips that Burubi Beach won Renae's heart. She bought a T-shirt there and wore it day in and day out, to the exclusion of all the others in her cupboard.

Cars were Renae's other passion, and from the time she could walk she could be found wedged under one of the cars her father, a motor mechanic by trade, was working on. She renewed her crush on them in her final years of school, when senior students were being prepared for the workforce. She needed to clock up some job experience hours, and before long was a regular at a local smash repairs shop. And she didn't just like it — she loved it. She would jump out of bed with a spring in her step and come home talking twenty to the dozen about all sorts of car things. After finishing school, she went back to work at the shop for a while, and by all reports was a valuable worker who colleagues labelled easily as diligent and reliable.

Turning eighteen heralds a new independence for most young people, and Renae was no different. She decided that her coming-of-age meant she now could dictate when she went out and when she returned home. Bob and Jenny Lawrence saw it very differently. Bob didn't care much whether his daughter was eight or eighteen — he worried just the same every time she stepped out of the house. She was his precious only child. Eventually he confronted his daughter, telling her that she had to abide by the laws he laid down while she was living at home — he expected her home at a reasonable hour.

Renae ignored him. She would leave the house at 8 or 9 p.m. on some nights with a group of girlfriends, not returning before 2 or 3 a.m. the next morning. And, before long, Bob Lawrence had had enough: 'I said, "No, not while you live here. I'm not going to lie at home in bed and worry about you being raped or whatever."' But it was the next sentence, delivered as much in haste as anger, that turned events so quickly. 'I told her to make sure she took everything [if she left] because she wasn't coming back. And she didn't come back.'

Within a short time, Renae was living with Tracie Sansom, her older and wiser lover and the mother of three young children. Renae quickly shut the door on her old world, cutting off all contact with Bob and Jenny. She had found a new place to belong. To outsiders, Renae and Tracie might have seemed the most unlikely of matches: a gullible teenager who had never had to fend for herself and an older woman who had experienced much more; a lonely young woman looking to belong and a mother busy with one son and two daughters of her own. Renae had never experienced a serious relationship, despite her family teasing her about the cute bloke at the smash repairs shop. But despite those odds, Renae fell desperately and fully in love with Tracie, insiders say. Tracie became her companion and lover, her mentor and teacher. And her partner in life.

Renae loved her instant family, too. She felt cared for. She fitted in, and the tribe of children who would so often fill the house with squeals and laughter made her feel important. Renae was a willing volunteer when it came to helping care for the children — she regularly offered to babysit them. And she frequently made mischief with them. The children, for their part, genuinely liked the young woman who had become such a big part of their family. They respected her, but also considered her their friend.

Life was full of fun and music and laughs, and the weeks quickly turned into months. And, before long, the months had turned into years. Renae met new friends, mainly through Tracie, and the pair of them would socialise easily, sharing a drink at the local club, sitting around Tracie's home playing music and just talking. They'd work, and look after their animals, go to parties and do the same household chores every other young couple did.

Bob and Jenny Lawrence were both pretty much forgotten after their daughter moved away, as Renae seemed determined to wipe out the years she had lived with them. That ate away at Bob. He believed he was owed the respect any father was, and that his daughter should acknowledge important events like birthdays and Christmas. But he played pretty much the same game, and never went out of his way to re-establish contact with the daughter who lived just across town and who, he now learnt, was a lesbian. He found her sexual preference pretty hard to take — not because he considered himself homophobic, but because he couldn't remember her showing any interest in females previously. He'd even gone on and on about the boy down at the smash repairs shop and she'd turned red with embarrassment, and he'd never had any reason to suspect that he would not one day have a son-in-law and possibly even a handful of grandchildren. But he'd learnt quickly — because word travels fast in a place like Wallsend — that she had shacked up with her girlfriend and started a whole new life. And it was clear that she did not want any contact with her father or stepmother.

'Jen kept saying she'd come around,' says Bob. 'I found it hard at first, and then I thought, she has her life to lead. I didn't contact her either — not while she lived with her [Tracie].'

Like so many parents, Bob and Jenny didn't like Renae's choice of partner — who wants to stay out of the public eye — and they made it pretty clear that while their daughter was welcome in their home, her friend was not. They might acknowledge that their daughter now shared a life with someone, but that didn't mean they were required to befriend the woman, or welcome her into their home. But that just served to push Renae further away.

Renae had been given a choice: her past life, where she was told what to do and when to do it; or a shiny new life in which she made her own decisions and was treated as an equal partner. It was an easy choice: Renae chose her partner, and, despite Wallsend being a small place, she severed all contact with her father and stepmother. She no longer visited Bob's parents either, and that really grated on him, as Renae was their only granddaughter. He could understand that their estrangement meant that she would no longer grace his home, but he couldn't understand why she would take that out on his parents. It showed a lack of respect, and that was not how he had brought her up.

The years came and went. So did family birthdays, anniversaries and get-togethers. Bob felt as though he'd lost his only child — but Renae was looking to the future, not the past. At least, until late 2004, when her relationship with Tracie, the basis for her future, came crashing to the ground. The break-up, friends say, meant that Renae lost her partner, her three young friends whom she saw as family, and her future.

She wanted to die. She needed to stop feeling like this. So, with no half measures, Renae Lawrence took a big handful of tablets and set off to a piece of deserted bushland up the road.

VII

Life in the Spotlight

Six months later, Renae Lawrence wanted to shut out life again. This time she was in an Indonesian police cell on suspicion of drug smuggling, crammed in her hot, stinky prison with no way out. And pills weren't so easy to access. So Renae plotted another way to end it all: she pulled the small ring off the top of a soft-drink can and then, wielding it as a blunt weapon, she set about slashing her wrists. Once. And again.

Like the time in high school when she wanted to dull the pain, and the time she tried to block out the world after her relationship breakdown, Renae couldn't fathom the way ahead. She didn't know what to do or how to do it. The pain was unbearable; the agony seeped throughout her body. She knew her future was now proscribed by a tough Indonesian legal system that wanted to crush the flourishing drug trade. It loathed traffickers and she now stood accused as one of them. She couldn't go on.

Last time she had got away with it. Last time, in October 2004 — according to information she provided early to police — she had tricked the sniffer dogs in Indonesia, sitting uncomfortably with heroin packed to her body for what seemed like a lifetime, and passed the vigilant Customs staff at Sydney's international airport. Perhaps it hadn't seemed that difficult, looking back now, but this time things had gone wrong. She and Martin Stephens had thought they'd made it, even shaking hands and congratulating themselves. But then things had turned. Someone had appeared. Everything had gone so fast, but time didn't seem to move. And now there was no way out.

So Renae Lawrence, a million miles away from Wallsend, tore the ring off the top of a soft-drink can and set about ending it all. It was her third — but would not be her last — desperate cry for help but, as in previous times, someone came to her aid. She had been saved each time, someone hearing her silent appeals for assistance.

This time it was a jail doctor able to prescribe a drug that promised to lift her mood. The black storm cloud which had hovered so ominously lifted, at least for a few weeks, then it came racing towards her again. The sadness descended with it. The desolation came back just as strongly. She was surrounded by black. Lost. Wounded. She had been set up and needed to tell the world. She was a victim.

Renae's life began to spiral out of control — really out of control — about the time her relationship broke down. She felt as though she didn't belong anywhere, and so she started the search to fit in again. She renewed contact with her father for the first time in many years. It was tentative at first, with both treading warily, but all the harsh words, accusations and counter-accusations seemed to vanish quickly. At least, on the surface. Renae told one of her friends that she felt her father was still unwilling to accept her lifestyle; that she found him harsh and uncompromising. But to Bob and Jenny she seemed to be pleased to be back on speaking terms.

They couldn't help seeing the change in her, however. She had disappeared from their lives close to a decade ago, when she was eighteen. She was now nearing thirty and so much had happened in between. She'd gone from being a child to an adult; from a thin adolescent to a stocky woman. Her clothes were different and so was her hair.

There was so much water under the bridge, on both sides. And neither Bob or Jenny — nor Renae, it seemed — wanted to travel too far down that road. Renae had stayed in contact with her mother and stepfather throughout the years and now Bob was just happy to have her back. Happiness was still eluding Renae though. She felt aimless, the only constant in her life her beloved border collie, Buffy. But even Buffy was unable to live with her after Renae was forced to bunker down with a friend.

At every turn there seemed to be a challenge for the young woman who had struggled through her childhood and adolescence. Now, with the masterful benefit of hindsight, friends and family can see that this period was a turning point in Renae's life — the hills higher than they seemed at the time, the journey more difficult than she made out. She continued to see both sides of her family and stayed in contact with her ex-lover's children, whom she continued to share an easy relationship with, even taking them out on occasion. She still worked hard too, turning up on time for her casual job at the Sydney Cricket Ground whenever she was rostered and going about it like a model employee. But no one really knew what happened during the in-between times, who she was mixing with and what she was doing. No one appeared to know what was happening inside Renae's head. No one. And so she was left to herself, although everyone who loves her now wishes that they had looked for signs — her occasional disappearances for a few days, for example. Or the clues that appeared not long before she left Australia for the last time. On one occasion she was with her father, who remembers a call she took on her mobile telephone. She sounded frightened and apprehensive, determined for him to not hear. She was trying to find excuses why she could not travel to Sydney that afternoon. Someone had been trying to force her, Bob Lawrence says. But no one suspected that she was in any real trouble.

She was, though. She was living a life destined to get her into trouble. Mixing with the wrong crowd, spending bigger chunks of time in Sydney with people her family had never met, and going about her week without any thought of what tomorrow might bring. She was in a fast-paced search to belong again — and once more it was an all-or-nothing proposition. She had to find a new place. The past was gone and she needed a future. *Now*.

Old friends lost track of Renae's movements during the months leading up to Christmas 2004, but didn't think too much about it. That was the good thing about friendship: it could be left a while and always rekindled. Renae didn't think too much of the consequences of not staying in touch, either. She was worried about today, not tomorrow. She would turn up for work and do her job, always punctual and hard-working, because that was the way she had been taught to act. But outside that she pretty much switched off, just focusing on trying to fit in.

Some of Renae's co-workers became her social circle, as she started to live life too fast. And Matthew Norman, her co-worker at the SCG, seemed to be doing the same — according, at least, to charges the pair were due to face in Australia soon after their arrest in Bali.

Police claim it was only an hour or two before dawn one morning in March 2005 — a week before the pair left for Indonesia — that Lawrence tucked herself behind the wheel of a car she did not own and, with Norman as her passenger, sped up the Pacific Highway she knew so well. She drove the highway several times a week, from Wallsend down to Sydney and back up again, and, like hundreds of commuters who did the same, she knew the stretch of road like the back of her hand. On this morning, she was feeling the need for speed and rebellion. Going too fast, according to police she ignored all police directions to stop. It wasn't the only perilous journey that Lawrence and Norman would take together.

Being told his daughter had been arrested in Bali on suspicion of carrying drugs through Bali's international airport almost stopped Bob Lawrence's heart. His daughter. Renae. In another country. Carrying drugs. The words mish-mashed around and around in his head. None of it made any sense, and the more he thought about it, the more he considered it not possible. Of course they had the wrong girl — Renae had never even been on a plane. Never been outside her home state of New South Wales, let alone in a foreign country. And she was broke, stony-broke. Bob knew that because her car had packed it in only weeks earlier and he had worried when she fell into a depression afterwards. She could not believe that something else was now going wrong in her life. First the relationship she depended on, and now the car she depended on. Her ticket to freedom, her transport to Sydney — she needed the car to get to work at the Sydney Cricket Ground. She was spending more and more time in Sydney and the car had safely transported her there time and time again. So she couldn't just go without it.

Renae called Bob, wondering what she could do. She understood cars, and knew her father did too, and they both knew it would cost dearly to put her vehicle back on the road. Certainly, there wouldn't be much change out of $800, if they were lucky. Renae didn't have a clue where she'd get that sort of money, and told her father exactly that.

Bob knew he could fix the car, but he didn't want Renae totally off the hook either. He believed in taking responsibility — all children should. She had to stand on her own two feet and take care of her own bills. He thought they might be able to fix it together, a bit like old times when the pair of them would muck about in the back yard pulling a car apart and putting it back together over and over. So he did a deal with his only daughter, who had recently come back into his life. He would help out, he told her — even give her a loan — and he would fix the car. Renae was genuinely grateful; her smile was his reward. Their relationship was being rebuilt, from the ground up, and in recent weeks she had felt able to pick up the phone and talk to her father. She promised she would pay him back, and they settled on the sum of $150. Renae said she'd need a couple of weeks to get that amount together; Bob understood that. And that's where they left it.

A couple of weeks passed, and Bob did not hear from his only daughter. He put in a call, and her phone went unanswered. So he left a message, asking her to call him back when she got a chance. And he waited for the phone to ring. It didn't, and Bob and Jenny wondered why. Things had been going so well. After they'd initially re-established contact, there had been a brief period when both of them could be a bit standoffish, but that had all passed now. Renae was dropping around, giving them a call, and asking for his advice.

A bit more time passed, and still Bob didn't hear back from his daughter. He wasn't chasing the money she owed him — he just wanted to make sure she was fine, that things were okay, and it didn't fit that she'd re-established contact and now disappeared again.

Then he received the phone call that would irrevocably change his life, the life of his daughter and everyone else in her family for ever. 'I didn't even know she was out of the country,' he says. 'I was devastated. I couldn't believe it.'

Back in her new Indonesian home, a jail she shares with bombers, pimps and prostitutes, Renae Lawrence desperately misses her family: her mother and father; her step-parents and stepbrother. She tells anyone who visits to pass on her messages of love. She writes them cards and sends letters. She wants to fit back in to her old life; she wants to belong back in Wallsend. But she can't, this time, and to survive she wears the armoury of a victim, even taking to the women's holding cell wall with a crayon pleading her case. 'Bali Four. 8.3 kg of heroin 2005. Innocent Victims' the message reads. That's matched by her other accusations: that the so-called Bali Four (Lawrence, Stephens, Rush and Czugaj) were pawns in a system. Duped by others. Tricked by Andrew Chan. Conned into the trip. Fooled.

Renae's attempts to take her own life are the sad and genuine cries of a young woman who needs to be heard; a young woman who struggled from early on to belong, to fit in, to find a place where she was the centre, despite both her parents loving her dearly. And when the sadness and fear descend on her, she hits out. Mainly at herself, rarely at others. That was what she was doing when she took her father's pills in high school. And again when her relationship faltered. That was what she was doing when she took to her wrists with the top of a soft-drink can, and that was what she was doing in the lead-up to her trial when she fractured her wrist, slamming her fist into the whitewashed concrete wall of her jail cell. She was crying out for help, for someone to take notice.

Taken to hospital, a fat and news-hungry media contingent in close pursuit, Renae gained more control: the attention of medical staff and the flash of cameras were handled with ease. They had chased the black storm cloud away.

Renae is smarter than she sometimes comes across. She is quick-witted and upfront — and very funny. Pleading for a feed from McDonald's recently, she told a visitor to the jail that she had contemplated skipping down to the local franchise herself, but feared it might not be met with approval. Her distaste for rice has her talking about McDonald's with anyone who will listen, and she even told waiting media her plan to ask the driver ferrying her to jail to go via the restaurant's drive-through window.

Her fairly new and close alliance with co-worker and co-accused Martin Stephens has given Renae a sense of belonging, at least for the time being. She feels less lost with Martin around. He has become her friend and protector, even giving up his meal to make her happy. They spend long and lonely hours together, Stephens not fully winning the battle to coax her into praying to God.

Together they've stood firmly, claiming they were tiny pawns in a big international drug-smuggling operation from the moment their secret words were captured on surveillance tape and played the world over. It's a mantra they've repeated at every opportunity since, along with some of their fellow travellers: they had no choice; they were forced to load themselves up with heroin — in Renae's case not once, but twice — and try to make it back through Sydney Airport on the promise of a wad of cash. Cash or no cash, they say, their families would pay with their lives if they reneged.

Trapped in a jail cell, contemplating a frightening death at the hands of an Indonesian law which does not treat drug traffickers with benevolence, Lawrence and Stephens are sticking together. She thinks she does not belong here, she knows she doesn't fit in. Neither does her new best friend, Martin. Nor the Brisbane boys she first met in the interrogation room after her arrest. Scott Rush and Michael Czugaj were part of the same evil plan of others. As was Matthew Norman, Renae's Sydney co-worker, who, only a couple of weeks earlier, was with her as she was screaming up the Pacific Highway, police in pursuit, and to those on the outside, not a care in the world.

VIII

From Illawarra to Denpasar

Martin Stephens's face filled the television screen as Renae Lawrence warned him, in conspiratorial tones, against co-operating. The two twentysomething workmates from Sydney didn't look like they were acting any more. With their disguises gone, their faces were drained of colour. It was a rare event, Stephens taking centre stage as he now did in the surveillance tape being aired across the globe. Mainly he seemed to always blend into the background. At least, that's how some people remember him. That's how it was in school, and at work, and in life generally.

Stephens lost contact with many of his fellow students at Corrimal High after his class graduated in the early 1990s, the born-and-bred Illawarra boy setting out on his own path in life just like the rest of the region's school-leavers.

It was an interesting time to be a young person stepping out into the world: Paul Keating had led the ALP to its fifth consecutive election victory; Bill Clinton had been inaugurated as the president of the United States, and a young Tony Blair had been elected to lead his party in the United Kingdom. The complexities of native title were being dissected in barbecue discussions; *Jurassic Park* and *Schindler's List* were big hits at the cinema, and Mariah Carey's 'Music Box', Bon Jovi's 'Always' and Bryan Adams's 'Please Forgive Me' were topping the ARIA charts.

Sydney was not yet claiming Wollongong as a dormitory suburb, although the big restructure of the steel industry would soon make that the case. Jobs were disappearing in the township, and its local economy was embarking on a brave transition. Boys at Corrimal High and the other schools in the area could no longer expect to blindly follow their fathers into the steel mills, as they had their fathers before them.

Across the small community and against that background, Martin Stephens's class spread like ripples in a pond. Some, like other teenagers the length and breadth of Australia, packed their bags and set off overseas to ponder how they would spend the rest of their lives. Some travelled through Europe, others through Africa, Canada and the United Kingdom, but almost all sent back regular updates of their travel tales. Others still, keen to make their mark, went straight to the big smoke, enrolling at one of Sydney's universities; one classmate eventually embarked on an honours program she would proudly complete in a decade. Some looked hard and won jobs in education, childcare, banking and tourism. Two tried the army. Many married over the next seven or eight years; some had children immediately, while others are still planning their families now. Not much differentiated this group of young school-leavers from any other. It could have been any class in any town in any state of Australia. But it wasn't: it was Corrimal High, where Martin Stephens was a student.

Martin never seemed as driven as some of his classmates, and many of them lost contact with him soon after the final bell heralded the start of their adult life. Tales of his school-yard years are marked more by him being unspectacular than anything else. Some classmates say he was known by his nickname, the same title given by mates to his brother before him: Vegie. That's all — no surname. Just Vegie. No one really remembers why he or his brother earnt the name originally, but it seemed to suit him and stuck almost immediately; one classmate was unaware of his real name before his arrest in April 2005.

The nickname wasn't meant in any nasty way, because most people remember Martin Stephens as fairly innocuous. Stephens says the name 'Vegie' had come from the Happy Little Vegemites song, but he says while some people tried to label him 'Junior Vegie', the name didn't really stick. His mother, Michele, also expresses surprise that some people had adopted the same nickname for her second-born as they had for Martin's older brother.

Perhaps they used it more behind his back than in front of him, and perhaps it was just a particular group that did, but either way Stephens was neither the best student, nor was he the worst. He wasn't loud, however if he felt comfortable, he certainly wasn't quiet. He wasn't the class clown, but nor did he shun a joke. That was Vegie, from primary school right through to high school.

'He was quiet, polite and nonoffensive,' remembers one young woman who shared a class with him through high school. 'He was left alone, never in any fights or in anything really ... just one of those kids who blended into the background.' And the last person tackled in the game of British bulldog too, she adds. That stuck in her mind — he stood out that day because he was the last person tackled in British bulldog.

Most days, though, Martin wasn't the last. Or the first. Classmates say he didn't hold a seat in the popular and cliquey school-yard crowd; neither did he seek one out. That just wasn't him. Stephens would come to school each morning and leave each afternoon, without offending anyone or leaving too much of a lasting impression. He was laid-back, but that didn't mean he always went along with things. And he could certainly fire up quickly if someone tried to pick on him.

'He pretty much kept to himself,' one friend, who was Stephens's classmate from day one to graduation, said. 'He had a little group of friends in high school, maybe three or four friends, and they pretty much stayed away from everyone else and did their own thing. He was quiet, but if someone picked on him, he liked to have a fight about it.'

Still another describes him this way: 'He was kind of a geek — not in a brainy way — but he never had a bad thing to say about anyone. He would talk to everyone and, even though he was never part of the popular crowd, I think he was well liked by most.'

Most people agree with that assessment: polite, courteous, fairly harmless. And they all agree that Stephens had a trademark naivety, and, as far as personality traits go, that one stood out. It was the first thing that came to mind when the telephone calls and email exchanges flooded computer in-trays upon his arrest.

'To all of us it seems so obvious that you're going to get caught that we can't comprehend how you'd have to be so stupid to do it, and then when they said it was Vegie ... we all went, "Well, there was one person in the year who was gullible enough to get roped into it",' one former classmate explains. And it's not said in a judgmental way — just as a statement of fact. Out of all of them, Martin Stephens could have been lured into it.

Of course, everyone sees others through slightly different glasses, and Stephens's parents should know him best. Michele says she never heard him called Vegie; that nickname had belonged to his brother. And she is aghast at claims her boy was the kind of bland person who blended into the background or who took a back seat in life. That's not her experience or memory of Martin as a little boy, at school or even now. Michele remembers Martin with a big group of friends, many of them not from his own school, but from other schools — which might explain the differences in how people characterise the young man now sitting in a Bali jail.

'Martin was always a fun, outgoing guy, he never blended into the background,' says Michele. 'I don't ever remember Martin being quiet; he certainly wasn't shy in coming forward. He has never been backstage, he has always had plenty of friends. He wasn't like an in-your-face sort of person. If you saw Martin in a group you would remember him. He would be funny, he might be slightly cheeky.'

Michele says her son would readily take centre stage on the dance floor where he was somewhat of a whiz, with girls lining up for the next dance. But she agrees with assessments that her son was a bit on the naive side.

'He has always been naive, everyone has always been his best friend. He always believed the best about somebody. He was willing to believe the best of people.'

After Martin's friends saw his face on the television after his arrest they were on the phone to the Stephens home in shock and disbelief. They wanted someone to tell them it was all an mistake. Drugs were just not Martin's thing.

Martin Stephens was born in Wollongong on 13 April 1976, to Bill and Michele, and his home remained at Towradgi, the small beachside suburb 5 kilometres north of the Wollongong CBD. His childhood was busy and his parents were supportive; sport took centre stage. Martin was a Towradgi Turtle junior lifesaver (from under-sixes to under-twelves, where his mother was president for about five years) and a Corrimal Cougar footballer (from under-sevens to under-elevens), and he would put up his hand for the chance to have a go at most sports. He also tried his hand at ballroom dancing, proving to be talented at that too, winning medals for both the cha-cha and the jive.

Martin played up like most teenagers, but his parents never worried about the path he would take in the long term. When he returned to Wollongong in 2004 after working for a catering company in Adelaide, they were thrilled to have him home again. He'd been gone for a couple of years, since 2002, and even brought home a steady girlfriend whom he planned to marry.

He'd started off working in a carpentry place in Unanderra making furniture, but he was to soon learn that hospitality, working in bars and clubs, was his true vocation — he loved it. He felt he had a knack with people and loved going to work at the various hospitality jobs he had over the years. 'I could spill a drink on someone and have them thinking happy thoughts when I left. To me, it's not a job,' Martin says now. He loved the fact that while working, doing things like cleaning the ashtrays in bars, he got to mingle with patrons and meet new people, chat and joke around. He couldn't ask for more in a job, he thought. He was good at doing the cocktail tricks too.

Stephens did a hospitality course and got the chance to work at the Royal Easter Show and the 2000 Olympics at Homebush in Sydney, as well as at a couple of other bars in Sydney. Hospitality gave him the chance to work in different places and travel. He went to Queensland for a while, to Adelaide and to Uluru.

It was in Adelaide that he first started working for Eurest, the company where he would end up meeting the people with whom he now shares the same fate and same jail. And it was in Adelaide that he met the young woman he thought he would marry. For a time he even managed a strip club there, until his female boss sold the place.

By late 2004, Stephens had been away from Wollongong for four years and it was time to go home; his fiancée went with him. Eurest had said they would give him a job in Sydney, so he made his way home. 'That's when my life turned upside down,' he says now. For it was while working in Sydney that Stephens met Andrew Chan.

As the curtain opened on 2005, Stepehens was working at the Sydney Cricket Ground. He worked a bit in Wollongong, too, because of the seasonal slowing at his casual job in Sydney. Bill and Michele Stephens, who had married as teenagers, didn't know everything about his life, but they liked the young man their son seemed to have become. They would sometimes join him for a beer down at the club, and were proud he would get up at 2 a.m. to catch a train to Sydney to be at work by 5 a.m. He had respect for others, and he was courteous and kind. He drank, but not to excess. His partner was a credit to him. And he seemed to enjoy life. There's not much more a parent can ask for.

Along with his trademark naivety, generosity seems to be a second hallmark of Martin Stephens's personality. One friend stricken with a serious kidney disease relied on him.

Andrew Albornoz first met Marty — as he called him — when he was fourteen. They went to different schools, but a chance meeting in the bush, where Andrew was camping and Martin was bushwalking, saw the beginning of a friendship that both knew would last for life. On weekends, together with their group of friends, the pair would don camouflage gear and play commandos in the bush. They were teenage boys, full of the bravado of adolescence, mucking about at pretend war games.

Andrew remains shocked at Stephens's arrest. He says it is so totally out of character for his best mate and the man he thinks of more as a brother. Diagnosed at three with kidney failure, doctors told Andrew he would be on a dialysis machine by the time he was sixteen. When it happened, Martin was there for him. On nights when Andrew struggled and most young people were out enjoying themselves, Martin proved to be a salvation for Andrew, passing up a night out to spend it with his mate, chatting, watching videos and keeping him company. He was part of the Albornoz family.

'He had no hesitation at all, he just wanted to help me out, that's what kind of bloke he was,' Andrew remembers. 'He is just warm and big-hearted. He wouldn't harm a fly. He has done so much for me, I don't know how I could repay him.'

It was Stephens who introduced Andrew to his fiancée, Kirsty Cockayne, six years ago. The pair planned to marry this year with Martin as their best man, but plans for the wedding are on hold until they find out their friend's fate.

Kirsty cries when she thinks of what will become of Stephens. She vividly remembers the period before the Bali Nine's arrest: Stephens seemed to have gone quiet; they couldn't get hold of him on the phone. Finally they found out that he had gone to Darwin and didn't think much more of it until 17 April. That's when the questions started and shock set in.

People are willing to come out of the woodwork with other stories of Stephen's generosity. A schoolmate remembers the party in senior year when he had far too much to drink — Martin, whom he had never been too pally with, carried him to the bathroom and cleaned him up. He hadn't asked him to; he just did it. Guards in the jail Stephens now calls home think the same: he's a gentleman, caught smuggling heroin out of Indonesia.

Like most parents, Bill and Michele adored their boy from the day he was born. And it's a feeling that is returned in spades. He cries sometimes now when reading a letter from his mother, and tells people that the worst moment in life was not his arrest on drug-smuggling charges, nor being thrown in jail, nor even fronting court in a strange country. Not even the spectre of the death sentence plays in Stephens's head as the worst part of this whole ordeal. The single worst moment in Martin Stephens's life was the instant he saw his mother's face, and his father's face, on their first trip to his Bali holding cell to see him. It was their thirty-second wedding anniversary and he thought he had broken their hearts. He never wants to relive that moment; playing it over in his mind is bad enough.

He wishes like hell he wasn't there, especially because of his parents, and he worries about how he has caused this unhappiness for them and whether they will cope. He worries about them getting older and spending their hard-earnt money visiting him in jail. He hates that, and he knows life will only get harder from here on. But at least he has God now. He always believed in Him, but, like so many others, in his own way. He didn't regularly turn up as a churchgoer, but he considered himself a Christian and liked to think he pretty much lived life that way. Now, in the long hours between dawn and dusk, and the long nights when the sounds of Bali permeate his jail cell, he prays, reading the Bible and searching for a way ahead. He wants the burden to be lifted from his parents' shoulders. The woman he loved and whom he was planning to spend his life with has now gone her own way, though they are still friends. She is young and it would be unconceivable to expect that she should wait so long for him. And he prays for his co-worker Renae Lawrence, who shares the same jail. He knows that Lawrence has come to rely on him, perhaps even to survive on him, some days, and he has a mission now. He must protect her. So he listens to her. Spends big chunks of his day with her. He likes her, thinks she's funny, but he also watches out for her and everyone knows that. The pair hated each other during those early days in Bali, before they were nabbed, but now Lawrence is his 'sister and best friend'.

This doesn't surprise people who have met Martin: his soft personality is obvious even to those who deal with him in jail.

Bill and Michele Stephens are proud of that, the way he was brought up. That's why they never thought that they had any reason to worry about where he was heading in life. Along the way he'd run off the rails a couple of times, which was fairly normal. But they had been happy with the big picture. So when he went off for a short spell in April 2005 — on a trip to deliver furniture to Darwin, his parents thought — none of his family or friends thought any more about it. That is, until they turned on the television news and saw his face fill the screen.

IX

The Quakers Hill Boy

Matthew Norman and his best mates at Quakers Hill High School in Sydney's west would have the girls in stitches over their juvenile Jackass hijinks. The antics made famous by the MTV prankster series would be played out in the school playground, or on the weekend, or at any other time, as long as there was an audience. Of course, Matthew and his friends didn't always have the props to deliver the same level of puerile pranks made famous by the real Jackass stars, but their show was just as funny. And it didn't need department stores or golfing greens or international travel to make it funny. It was never cruel, either — just a few dumb stunts and a dose of good-natured fun to pass the time. They developed a bit of a following over it, and as long as there were witnesses, Matthew and his mates were happy to perform.

Matthew's friends came from two different years at the local high school, with a big casual group of girls and boys mixing easily. Everyone pretty much got on, and were open to new people joining in. A few of the girls thought Matthew was a pretty good catch. He was open and funny, easy to talk to, and he seemed really genuine. But he only had eyes for one young teenager, Jess, and her friends thought she was pretty lucky. They also thought that Matthew spoilt her rotten.

'I keep thinking of the way he treated his girlfriend and how caring he was towards her,' one of Jess's friends says now.

Matthew would buy Jess presents, sit and talk to her during recess like she was the only person in the world, and he even planned to take her up to the NSW Central Coast to live when they were a bit older. Jess was a year younger than Matthew, and her friends liked him from the start, and looked up to him. In a way, that's what brought the two school years together.

Jess's friends thought Matthew Norman was gregarious, but he wasn't loud. And he didn't get embarrassed talking to the girls. Some of the other boys did, and that was a real turn-off. But Matthew was great for a laugh.

Like most of his mates, Norman didn't rate school too highly, or take it too seriously, and English, especially, was well down the list. He didn't read much, but he knew what was going on. Sport, on the other hand, made turning up each day well worth the effort. He loved sport — any kind — and now, sitting in an Indonesian jail cell, he still misses it madly. So much so that the first sentence he uttered to a group of waiting media late last year was a plea for them to find out the score in rugby union's Bledisloe Cup.

At school, Matthew liked recess too — the time when they would all sit around and have a laugh. Whether it was fake fights he staged with his friends, or other *Jackass*-inspired stunts he and his mates would play, Matthew always looked like he was having a ball. He rarely talked about his home life; no one really asked and he never really offered much. So few, including many of his and Jess's good friends, knew of the enormous upheaval and drama that had characterised his early years.

* * *

Matthew Norman was born in Westmead in Sydney just after his twin, Cheryl, in September 1986 and life was a minor struggle from the start. Born weeks premature, the twins endured some early scares and a prolonged hospital stay before joining their mother, Robyn Davis, and their father, Michael Norman, in their Quakers Hill home. The couple already had one little girl, and the twins were a welcome addition to their family.

However, things turned sour for the couple, who had married only a few years earlier, and within a few more years they separated, with Davis and all three children initially moving out of their home. That's when things went from bad to worse — and they kept moving in that direction.

Michael Norman didn't see his children for huge blocks of time that stretched into years. The bitter and acrimonious separation was coloured by nasty accusations, claims and counter-claims, legal accusations and Family Court involvement, before all three children came to live full time with their father.

The effect of that period on Michael Norman remains. 'I ended up with the children, but it cost me a lot of money. About $80 000 I lost,' he says, along with all respect for a court process that is supposed to determine the best outcome for the children of a broken marriage.

The impact on the children, being the subject of such a nasty and prolonged fight, must also have been great, and Michael admits that behavioural problems dominated their early time together. 'They [the children] were sort of immature for their age . . . because of what they'd been through. They didn't know how to make decisions for themselves and they didn't know how to handle things. They used to have tantrums and this sort of thing.'

Robyn Davis now lives in Port Macquarie on the NSW north coast, and she deflects all public interest in her family. She stays in contact with all her children, and frequently sings Matthew's praises to those who will listen. She has told people of how Matthew helped her when she was sick a few years back, and undertook repairs on her home. He was a good son, even becoming a member of the Salvation Army when he was younger.

Michael Norman found looking after three young children a full-on task, especially when he was also trying to hold down a full-time job. He took long-service leave for several months, and tried to get to know them all over again. The children were still a few years off becoming teenagers, and they had to learn who their father was again too. Some days were tough; others almost impossible. Matthew could be hesitant, withdrawn sometimes, and didn't always trust people easily. But other days were action-packed with fun, and as time went on, the fun ones dominated.

Michael, his two daughters and son would go on family outings and share all the household chores, even the cooking. That was, until his daughters thought his kitchen creations weren't quite as good as their own, and Michael escaped that task from then on. So did Matthew, who burnt almost everything he set about to cook — none of them really sure whether or not it was intentional.

Time passed quickly as the children raced through upper primary school and into high school. Matthew never stood out in any bad way. He was a respectful child, built his spare time around the sport he played, and was a fairly accommodating brother to his sisters. After the initial settling-in period, the three children gave Michael only rare moments of worry. Indeed, the pivotal moments in their teenage years proved to Michael that they had been brought up to know what was right and what was wrong. And they would never be involved in taking drugs.

* * *

When Matthew was just fourteen, a friend's mother almost died of a drug overdose. It was a terrible thing for a young teenager to witness, Michael Norman says: 'Matthew and this other guy saved this woman's life. That's where Matthew got introduced to hard drugs, and from that day he's had nothing to do with drugs.' Michael's trust in his son is absolute. He says he can read him like a book, and knows when he is telling the truth. For that reason, the controversy surrounding Matthew's friendship with Leif Ibrahim, the young man who sold the ecstasy tablet that killed Sydney teenager Danielle Chalon — a revelation outed in the media as Norman sat in his Indonesian jail cell — riles Michael. Sure, he says, his son had struck up a friendship with Ibrahim, whom he had also met several times. That's what children do at school — mix with other boys. But that friendship died ages ago, he says, with Matthew not having seen Ibrahim for more than eighteen months.

Matthew and Michael seemed to share a similar relationship to most other fathers and sons, with ups and downs usually generated by household budgets, curfews and meeting family obligations. Michael met many of Matthew's friends as he passed through his teenage years, eventually moving out to live with friends. But he still had a room in the Quakers Hill home his father shared with his two sisters, and he would pop home at least twice a week. They would all look forward to that. But sometimes that, too, would be a bone of contention, when Matthew would use the home phone to dial up a costly phone bill. Early in 2005 Michael had to chip his son over his phone use. Matthew was spending between $60 and $100 a month, and while he did contribute to the phone bill, he didn't pay rent for any of the times he crashed there, and that was far too much money being wasted. Michael Norman told him so — all youths need to take responsibility.

It was another phone call, though, that shook Michael, his ex-wife and their daughters to the core. Michael was out at a first-aid course in Parramatta, in Sydney's west, when his daughter Cheryl took the call. She gave her father the message late that day, soon after he arrived home: someone from the government was trying to contact him. Michael thought it related to a query over child support. Things relating to custody and children seemed to drag on for years and years, and he had no reason to suspect the call would be for any other reason. Certainly, in his wildest dreams, he would not have thought that the call would tell him that his son had been arrested in Bali with eight other young Australians, three of them his co-workers. None of that made sense. He knew Matthew better than that. He also knew one of his co-accused, the young woman by the name of Renae Lawrence. She had even been to his house once.

It was on a Sunday, around Christmas time, and Michael and his daughters were heading out for the day. They'd packed the car and were ready to take off when Renae fronted. She had come around to look for a bag that belonged to her; she thought it might be in Matthew's room. Michael Norman walked her up the stairs to check whether any bag had been left there. He remembers how boyish she looked, and how he really had thought, at first, that she was a man.

At the top of the stairs, Renae looked around but couldn't find the bag, then left. And Michael Norman didn't see Renae Lawrence again until her face filled the same television news bulletin as his son's. Both of them, along with a handful of others, had been arrested in Bali on serious drug charges. Michael had also heard of one of the other young lads, but that was all. Even though Matthew worked with three of them, most of their names did not ring a bell. Certainly, with the exception of Renae, they'd never been to his house. Something just didn't add up.

X

The Brisbane Connection

When the 10.46 p.m. train from Graceville slides into Chelmer station on time, the young bloke hanging onto the back is met with the drunken applause of his mates drinking nearby. Others are focused on the middle of the train as a lad appears from nowhere, deftly using his spray can to sign his moniker on one of the carriages, before the train chugs off towards Indooroopilly and beyond. Others are too lazy for the short journey to the platform, knowing that, if they want, their turn will come later. A train runs between the two Brisbane suburbs pretty much every thirty minutes until 1.16 a.m. on this night, and there's plenty of time to go for a B-ride — back-ride — or use the spray cans hidden nearby to put their tag on a train.

It's Friday night and Scott Rush, Michael Czugaj and a gang of other youths are drinking and smoking in a little park snuggled in under the Walter Taylor Bridge in Indooroopilly, in Brisbane's west. Not everyone in the group of twenty or so knows each other, but that doesn't matter. Not everyone is drinking, either, but certainly most are. Nor is everyone smoking, but groups of them are passing around a joint. Everyone knows someone in this big, broad group of teenagers, almost all boys, from some of Brisbane's best schools. There's a couple from Marist Brothers Ashgrove and Marist Brothers Rosalie. St Lawrence's is in there too, and Kenmore State High School, Corinda State High School. And other schools, either based in the local area or a quick train ride away. But, without uniforms, there's not much to identify what school most of the young lads attend during the week. That's not important here, anyway, where school books are forgotten and people's school identities along with them.

The ages of the boys sitting around run from fourteen or so to seventeen, although you can't rule out someone a bit younger or older sneaking in. No one stands out on these nights and everyone is dressed in similar gear. Tracksuit pants, polo shirts, runners and the odd hat are the uniform of choice. But the few girls who dot the circle of teenagers certainly stand out. Tonight there's only a couple of them, and they are wearing short skirts and body-hugging tops. They seem to want the attention the boys don't. But the boys aren't entirely aimless — the school week ended six hours ago, and most of them planned to drink until they were drunk and school was a hazy memory. They looked forward to having a laugh. Perhaps sharing in the joint that would be passed around. Maybe even kiss one of the girls, if they were really lucky.

The group had met a few hours earlier, as they often did on a Friday or Saturday night — sometimes both — outside the neon-lit convenience store not far from the railway station at Indooroopilly. That was always the deal, and they'd reiterate it to each other at the bus stop each Friday after school. Meet there, not too early: sometime after 7 p.m. Then they'd decide what they needed to buy and who would buy it. And then, where to head to. But it usually came down to a choice of two places: the small, dimly lit park sandwiched between McDonald's and the Indooroopilly shopping centre, or the park they were sitting in now, just over the bridge and between the big white pillars that allowed them to practise their graffiti, or get lucky with a girl.

On this night they'd actually started at the park on the other side, near the shopping centre. Laden with supplies they'd either pilfered from their parents' liquor cabinets or conned someone older into buying or been brash enough to buy themselves, they'd dawdled down the street, around the corner and into the park bordered by the imposing centre.

The red and yellow lights of McDonald's framed the other side of the park. They'd often drop by there, sometimes to grab a bite to eat and sometimes to hide from police after complaints from passers-by. The manicured greens of the local bowls club sat on the other side of McDonald's. But tonight they'd settled early in the middle of the park, on the grass, and opened their beers. Others lit a joint. Some claimed to have popped a pill or two, but most didn't. And all of them toasted the end of the school week, and the beginning of another weekend.

Scott Rush's family lived only a hop, step and jump away in the well-to-do suburb of Chelmer, in a leafy street that played T-junction with the river. The Rush home was not one of those with a Prado or BMW parked outside, but it was neat and tidy, and had been home to Scott and his brothers for a long time. Scott was born in December 1985, the third child for Christine, a teacher, and Lee, who worked for Telstra. Christine and Lee were nice folk and they took pride in themselves, and the home in which they'd raised their children.

Scott went to the upmarket Marist Brothers college in Rosalie, where he played in the rugby union team. He was toned and athletic and very good-looking.

Michael Czugaj had gone to the same school, but now was at Corinda State High School, part of an effort by his mother and father to stop him playing truant. They'd tried most other things, so changing schools was the next step. Michael, or Mikey to his family, lived with his father and a handful of brothers and sisters a little further away from the Rush family, in the working-class suburb of Oxley. He and Scott weren't good friends, but they had sport in common — like so many others there — and on nights like this, that was enough.

Scott Rush passed a beer down the chain of hands to one of the others, a student at Marist Brothers Ashgrove. The two didn't know each other well, although they had their Friday and Saturday nights in common. So handing over a beer was a pretty generous gesture — but that was the thing about Scott, who had at least two girls vying for his attention at this time. Scott could be generous to a fault — until you crossed him. Then he could turn on you. And few wanted that to happen. He was muscly, and fast; stocky, really. And he wouldn't back away from a fight.

As the night wore on, and the alcohol numbed memories of a school week during which many of them felt out of place or alienated, some of the group would get up to their regular weekly tricks. They might pick up a few sticks and venture the short distance to the bowling green, where they'd set about trashing the lawns, vandalising the club and breaking windows. They knew that the club's managers would be hard at work before the school bell rang out on Monday morning, fixing it up.

It had become a bit of a game over the past few months. The gang of youths would wreak havoc, ripping up the lawns, kicking in walls and even painting graffiti on the roof. By the next week, though, the lawns would be once again manicured to within an inch of their lives; the broken glass would be fixed, and the roof no longer host to their amateur artwork. They'd consider that a challenge, and the very next week they'd set about wreaking the same havoc, determined not to blink first. It was the same with Queensland Rail. The government authority would get rid of the graffiti straightaway, and that would just spur the boys on even more.

On the way back from the bowling green to their mates who'd remained drinking in the park, the youths would throw a few rocks, causing a bit of trouble for passing motorists, or even try to break into a car or two. No one can remember Scott joining in a lot of that mischief though. He would just sit quietly, having a drink on some occasions, holding court on others. He certainly had an air of authority about him; he was charming, but in an aloof sort of way.

Stealing was part of the scene, and you could tell who had souvenired their clothes by the gaping holes near the neck, caused by the security tags being ripped off. Getting spare change out of cars also helped finance some of their drinking and dope binges. The Indooroopilly and Chelmer train stations acted as honeypots to those workers who drove as far as the western suburbs before commuting into their jobs in the city. And on a Friday night there were plenty of cars not expecting their owners back for hours, just as there were on a Saturday night when the local cinemas attracted a good crowd.

Some of the boys would take their shirts off, wrap them around their hands, smash a car window and rifle through the glovebox. It was a low-grade break-in, with most unable even to pick a lock, but it always seemed to net something worthwhile.

However, it certainly wasn't as lucrative as stealing mobile phones, which could net some serious cash, as some of the group could attest. It seemed everyone at school now boasted the latest model, and to swipe one and sell it for $150 was no big deal. No one got much more or less for a phone. That was the going price, as one of the guys who worked at the local cinema had revealed. With access to the lost and found boxes, he had a really good deal. Each session would result in some patrons leaving behind their mobile phones. He would record the finds, and put the phones in lost property — but not before phoning his friends and providing detailed descriptions of the handsets. One by one, other lads would turn up, explain to the manager that they had left their mobile phone behind, describe it and walk away. For a while, that group budgeted on finding and selling two phones a day. That was $300 each day — and the racket went on for weeks.

As Friday night wore on, and lights in the homes around the parks were turned off, the boys would discard their mess of empty bottles and cigarette packets, gather up what remained, and head off on foot for the short walk across Walter Taylor Bridge. The park under the bridge was even more dingy, and unless the residents of the houses just nearby called the police, the group would pretty much be able to run amok. That's where some of them would go for a B-ride on a train heading to the next suburb or Graceville. While the trip took only a minute or so, it got the adrenaline flowing, particularly on a bellyful of beers.

It was important to concentrate, because the train worked up a pace; by the time they alighted at Graceville station, their knuckles were a deathly white. But they'd be keen not to miss the return ride back to their open beer at Chelmer. So they'd wait until the guard was looking the other way and jump back onto the end of the train, pulling into Chelmer station to accept the applause of their mates. It was worth the risk, showing off that way. And it filled in time.

The graffiti gang got the same buzz practising its art on the trains heading from Chelmer into the city. No one seemed to boast too much talent, but that didn't stop them giving each other tag names and seeing who could own what carriages. They called the gang BDR, after 'Bring Da Ruckus', a song made famous by the Wu-Tang Clan, a rap group which helped move hip-hop from inside the clubs to the street corners of New York. The name suited this crowd of schoolboys who were struggling to find their way ahead, and whose parents paid thousands of dollars each year for a good private education, but who would spend their Friday and Saturday nights looking to belong.

For the most part, the trouble the group caused was along the lines of small-time break-ins, a bit of vandalism and the odd bin set alight. And, certainly, it was aimed more at filling in time than hurting anyone. But the odd fight would occur. Sometimes, after a joint or two, Michael would hit out at those he knew. One night he was sitting down, sharing a bong with two other boys, when he asked whether he'd had one or two cones. When neither of the other two boys could answer, he grabbed one of their hats, threw it to the ground and tried to pick a fight. And then, just as quickly, it was over, and he apologised.

Many of them were into a bit of showing off, too. One week, a small breakaway group decided to end their boredom by forming the 'goon kings', a small clique of drunk boys who would buy a cask of wine each, wear the cardboard on their head, the goon on their belts, and walk around the nearby shopping centre. The more people laughed, the more they enjoyed it.

Sometimes, though, it could get a bit reckless, especially if Monday was a public holiday and they decided to meet on a Sunday night when movie marathons swelled the number of people pouring into the shopping centre. On those nights, up to forty teenagers might gather in the group, and that's when things could get out of hand. On a dare, some would walk over the rails between the wooden planks on the train tracks, knowing that there was no easy escape if they had misjudged the timetable. On another night, a couple of smart alecks decided to set fire to a shading cloth that covered part of the park adjoining the bridge. A lightning rod for other disaffected youths, more joined in and soon bins were being set alight, trees pulled out and fights started. The police arrived quickly that night, but not quite quickly enough: the youths disappeared into the night. Those caught had their names taken, but they didn't hear anything more from the police.

Perhaps more through luck than good fortune for those concerned, police were not around on the night one of the boys brought along his older brother in a souped-up car. The older boy opened the car boot, proudly pulling out a gun, before running around the park pointing the weapon indiscriminately at others.

'I remember this one guy who was absolutely pissed,' one of the youths who attended that night said, 'and he went up to one of the guys holding the gun and put it in his mouth and said "Shoot my brains out. I'm that pissed". They said it was unloaded, but I'm sure they never really checked whether it was or not.'

While older youths dropped by now and again, these Friday and Saturday nights were usually the domain of the high-schoolers. When the older youths did arrive, it was usually because they were up to no good. They'd pull up in their shiny cars, revving their engines, before one or two of them would venture down into the darkness to do a quick drug deal. And then they'd be off again, and few would remember them being there.

There was another group of older youths whom it was good for the younger teenagers to stay away from. They were all in their twenties, and had met at school. One night, one of the regulars had $1100 in his pocket. This older group arrived and fronted him, accusing him of moving in on some of their territory. They said he was becoming too successful, and as punishment they took him aside, bashed him, and walked away with his hat and his shoes.

On occasion, if someone was desperate for a marijuana hit, a small band of the youths would walk back across the bridge and into Indooroopilly, where they would meet, after a quick phone call, an Italian man in his forties. He seemed to be able to supply any of their needs. No one knew his name, nor remembers how they were put in touch with him in the first place.

Most of the teenagers didn't get mixed up in all of that though. No one touched heroin. Most of them, including Scott and Michael, just yearned to fit in, to find out where they belonged. Content with the alcohol they'd brought along, and the joints that were passed around, they'd have their night out, and turn up, mostly anyway, for school on Monday.

As time wore on, the group which swelled to forty members on big nights gradually disbanded. Some parents, previously clueless to the exploits of their young sons, launched a crackdown on their behaviour. Kevin, the guy who'd started the BDR graffiti gang, thought it had all become a bit too serious. He pulled up stumps and ventured north. So too did another lad, caught by his parents one night in a comatose state; he was sent to relatives in the Northern Territory. A girl who, at least one regular says, fell victim one night to a vicious sex attack by an outsider, also left town. And there were others who departed. One of them, known as Brunswick to his friends, believes he had a narrow escape. His best friend was expelled, and he went in search of other friends.

'That was the biggest wake-up call for me personally,' he says now. 'It kind of put me on the spot and it made me realise they were all wankers. It just started all getting so serious and I took a step back. It wasn't what it was when it started off, which was just a little rebellious group where you had a few drinking mates and running away from police was part of the fun. You'd still go to school on Monday.'

That was certainly the case for Scott Rush, who, despite whatever else was happening in his life, went on to graduate from Marist Brothers Rosalie, his family proudly by his side.

XI

Let Me Follow

Michael Czugaj and school just didn't mix. Right from the start. He didn't like it, and he didn't bother trying too hard — except at sport. He loved his sport, no matter what kind it was; he played cricket and was on the school football and swimming teams. And he'd play anything else offered in the lunch hour and after class. On weekends he'd never pass up the chance to go for a surf or try his hand at fishing. And he had some pretty good catches to his name. But no matter how much time he spent on the school oval, that never made up for the Monday to Friday, 9 a.m. to 3 p.m. drudgery of class after class.

Sometimes — often, in fact — Michael would leave home with his schoolbag slung over his shoulder, having no intention of walking through the school gates. He'd skive off to sit in a park, wander the local suburbs or hit one of the local shopping malls until the time came to go home again.

Michael's parents, Vicki and Stephan, would shake their heads, wondering what they could do about their sixth-born. He was such a good son in so many ways, but he just didn't like school, and no matter what encouragement his parents offered or punishment they dished out, he wouldn't listen. It even reached the point where the Czugajs made the decision to move him from Marist Brothers back to the local Corinda State High School, hoping that he would be more inclined to go to school if it was just down the road. They were prepared to try anything, really. But that didn't work either.

Vicki knew that one of her other sons held a strong influence over Michael and that it was part of the problem. Richard was Michael's hero, and there was no one Michael wanted to be like more than his big brother. Richard was his role model and mentor, and Richard liked to wag school too, so there wasn't much chance of getting Michael through the school gates if Richard was doing otherwise. Richard was the leader, and Michael the follower. The two of them would put their heads together and plot their day outside the school ground, wandering around Corinda and Oxley, catching up with friends and hanging out. And there wasn't much Vicki or Stephan could do about it.

Vicki used to worry about what this behaviour meant for Michael's future, but one day she sat down and considered what type of son Michael — or Mikey, or Mick, as he was known variously amongst his seven siblings — was. Sure, he didn't front class enough, and his grades left a lot to be desired, but that wasn't the be-all in life. Michael was a good kid with a compassionate personality; he was a good brother and babysitter — teachers remember him rocking his baby sister until she fell asleep. He'd also always be the first to put up his hand to help around the house. As a child, he had an abundance of smiles and friends, and even as a teenager he wasn't too proud to show his mother how much he loved her. After a hard day at work, Vicki would come home and sink into the family's couch. Unprompted, Michael would massage her feet and shoulders for thirty, sometimes forty, minutes. He just wanted her to feel a bit better. So, while his truancy played on her mind, it didn't seem too big of a deal.

* * *

Michael was a bit of a family favourite. The Czugajs — Michael was the sixth of eight — were used to fending for themselves, but Michael could always get himself out of a sibling bind with his big, open-faced smile — just ask his sisters. He stood out as the funniest, and certainly the cheekiest. And, with his shirt hanging out the back and his habit of tugging at a clump of hair near his forehead, he was perhaps the most laid-back as a child. And at nine pounds seven ounces, there was little doubt that he was born the chubbiest. A Gemini, he was given Michael as his Christian name, and his grandfather's middle name, William, as his second name.

Michael's big sisters adored him from the moment he came out of hospital and he became their Chubby Bubby, as his Mum would say. They'd cart him around the house, playing happy families, and he'd join in their games, taking in his stride all their doting attention. His big brothers, too, would let him tag along, and Michael enjoyed their company even more than the straggle of school friends who were a constant at his home, especially during his primary school years. He particularly liked following Richard around; that made him feel important.

The Czugaj home was always loud and filled with the colour and drama of one big family where the age difference between the youngest and the oldest child stretched twenty years. It was only when Michael became a teenager that he began to test his parents' patience occasionally. And that usually related to his wagging school. But he never missed the big family occasions, and, like the rest of his siblings, he would come and go, always welcomed back into the family's home, a modest house nestled in a cul de sac in the working suburb of Oxley.

To Vicki Czugaj, it came almost as a relief when Michael finally quit school, despite him not finishing Year Ten. He just wasn't meant to be there, and the pre-vocational course he embarked on at TAFE seemed proof of that. He quickly found an apprenticeship as a shopfitter before moving on to glazing. He dumped some of his friends, more because his life had taken a different turn now. He had to turn up to work on time, and alert. He'd half-heartedly looked around for a job originally, but now he had one he wanted to keep it. Besides, he liked what he did, and enjoyed his pay packet even more.

Michael finally felt a sense of achievement and a sense of belonging that had eluded him for so many of his high school years. Of course, he kept up the drinking, and certainly still enjoyed a bong — some say too much — but he seemed to have escaped the grip of the group of youths who would spend their Friday and Saturday nights getting wasted. He was pretty much living the life of many other Brisbane teenagers let loose with their first pay packets. Everything seemed under control.

While Michael flatted elsewhere, he made sure he regularly dropped by to see his little brother and baby sister, who were both still at school, often bringing a friend or two with him. His parents lost track of many of his friends as they came and went, but neither remembers Scott Rush, whom Michael had met through the school football team, visiting their home.

'He went to school with Scott but I don't think they were close friends,' Vicki Czugaj says now.

Scott Rush and Michael Czugaj had shared the same big circle of friends who would meet in Indooroopilly each Friday and Saturday night, and that association continued after Michael had swapped schools. Trains ran regularly through Brisbane's western suburbs, and he would continue to meet up with the rest of the crew at Indooroopilly at the appointed time each week. But once Michael left school altogether, did his apprenticeship and started work, he seemed to move outside that circle more. Most in the group still attended school, and while that was irrelevant to their weekend escapades, Michael didn't make it to the gatherings quite as much. He remained a follower more than a leader, but he seemed to be getting on with his life without the same heavy influence of those who had been his mentors along the way.

One friend remembers telling Michael that he had to look forwards, not backwards, and make a go of his life; that it was up to him who he hung around and what course he took. And Michael would nod his head in agreement, despite continuing to drink too much and smoke dope too regularly. He'd while away some of his spare time listening to hip-hop music on the few CDs his friends say he owned.

Early in 2005, though, something changed. One friend noticed it almost immediately. As quickly as Michael had focused on his new life, he turned on his heels and walked away from it. Work was no longer the routine that offered him a direction; it had become a millstone, cutting into his time with friends, and getting in the way of him doing what he wanted to do. He started going out during the week and going home late. And then he started going out all night, friends say. He didn't seem to care any more about next week, or next month, let alone next year. The only thing that mattered was today.

A few months earlier Michael had renewed his acquaintance with Scott Rush, the smooth-talking, good-looking boy from upper-middle-class Chelmer. Rush had graduated from school in 2002, working in a fruit shop and cargo-carrying company, and as a carpenter, before his arrest.

Rush had also stayed in touch with some of the Friday and Saturday night crew as it whittled its way down to a handful of youths. And despite his private school education and the love and support of his family, Rush also couldn't see his way forward. His adolescent penchant for alcohol continued, and his life seemed to slip out of his control. He started to mix with a bad crowd. Despite this, people could be forgiven for thinking that Rush was a good influence on all his friends. He always looked good, was charming to everyone he met, and at least one friend joked that he always came across as the perfect son, friend, boyfriend or potential son-in-law.

'He's the sort of young fellow who butter wouldn't melt in his mouth,' says the friend. 'He'd pull one over you and you wouldn't even know it's been done.'

The rekindling of the friendship between Rush and Czugaj could only be bad news for both of them, but probably especially the naive young lad from Oxley who would always find it easier to follow than to lead.

Rush, another friend and Czugaj started to hang out together, frequenting Fortitude Valley's clubs and mixing with Brisbane's underbelly. They met new people, and trusted them probably too much. No one ever saw Michael take drugs other than marijuana, but he would stay out to all hours of the night, often with Rush and a couple of others in tow.

After one night out, when Michael finished up at about 4.30 a.m., a friend tried to find out where he had been and what he was doing. 'You couldn't get much out of him; he just wanted to go [home] to bed, you know,' his friend says now.

Police were also told about the small group of youths who would walk around at all times of the night and day, swearing and carrying on. At least one complaint was aimed directly at the trio, who witnesses say soon became inseparable. Rush and his friend had earnt themselves a bad name, with claims Rush even tried to attack a colleague, whom he believed owed him money, with a pool cue at an inner-city club late one night.

Michael's life began to lose all direction. One night, he just disappeared. Friends asked around, worried about where he might have gone and whether he was in any sort of trouble. And, like the Czugajs, they were told that Michael had gone to Cairns.

XII

Recruitment over Karaoke

Every big city has a suburb a bit like Brisbane's Fortitude Valley. It's brusque and brash and home to anyone and everyone: the pimps and the prostitutes, the touts and the homeless, as well as the new wealthy who have chosen its homes to gentrify and renovate. Perhaps for that reason, or perhaps because it's only a bus stop or two from the city centre, the Valley has also become the Friday night host to the young urban set who have spent the week toiling in the nearby offices. The modish clubs and pubs that stretch down Brunswick Mall and hug the surrounding streets are loud and dark, strobe lights playing hide-and-seek with the identities of their young patrons.

Some of the clubs have tough entry standards now, and you have to look the part before the bulky bloke at the front door steps aside and lets you pass. No one with a tie is allowed in this one, a particular look is not welcome in another. Of course, they don't say that; everyone just knows and fits in accordingly.

Young people have their favourite venue, and might meet at their regular soon after their office doors close for the week before migrating for a bite to eat in the open mall or one of the many Chinese restaurants that fill the area. After dinner, the clubs swell with sinewy bodies and talk of weekend plans as mojitos, cosmopolitans and Manhattans are downed alongside light beers and house chardonnays.

On this Friday night, in the middle of the Brunswick Mall, a lone busker strums his electric guitar, trying to ignore the light rain as well as the solitary drunk who is standing in front of him, dancing by himself. Young women in skin-tight black dresses, and their partners, in office-issue suits and white shirts now rolled up to the elbows, make wisecracks as they pass by on their way to the next club. They'll soon pass one of their own — a young, well-dressed twentysomething who forgot to pace herself, stumbling out in search of fresh air. Less than 100 metres away, a group of young people probably the same age sits drinking out of clear plastic bottles, proof of the chroming and methylated spirits drinking problems that have been challenging the local politicians.

In the other direction, a similar distance away, a police shop front stands out, its bright lights in contrast to the darkened pubs and clubs it sits with. Inside, about half a dozen officers — the same age again — stand around deciding their night's plan. In just a few minutes they will all go off in pairs, in different directions, stopping the youthful to check the age identification they are carrying, telling the two blokes who have discarded their shirts to dress, and hoping their presence keeps in check some of the exuberance that can challenge them on some nights.

Michael Czugaj, Scott Rush and their friends wouldn't look out of place here on Friday night, or any other night — it's young, it's hip and it's happening. Neither would Tan Duc Thanh Nguyen, the baker from a family of bakers who lived across the other side of Brisbane.

Wellington Point is a newish area of Brisbane, one of those suburbs hugging a big capital city, where voters targeted by the Liberal government of John Howard in the mid-1990s are making their mark and moving up. This is mortgage-belt country, where the houses are mainly brick and new, and the boats in some of the driveways are testament to the suburb's growing affluence. The average wage of those living here has been steadily growing, although it still only hovers above $40 000 a year — but many are young and only starting out.

Each year more than 3000 people move into Wellington Point and other suburbs in the local shire area, and the number of babies born in this one suburb in recent years is three times as many as the number of deaths recorded. Young children ride their bicycles to school during the week and play with their friends in the manicured parks each weekend.

Tan Duc Thanh Nguyen's family lives in a good street here, in a house like many of the others. The asking price for a house up the street was $417 000, and while it offered ducted air and split-system air conditioning, was much roomier, and boasted Smeg appliances, it was an indication that the Nguyen family had chosen a good street in a good suburb in which to to raise their young clan. They stuck pretty much to themselves, though, their understanding of English much better than their ability to speak it, but they looked the part, coming from and going to work, ferrying their children to school and doing the weekend chores. They just fitted in like the other families who had chosen Wellington Point as their home.

Their eldest son, Tan Duc Thanh, was helping out in the family business, his siblings still at school. Tan Duc Thanh's car was his pride and joy. He had taken out a loan to buy it, but the flashy, blue Nissan 2000 SX was worth every cent he had, and took pride of place in the driveway of the family home. It was done up within an inch of its life, and every six weeks or so the car would undergo further enhancement: new side panels, a big stereo, 19-inch wheels. Some of the neighbours wondered what else could be done to it.

That was the picture of the Nguyen family, from street level.

Close up, things were not quite so neat and tidy. The lawn didn't always get mowed when it should have and the local throwaways would often remain on the lawn for days; so would the odd cigarette butt. The back yard, too, was littered with children's toys, and the house was often unkept and untidy. Appearances within the Nguyens' Vietnamese community were of paramount importance; at home they were not such a high priority.

There were other incongruities in the Nguyen home. One neighbour noticed that a big plasma TV screen filled one wall inside the house, but it seemed out of place against the basic lounge and chairs it surveyed. It looked so new, and so much else looked so old; it was squeaky clean, in contrast to everything that lay around it. But none of that worried the neighbours, who found the Nguyens to be a quiet and courteous family. Their children, especially their well-spoken and respectful daughter, were a credit to their family and didn't give anyone cause for concern.

As the busy little suburb went about its daily business, neighbours would say hello to each other, the Nguyens joining in the civility. Or sometimes they'd just raise a hand in acknowledgment. They fitted in here, in Wellington Point in Queensland, and, like the hard-working families around them, it had become their home.

Tan Duc Thanh Nguyen was born in the Philippines in 1982, and his family mirrored many others in Brisbane's ethnic community. His parents worked hard, with the aim of giving their children a fresh go in a new country. Nguyen's parents were keen for him to do well, as individual success was considered important among Brisbane's 18 000-strong Vietnamese community. There, accolades were crowed about by proud parents keen to show off their children.

On the other hand, problems were rarely aired. Sometimes, that made life difficult for Vietnamese youths, pulled between the cultural expectations of their parents and the path chosen by many of their young Australian friends. Many lacked a sense of belonging as they struggled to find their place in the melting pot, and were lured by the sense of freedom others in their school classes seem to boast.

Some people in the Vietnamese community suggest that this is how Nguyen felt. And he might have been like that — or he might not. The Vietnamese community is a closed shop, and parents and children don't usually speak about their dreams and their fears. The expectation of success is what counts.

As a teenager, some say, Nguyen did not boast the potential of his confident and diligent younger sister, whose maturity and respect for others seemed to stand out. The lure of peer pressure was always greater for Nguyen than for his sister, and his focus in high school drifted. His parents might not have chosen the same friends he had at times, but they believed he was doing well enough and that he tried to be a good son at home. He was quiet; never held big, loud parties; seemed respectful of others; and helped out in the family baking business.

Neighbours watched him come and go in his Nissan 2000 SX — it seemed like his best friend. That's the way he treated it. Sometimes the music blaring out of its stereo could be heard along the street, but that didn't really upset anyone. Tan Duc Thanh always acknowledged his neighbours as he pulled up outside the family home, before disappearing inside to his parents and younger siblings. He'd give them a quick salute, a friendly wave — but he rarely stopped to start a conversation. He was content as long as he could spend as much time as possible with his prized car.

If his parents suspected something was wrong with their son, it was not something they shared with others.

As the crow flies, the Nguyen family lives only a stone's throw from Kay Danes who, with her husband, Kerry, spent eleven months in a Laos jail after being convicted on trumped-up charges of gem smuggling by a closed court — charges they always strongly denied. The Danes, who were only released and pardoned after intense lobbying by Foreign Minister Alexander Downer, now devote enormous energies to the foreign prisoners' support service, and Kay has spent time talking and counselling some of those families coming to terms with their children's black futures.

It was in that capacity that Kay Danes recently went to see the Nguyens and check how they were faring. They had moved out of their home, driven by embarrassment, shame and disappointment, and were staying in the home of an extended family member. But on this day they had ventured back, to their old life in their old street, to spruce up their house. They planned to sell it. Kay found the Nguyens to be guarded as she approached, not willing to let anyone else into their tormented lives. But she could almost hear their sigh of relief when she explained her role and offered them support. It was an offer, though, that Danes knew probably would never be taken up.

Tan Duc Thanh Nguyen was far from reserved the night he met Michael Czugaj in a Fortitude Valley nightclub. He had met Scott Rush six months earlier, and on this night, while other people in the club tried their hands at karaoke, Rush introduced him to Michael Czugaj. Almost straight up Nguyen asked the Oxley teenager whether he'd ever been abroad.

'Next, he offered me to come to Bali and I agreed,' Michael later told investigators.

A few days later, Nguyen came to Michael's home and asked for his identification, so he could have a passport processed.

After Michael and Scott had obtained one in the city, they were driven home to get some clothes and taken to the home of someone in Sunnybank called Chicken. Czugaj took the Bali offer at face value — a free trip at Nguyen's expense — and listened as Nguyen talked about it over dinner.

They stayed with Chicken for four days and then, again on the generosity of Nguyen, flew with Nguyen to Sydney. They caught a taxi to Strathfield railway station, and were then driven to the Spanish Inn by Myuran Sukumaran. It was the first time they'd met him.

XIII

Planning Ahead

With a two-star rating, the Formule 1 Hotel in Sydney's Enfield is not the flashiest joint in town. But it offers a good deal, with a standard room available for just under $70 a night. Not that Martin Stephens and Renae Lawrence were paying — the bill was being fixed up by their co-worker Andrew Chan. The rooms weren't anything special, but they were clean and tidied daily, and each had a queen-sized bed with a single overhead bunk, which allowed for three adults. Only Stephens and Lawrence were in room 126, with Matthew Norman and Si Yi Chen nearby in room 129, so there was plenty of space for their luggage. Not that they needed much of that, either — Chan's girlfriend, Grace, had come around the day before and removed much of it, replacing garment after garment with other items. Bandages, fabric bands, a pair of tight, short adidas pants — an item unlikely to have found a place in Renae's closet — adhesive tapes and a waist belt. Grace had then carefully repacked their suitcases.

Stephens and Lawrence now carried the suitcases out the door and down to the waiting taxi. It was only early, and the 5 millimetres of rain that had fallen the day before had cleared the skies. The low cloud had put a lid on the city then, seemingly dampening its spirits, but the cloud had since vanished and the mild easterly wind turned into an even milder westerly. The temperature was already climbing to the maximum of 25.5 degrees Celsius that Sydney would enjoy this day.

Everything seemed promising as Stephens and Lawrence put their luggage into the taxi, checked they had their passports and sped off in the direction of Sydney's international airport. Matthew Norman, the young lad from Quakers Hill, and his friend Si Yi Chen were in a second taxi not far behind, and they were also headed for the airport. It was 6.30 a.m. on Wednesday, 6 April 2005.

On the same day, not far up the road in the neighbouring suburb of Strathfield, Scott Rush and Michael Czugaj were enjoying the hospitality at the four-star Spanish Inn Motor Lodge. They had flown down from Brisbane — Rush for the second time — on the invitation of Tan Duc Thanh Nguyen. Rush's first visit had been only a few days earlier, when he had joined in the birthday celebrations of Nguyen's friend's girlfriend. They'd partied in a club, and he'd flown back to his home town a couple of days later.

Now he was back in Sydney with Michael; they were picked up, taken to their motel and told the bill would be looked after. That wasn't a bad way to start their sojourn: room 204 at the Spanish Inn — a colour television which offered Foxtel, a video and DVD player, along with a refrigerator, toaster and microwave, all at their disposal, as well as the services of the Lodge's 24-hour reception. The drudgery of their Brisbane lives seemed a world away as they enjoyed a fine Sydney day. And things seemed only to get better when, a little bit later, they met up with Myuran Sukumaran.

* * *

Sukumaran had an order for Rush: he was to do a job for him in Bali. Sukumaran would fund the trip for both Rush and his Brisbane friend, so they should go and buy a travel package. Stories vary on whether it was Sukumaran or Nguyen who then gave Rush a wad of cash. But Rush took it, the fat stack of dollars no doubt promising something new and exciting. Three thousand dollars. In cash. And it had just been handed to him.

The money was to cover both the cost of an airline ticket to Indonesia and accommodation in Bali, and Rush was told to buy the travel package at the local Flight Centre travel office. It wasn't long before Michael Czugaj and Scott Rush were booked onto an Australian Airlines flight to Bali, leaving on Friday, 8 April 2005 — just a day away.

Rush and Czugaj didn't know Stephens and Lawrence, who had already travelled the skies above Australia, but all four were heading for Bali's Ngurah Rai international airport. It was where they would all eventually meet, eleven days later, when their lives would become inextricably linked in life and, perhaps, even in death.

Two different groups, on two different flights: it wasn't chaotic planning, but a deliberate strategy. Indeed, both trips had been plotted, and re-plotted, the operation schemed to the nth degree. Every I had been dotted, every T crossed. And then checked. And re-checked. This trip had to be a good run. Sure, it was a practised track now — Sydney to Bali and back — with previous trips in December, October and August. Not necessarily for this bunch, but others had done it. And while there had been successes, one of those trips had been a complete waste of time and money. That trip took place only a few months back, in December 2004, and this new trip had to be different: it would run like clockwork.

It was the first trip to Bali for the two Brisbane boys, the dashing and charming young Rush and his quieter, younger-looking friend who didn't boast the same confidence but seemed willing to go along for the ride. The two of them looked the part — they could have been any of the hundreds and hundreds of young men who venture over to soak up the sun and the surf on the island each year. They were young and athletic and in search of a good time, like the hordes of others heading in the same direction. There was no doubt that they would blend into the streets of Kuta, where bars fill early each night with people just like them.

The couple of ordinary-looking, twentysomething friends from Sydney — one of whom had already been to Bali a couple of times before — fitted the part too. Nothing about Renae Lawrence or Martin Stephens really stood out. They were not stunning-looking but they weren't unattractive either. They wore clothes similar to those of the rest of the Bali-bound holiday-makers. Not that that mattered — one of the good things about Bali was the fact that anyone could mix in. It offered a good time to everyone, as long as you went there with enjoyment on your mind and a spring in your step. And there was no doubt that the recruitment for this sojourn had gone particularly well.

Now, with one group on the plane and the other with tickets at the ready, every detail had been taken care of. Flights: check. Times: check. Places: check. Accommodation: check. The Job: check. And then they were checked again. And again. Scott Rush and Michael Czugaj; Renae Lawrence and Martin Stephens. They didn't need to know about each other. Not now. Not ever, really. They were on an all-expenses-paid return trip to Bali. And it was looking mighty lucrative for everyone involved.

Martin Stephens thought it was Andrew Chan's mother and sister who had been at home when he pulled up outside the Enfield address about a week or two earlier. Of course, he knew

Chan from work, but not too well. They did the same kind of job at the Sydney Cricket Ground, but both were casual employees and not always assigned to the same events on the same days. And Chan had been there for a while, having joined the catering company almost two years to the day before Stephens started only months earlier. But today, at his home, Chan was all about another sort of business.

Chan sat down and talked to Stephens, who remembers the menacing tone in his colleague's voice and the warning that stuck in his mind: he was not to talk to anybody, not a single word. Stephens's task seemed simple enough: he was to do everything asked of him by either Chan or Sukumaran. *Everything*. And that was the end of the conversation — it stopped as abruptly as it had started. Renae Lawrence walked in; Chan asked Stephens to leave. And he did.

Lawrence, too, was given similar instructions — to be prepared to do exactly as she was asked. First up, that meant pretending that she did not know her co-worker Matthew Norman, or Si Yi Chen. If Lawrence wanted to find out more about the trip, it seems she did not ask. Besides, she had done this once before. She had been roped in once again, this time with Stephens, and was going along for the ride.

A day or two later, on Wednesday, 30 March, Lawrence and Stephens met up with Chan again at the big and busy four-level Roselands Shopping Centre in Sydney. Here anyone can fade into a crowd, as thousands of people use the one big centre to do their weekly shopping and banking. Myuran Sukumaran, Si Yi Chen and Matthew Norman were also there this time, and the group of six Sydneysiders sat down and, according to their accusers, designed and planned the heroin run from Bali to Australia.

That's not the story Lawrence and Stephens tell, though. They say they were told that they were required to do something in Bali, but it was never fully explained to them what that was. Stephens says that when he specifically asked, he was threatened and told to wait for instructions.

Regardless of who is to be believed, it was on this day that at least part of the plan was shared. The group was to go to Bali, almost straightaway. They would all leave on the one flight, it was explained, and Chan then took Stephens down to one of the ticket agencies. There Chan inquired about flights and fares and, armed with that information, went off to his bank, withdrew the required amount and handed it, in cash, to Lawrence. It was more than $2000 and it was to cover airfares and accommodation, she was told. Carrying the wad of cash, Lawrence and Stephens then went back to the ticket office and bought their seats on Australian Airlines flight AO7829, leaving Sydney for Bali on the morning of 6 April. It was less than a week away.

A few days later, Andrew Chan himself headed for Sydney's international airport, and a flight to Bali. The young Sydneysider had booked an eleven-day holiday, to be filled with jet-skiing, parasailing, snorkelling, shopping and drinking, and his base would be room 5314 in the Hard Rock Hotel. As Chan booked in there, Lawrence and Stephens were preparing to stay in the Hotel Formule 1 in Enfield, room 126 — their home until their departure a few days later. But that time flew as they ran errands, held meetings and caught up with a colleague for a drink. The day after they moved in, Lawrence remembers being given an extra $500 in cash by Sukumaran, along with a grey Nokia 1100 mobile phone. On the same day, Chan's girlfriend, Grace, came to repack their luggage and Lawrence had to run errands, like picking up Si Yi Chen and Matthew Norman from a local train station. Stephens remembers receiving some advice from Sukumaran: to not let on that he knew Chen or Norman, despite the fact that he sometimes worked with the latter at the

Sydney Cricket Ground. Stephens has since said that he was told the consequences would be severe if he broke that or any other instruction: he and his family would die.

Late that night, at about 11 p.m., with their plane set to take off less than twelve hours later, Lawrence and Stephens went for a drink.

Lawrence, Stephens, Norman and Chen didn't know that another group of young people would embark on the same journey only two days later. On 8 April, when Rush and Czugaj headed for Sydney Airport and their mid-morning Australian Airlines flight, the temperature was just tipping 19 degrees Celsius, and a light westerly wind was blowing. They seemed like perfect flying conditions. The boys joined the throng of others in Sydney's departure lounges, booking their luggage in and being assigned a seat before heading through security and immigration.

Sukumaran and Nguyen, who had first met Rush in Brisbane a short while ago, were heading for the same flight. The date: Friday, 8 April 2005. Destination: Bali's Ngurah Rai international airport. Estimated time of arrival: 2 p.m. local time. The 'holiday' was about to begin.

XIV

Bali Bound

Like everyone else in the line, Scott Rush handed his passport to the Customs officer on his way to board Australian Airlines flight AO7829 to Bali. It felt brand new, having just been issued four days earlier in his home town of Brisbane. As his passport number, M2456566, registered in the computer at Sydney Airport, it triggered an alert for the on-duty officer processing it. The pass or PACE alarm is owned and maintained by Customs but used by loads of enforcement agencies, from the Family Court to State and Federal police bodies.

The officer, trained to follow instructions meticulously when a warning was set off, read the note on the screen in front of him. He knew that the alert was used for one of two reasons: either to gain intelligence on someone, or to prevent a targeted passenger from entering, or leaving, the country.

If Scott Rush knew that the officer behind the screen was about to make a phone call and check the origin of the alert, he never let on. He was less than an hour away from boarding his flight to Bali for an all-expenses-paid sojourn. Take-off was scheduled for 10.15 a.m. He waited patiently, just like the others in the queue. The Customs officer behind the screen no doubt looked at the young lad in front of him before putting in a call to Paul Collins, an AFP investigator at Sydney Airport. Collins had arrived at 7 a.m., and it was 8.55 a.m. when he took the call alerting him to the fact that the name of Scott Rush had just been activated for a flight that was to leave in eighty minutes' time. Collins followed the rulebook: he put in a call to the AFP officer in Brisbane who had requested the alert.

The officer had received a telephone call from Bob Myers, a friend of Scott Rush's father, Lee, the previous night. Myers had told the police officer that Lee Rush had found out that Scott was scheduled to leave the country, and he was worried that his son might be up to no good. He wanted him stopped. Myers, a Brisbane barrister, offered to call someone he knew in the AFP.

Once he had spoken to the officer, Collins also called the Queensland Police seeking information on Rush's bail conditions. These things take time, finding the right person and accessing the conditions of bail. Collins waited patiently. Meanwhile, Scott Rush carried on, unaware that the details on a screen he couldn't see might prevent him joining his friend Michael Czugaj and others on the flight.

Rush sauntered to the gate and began boarding the plane, along with all the other excited passengers. It was 9.45 a.m., and Collins finally had his information: there was no reason to detain Scott Rush under any bail conditions. Collins also believed that, despite the concerns of Lee Rush, Scott was an adult, and there was no basis for detaining him.

He ran his decision by his supervisor and then called Customs back. The AFP would not be taking any further action. The Customs officer had done his job. Collins had done his job. And Scott Rush sat in his seat. Within hours, he and Michael would be landing in Bali.

* * *

Sukumaran and Nguyen soon boarded the same flight, taking the same path through the departure floor of Sydney Airport. As they moved through Customs, the pass alarm was triggered again. This time, when the officer investigated, he found that he had to alert the Australian Federal Police again. He picked up the phone and dialled through. Officers listened as they were told that one of their suspects in an international drug-smuggling operation was attempting to leave the country. It was a piece of gold in their ongoing investigation, a clue that allowed them to build a bigger case, the piece of the jigsaw that would help show the complete picture of what they were up against.

The AFP investigators wasted no time — they quickly started checking their files, making telephone calls, and finding out who their target was travelling with, all the information adding to the profile they had already built of several other suspects.

At the same time as the Australians' Bali adventure was being planned and they were boarding their planes, the award-winning film *Maria Full of Grace* was being reviewed in Australia to critical acclaim. 'Once a decision is made, there is no turning back' — it's just one line in the film, delivered to the star character, Maria Alvarez, but it signals the start of a young woman's desperate journey to escape rural Colombia. She is still in her mid-teens when she makes the life-changing decision to act as a drug mule; to stuff her stomach with handfuls of heroin pellets which would sit alongside her unborn baby. Each pellet was weighed exactly, coming in at 10 grams. Each was measured meticulously: 4.2 centimetres long and 1 centimetre wide. And each one had to be swallowed whole. There was a risk one would burst, and that she would die as a result. Perhaps even a greater risk that she might get caught. But that risk seemed to diminish with the promise of money and the new life it would bring.

Learning to swallow the pellets was hard, but before long Maria shut her eyes, and the plane took off. It was her first-ever flight and it traversed the skies from Bogota in Colombia to New York City. Ensconced in her seat, the sense of hopelessness and endless poverty that coloured Maria's childhood seemed forgotten, replaced by the escape plan offered by the once-in-a-lifetime opportunity.

Maria saw her friend Lucy on the flight. It wasn't Lucy's first time — she had helped Maria learn to swallow the pellets. Maria saw her other friend too, but none of them acknowledged each other. These were the orders. And she took the orders seriously.

'One more thing,' the supplier told her after watching her swallow pellet after pellet of heroin before boarding the plane, 'if anything of what you are carrying gets lost along the way or doesn't show up, we'll go and have a little conversation with your grandmother, your mother, your sister and little Pachito. We know exactly how much each one of those sixty-two pellets weighs. Understood?' Maria knew there was no turning back, and when nature expelled one of the pellets, we see her in the plane toilet swallowing it again.

The movie is dirty and gritty and real; based on 1000 true stories of young mules, chosen for their innocence and naivety. Maria is just one of them. As the flight droned on, we saw her friend Lucy become very sick. We saw Maria saved from an X-ray on landing in New York because, while suspicions prompted investigators to question her, the X-ray could damage her unborn baby. Maria walked out into a city as foreign to her as her future. Others weren't so lucky. One mule Maria didn't even realise was part of the same racket was arrested. Another went back, no doubt to do it again. Her friend Lucy died an agonising death, her stomach later cut open to extract the heroin.

Lucy was the pretty young girl who had taught Maria to swallow the pellets. 'It's not easy,' she had told Maria. 'But it's not difficult either.'

* * *

The lure of an all-expenses-paid trip to Bali, with or without the knowledge that they would be used as dispensable mules in a risky drug-smuggling operation, could have been the ticket to freedom for many of the young Australians heading for Bali in that first week of April. It might have been an escape from home, a chance to forget the unrequited love of a partner, or the opportunity to make some money and a new start. Or it might have been plain greed, the chance to pocket a few bucks and have a holiday on someone else. Or perhaps plain ignorance as to what they would truly be expected to do, once there.

Whatever their motivations, nine young Australians were on their way to Bali, and it was a journey destined to go the same way as that travelled by Maria Alvarez in *Maria Full of Grace*. Maria was just seventeen, and the Australian lot were not much older. Matthew Norman was only eighteen; Michael Czugaj just nineteen. So was his friend, Scott Rush. Si Yi Chen was twenty. Renae Lawrence was a few years older, at twenty-seven, and so was Martin Stephens, at twenty-nine, but the two of them seemed younger than their years. Andrew Chan, who had led the delegation heading off to Bali by himself on 3 April, was only twenty-one. And Myuran Sukumaran and Tan Duc Thanh Nguyen, who now sat a row apart but on the same flight as the two Brisbane youths, Rush and Czugaj, were only twenty-three and twenty-two respectively. Nine young Australians; a secret plan to smuggle chunks of heroin back into Australia; and a gamble that, if they won, could earn each of them thousands.

On 3 April 2005, Andrew Chan's flight from Sydney landed at Bali's Ngurah Rai airport. He grabbed his bags, jumped into a taxi and headed off in the direction of Kuta. It was a drive he was becoming used to, having previously been to Bali a couple of times. At the Hard Rock Hotel in Kuta, he booked into room 5314.

Three days later, Renae Lawrence and Martin Stephens walked off their flight at 2.30 p.m. local time and into the tropical climes of Indonesia's playground. It was Lawrence's third trip to Bali and Stephens's first, so she was able to take the lead. The two of them shared a taxi, going straight to the Kuta Lagoon Hotel, where they were handed the keys to room 126. Si Yi Chen and Matthew Norman had shared the AO7829 flight with Lawrence and Stephens, but they didn't acknowledge each other at any time. That had been the instruction — pretend you have never met — and that's what they had done. Chen and Norman picked up their bags, hailed a taxi and ordered it to go to the Hotel White Rose. Room 1022 was prepared for them.

Two days later, on Friday, 8 April, the remaining contingent of young Australians on this journey finally arrived. Scott Rush and Michael Czugaj joined the crowd of other holiday-makers leaving the airport in search of their accommodation. They were headed for the Hotel Aneka in Kuta, where they were told to dump their bags in room 404. Their Brisbane friend, Nguyen, who had recruited them for the holiday, stepped off the same plane but didn't join them at the Hotel Aneka. He grabbed the two backpacks he had brought, one red and the other black, and headed for his hotel. He was booked into the Hard Rock Hotel, the same place as Andrew Chan and Myuran Sukumaran.

Sukumaran had been on the same flight, and had even sat next to Nguyen for part of the journey. Sukumaran had originally been allocated a seat a row away from Nguyen, but the seat next to him was vacant; during the flight, Nguyen, annoyed by the person snoring next to him, ducked over and sat on the seat to the right of Sukumaran. But, off the plane, they were strangers again, just as Nguyen was to his Brisbane friends. Sukumaran ordered his own taxi to go directly to Kuta. And he, too, booked into the Hard Rock Hotel.

Back in Sydney, AFP investigators were working fast, putting the final touches on their request to the Indonesian National Police for assistance. They had already built a detailed picture, and pieces were starting to fit into the giant drug-smuggling jigsaw. As in any investigation, there were two steps forward and one step back, but everything was beginning to pay off.

Several names appeared on their list, and eight had left the country in the past five days. It was all panning out as expected: the eight had all been linked through ticket purchases, holiday bookings and information supplied during the AFP's investigation and through telephone calls. Andrew Chan. Renae Lawrence. Martin Stephens. Matthew Norman. Si Yi Chen. Tan Duc Thanh Nguyen. Michael Czugaj. Scott Rush. As well as a few others.

The AFP drafted a letter and sent it through to their counterparts in Indonesia on 8 April, the same day Rush, Czugaj, Nguyen and Sukumaran left Australia and landed in Bali. 'The AFP in Australia has received information that a group of persons are allegedly importing a narcotic substance (believed to be heroin from Bali to Australia),' the letter began.

XV

On the Trail

Australian Federal Police officers were trawling through the life of Andrew Chan, attempting to build a profile of the young Sydney lad who lived with his parents in Enfield. He was twenty-one years old and had held four different jobs since leaving school in 2000. He'd gone to Bali a couple of times, and knew the three other young Australians whom officers were working equally hard to profile. Renae Lawrence had been put on the profiling list too, and she was a bit older than Chan. Her parents lived up near Newcastle, but she worked in Sydney. Martin Stephens and Matthew Norman were also on the officers' to-do list.

Did these four young Sydneysiders know each other? Who else did they mix with? Telephone records were invaluable as officers painstakingly and meticulously started to assemble a criminal portrait of the four young Sydney targets in their operation.

The profiling had begun a few months earlier, after a telephone call from an informant in Brisbane to the AFP. The report was brief: a group of young Australians was planning to travel to

Bali to pick up some heroin and transport it back here. There were no names given to police and no details on when the group would leave Australia. But it didn't seem like a piece of idle gossip — the informant was known to police and the information was soon backed up by another police agency. Still, as far as intelligence went, it was pretty raw.

The AFP were used to getting hundreds and hundreds of tips of potential wrongdoing each year: someone planning this, someone else planning that. This was just another one, without a lot to go on, but it warranted a follow-up, and officers began a regular intelligence investigation. Soon a couple of suspects came to the fore. One stood out. And then, by looking at who he mixed with, another one emerged.

Police didn't know they were really on the track of an international drug-smuggling ring, but kept working away, building profiles and piecing together friendships, meetings and travel plans over the past six months. One person had travelled overseas and bought the ticket with another person. That person then joined the profilers' target list.

Reams of paper soon built up into folders of information. A big wall chart was started, and that was often a helpful tool in connecting one young life to another. It continued to grow each day as one name led to another which led to another. That didn't mean everyone put on the chart was involved in illegal activity, just that they could be linked through associations. At least, that was the case at the start.

Investigations into drug running are the bread and butter of the AFP's work in Australia, especially since the big heroin drought a few years back and due to an increased focus on border protection. During the 'drought' some of the smugglers became even more sneaky, diversifying what they ferried into the country and how it was carried. The big, risky ventures by international drug cartels slowed, replaced quickly by a strategy of attempting to slip in smaller amounts more regularly. Officers would often come across drugs sandwiched between sheets of wonton pastry, or funnelled into the buttons of women's dresses, soaked into pairs of designer denim jeans, inside fish fillets or candlesticks or even car parts.

The big crackdown on drug importation also meant that sometimes drug lords would attempt to sneak their cargo into the country via sea, usually in cargo, and occasionally by air. And sometimes they'd mix it up to spread the risk.

The drug lords were trying a bit of everything now in order to keep up the supply, and drug mules were an important part of that mix. Young, single and white: that was the target recruit. Backpackers were invaluable, as shown by the drug recruitment styles of the West African organised criminals trying to import cocaine into Australia in recent years. They would actively search for backpackers, with the most appealing coming from Australia, Canada and Britain. Law enforcement officers around the world would know why: young, white and single travellers would pass through Customs without a hitch nine times out of ten.

Cartels would always look for the type of people who would never attract attention through either their looks or their behaviour. It was important that they looked the part of a tourist or business traveller, and if they knew another mule on the flight, it was crucial that they didn't acknowledge each other. Airport security staff were trained to look out for suspicious activity, and the fewer risks, the better.

Drug mules were also invaluable in spreading out the risk. If ten mules were employed to carry in chunks of heroin and one was pinged, nine-tenths of the heroin would still find its way through; if three were pinged, seven-tenths would make it through. It was a gamble, any way you looked at it, but drug lords knew the market in Australia and how lucrative a haul of good heroin could be.

Australian Federal Police officers knew how it all worked; they'd seen it time and time again. And, as they advanced this operation, a sharper picture began to emerge. They had a group of young Australians, slowly growing in number, who appeared to be part of a planned drug importation. Nightclubs seemed to be a crucial part of the recruitment process, with youthful-looking Australians offered free holidays and wads of cash to take the risk and keep their mouths shut. In the melting pot Australia had become, the requirement of some overseas networks for mules to all be white wasn't that important, and in a tried and true illustration of six degrees of separation, recruitment efforts in Brisbane and Sydney nightclubs fanned out to net a group of young people from different socioeconomic backgrounds, cultures and demographics. As March 2005 marched into April, the list being drawn up by federal police agents covered people from the eastern suburbs of Sydney to the western suburbs of Brisbane and beyond.

Scott Rush's parents were worried. By the time Lee Rush arrived home from work at 7.30 p.m. on 7 April, his family had received several calls from a Flight Centre travel agent in Sydney. Their other son had taken one call, and messages had also been left at 2.30 p.m. and 3 p.m. and again at 6 p.m. The person making the call said they were a consultant for Flight Centre and needed Scott to pick up his ticket. To Bali. Lee was stunned. He told the consultant that his son, whom he hadn't seen for several days, would not have had a passport or the money for such a trip.

Lee sat down in the family's Chelmer home and felt desperate. Fearful. The consultant had said the flight left the next morning. Lee worried about what to do — he thought his son might be up to no good. So he picked up the phone and dialled his friend, Brisbane barrister Robert Myers.

Bob Myers is a good listener, and he paid attention to what his friend was saying. Lee Rush was worried that his son might be travelling to Bali to be involved in illegal activity. Could he be stopped? It was a father's appeal, driven out of love rather than punishment, for someone to step in and help. Myers knew an Australian Federal Police officer, he told Lee, and he would put in a call and see what could be done. Scott was due to fly out within hours, just after 10 a.m. the next day, so there was no time to waste.

Myers called his contact — a Queensland police officer on secondment to the AFP. It was Thursday night, 7 April 2005. It wasn't the officer's area of expertise, so he consulted other officers. Myers was told that the AFP might not be able to stop Scott Rush, but that a passport alert would be activated. Myers asked for Scott to be warned, if he could not be stopped, that his every move would be watched in Bali. The phone call left the lawyer with the strong impression that Scott Rush would be pulled aside and warned in no uncertain terms that someone would be watching him the whole time he was away; and he hoped that an in-your-face warning not to look sideways by some burly law enforcement officer would act as the red light to any dodgy plans the young man might have.

Myers conveyed the content of the phone call to Scott's parents, Lee and Christine, and they all believed that if Scott boarded the Australian Airlines flight he was booked on the next morning, it would be after a tough talk with a police officer at Sydney's international airport.

Friday morning, 8 April, dawned, and true to his word, Myers's AFP friend called him to confirm that the pass alarm had been activated. Myers passed on the news to Scott's parents, all of them believing that Scott would have been issued a no-nonsense police warning on departure. No one really believed that Lee and Christine's nineteen-year-old son would do anything silly — let alone risk bringing wads of heroin into the country, strapped to his body with cheap packing tape.

* * *

As each day in April progressed, the AFP began to — as one officer puts it — trap more rabbits down the one hole. Up to fifteen mules could be employed by this drug syndicate, some officers thought. Previous attempts to carry heroin into the country by some of the same targets had been made over the past eight months and it appeared that one or two of the trips had even been successful. Checking previous travel bookings proved worthwhile: three of the young people now under investigation had travelled to Bali in October 2004; another trip in December seemed to have been aborted, and a trip was also made in August 2004, although that introduced different people onto the list of names the AFP was building.

Officers working on the case started to draw arrows from one person to the next. Names kept popping up, and that would open a new line of inquiry. One step at a time and another piece of the puzzle was found. Investigators knew that well-oiled drug syndicates — and this looked like one of those — needed money, people and planning. When chunks of heroin arrive at Sydney airport, the drug lords rely on a sophisticated network of suppliers at different levels to deliver the heroin to Sydney's west and beyond. But it works the other way too: the drug bosses also need to know how to source heroin coming from Burma and elsewhere. In the slimy underbelly of Australia's drug trade, they had to know who they could trust and where to put their hands on the financial backing to make it all worthwhile. And they were the same questions officers set about trying to answer.

By the time Rush, Czugaj, Nguyen and Sukumaran boarded their Australian Airlines flight to Bali on Friday morning, 8 April, investigators were flush with intelligence. They had a list of names. They knew these people had planned an earlier operation but had not had the money to fund it. They also had enough detailed information to know that the young mules had been ordered not to smoke for two weeks before departure, because they might look nervous not being allowed to light up a cigarette on the way home. The body packs of heroin would be attached to their legs and backs, hidden under oversized clothing, and sandals that would avoid metal detection. Pre-paid mobile phones would be used to keep in touch with each other, and Customs searches would be avoided by focusing attention on the big wooden objects they would carry in their luggage back to Australia.

The AFP's investigations pointed to Andrew Chan being the organiser, his travel itinerary even leading officers to the hotel he had booked for accommodation.

The AFP sat down and penned a letter to their Indonesian counterparts. And they weren't shy about asking for help. Australian Federal Police officers sought an information swap, asking the Indonesian National Police (INP) to take secret snaps of any meetings between the targets, furnish any phone records that might help, and gather as much evidence as possible to identify both the ringleaders in Australia and the source of the narcotics in Indonesia.

Four days later, the AFP sent another letter, again listing dates of birth and passport numbers, and also likely return dates. They kept working away in Australia, building links between the groups of young Brisbanites and Sydneysiders being kept apart by their bosses. Within a couple of weeks — by 28 April — they would boast a wall chart that looked like an enormous pyramid: dozens of names all linked by arrows. The names of eight of the Bali Nine had been put down over time, as had the names of others. And the last one, on information given back to them by the INP, would soon join the others, right up at the top of the chart: Myuran Sukumaran. The AFP officers working on the case had never heard of him.

XVI

Chan's Bali Adventure

You never forget the smell: a mix of incense and greenery — hard to describe and even harder to forget. It's the smell of Bali, wafting around the atmosphere as soon as you get off the plane on the Indonesian holiday isle.

It is the Balinese way to pay homage to their Hindu gods and ward off evil spirits. They place offering baskets everywhere, from the sidewalk to tiny shrines in offices, public places, homes and big temples. Little baskets made of woven banana trunk with anything from biscuits to eggs to lollies inside, along with burning sticks of fragrant incense. Walking down the gangway after a flight from anywhere, the aroma acts like a beacon — welcome to Bali, Island of the Gods.

Now another welcome beacon has become just as prominent, near the X-ray machine that scans hand luggage after passengers have come through Customs. Right next to the machine is a gleaming sign that states, 'Welcome to Bali, death for drug traffickers'. Andrew Chan must have seen it — he couldn't have missed it, really. The message, in English, is blunt and clear: get caught with drugs here and you could well find yourself lined up before a squad of armed men who will aim their rifles at your heart and pull the trigger. On 3 April Chan walked within metres or even centimetres of this frightening warning. Did he even look at it? Did it mean anything to him?

Only Chan knows for sure, but it's a pretty fair bet that he would have seen the sign. Especially since at that time it was only six weeks before the Schapelle Corby verdict. The story had been big news since the young Queensland woman's trial had started, and by the time Chan arrived in Bali there weren't too many people who hadn't heard that the Gold Coast beauty student faced a potential death penalty for attempting to smuggle marijuana into Bali. But the words on the sign couldn't have meant too much to Chan — perhaps he thought they would never apply to him. After all, he'd gambled with these authorities once before and won. Sign or no sign, law or no law, he knew he could smuggle drugs through Bali airport, and through Sydney airport as well.

This was Andrew Chan's third trip to Bali in six months. In October 2004, he, Renae Lawrence and others had taken a shipment of heroin back to pollute the streets of Australia, without a hitch. And members of the syndicate tried it again in December, thwarted only by a lack of money or heroin, or both. It was going to work this time.

Chan headed back to his old stomping ground, the Hard Rock Hotel, right on the beachfront in Kuta. Why he chose the Hard Rock on this and the previous occasion is a mystery. Perhaps the very reason why some tourists shy away from spending their Bali holiday in such a commercialised Western establishment was what drew Chan there. Many of the other hotels are smaller, more quaint and brimming with Balinese tradition. The staff, in traditional Balinese sarongs and *kebaya* tops, tend to know their guests' names, say good morning and good evening, and generally hang around for a chat with holiday-makers. This would not have worked for a man in the midst of organising a drug shipment. He needed a place where he could be much more anonymous, draw little attention to himself and become lost in the sea of Asian-looking faces similar to his own.

The middle to higher echelons of Indonesian society like it at the Hard Rock. It's not unlike Hard Rock hotels anywhere around the world — guitars of musical icons past and present lining the walls, gold records and loud music everywhere, including piped through the hallways of the guest areas. The staff in the accommodation section wear overalls, and there is a big bar area, along with a separate nightclub section.

Chan needed to come and go without drawing too much attention to himself, so the bustle of the hotel suited him. Moreover, it was close to the shops and nightlife, and to some of the hotels in which his recruits would be staying. He knew that because he had been involved in arranging their hotels as well, ensuring that the two groups of mules were kept well away from each other. Chan also didn't want anyone to know where *he* was. He told front desk staff at the Hard Rock not to tell a single person that he was there. Not something most tourists would care much about, because who would be asking anyway?

Three days to go before the first group of recruits would arrive and five days before their cargo would be here. Trying to portray a picture of innocence, Chan later told police that while he was in Bali he did what many true tourists do — he went jet-skiing in Nusa Dua but had to cancel the parasailing because the weather was no good. Instead, he said, he went banana-boat riding and snorkelling, but that that only lasted twenty minutes because of the weather. And, of course, he indulged in the staples of any Bali holiday — shopping and drinking. Except that this wasn't just any Bali holiday, and the leisure and recreation activities were a cover for something far more sinister: most of his time was spent planning and detailing what was to come once the recruits turned up.

Five days after Andrew Chan arrived in Bali, the letter from the Australian Federal Police was waiting in the office of the Australian Consulate in Renon, the business district of Denpasar, Bali's capital. It seems that the letter was not collected by Indonesian police until 12 April, and the first meeting between a team of surveillance officers from Polda, the police headquarters in Denpasar, who had been assigned to watch and document every move of the group, took place the next day.

By this time the first group of Chan's lieutenants in his illicit business were already in Bali. Renae Lawrence and Martin Stephens had gone straight from the airport to their hotel. The Kuta Lagoon Resort in the heart of Kuta, just a stone's throw from the bustling main street of Jalan Legian, would be their home, free of charge, for the next eight days. The accommodation had been arranged and paid for by Chan, the man who would later be painted as a supreme organiser.

He could have chosen worse places for his mules to stay. The Kuta Lagoon falls into the category of one of those quaint hotels where Balinese tradition abounds. Far enough off Jalan Legian, down a laneway, it is peaceful, unaffected by the noise of the traffic and beeping horns that characterise Kuta's main thoroughfare. But it is close enough to enable guests to walk to everything — the bars, the shops, the markets and even the beach. And, importantly, close enough for the mules to get to the meetings arranged for them by Chan.

The gardens and swimming pool are framed by frangipani trees. Dubbed the Cool Blue Lagoon, the pool could be described as the hotel's crowning glory, weaving the entire length of the accommodation area. Guests on the ground floor need only walk out on their balcony, down their steps and dive in. The rooms are older and a bit tired looking compared with the classy new resort and villa complexes that have spawned in recent years, but when you're not paying personally there is no need to be choosy. And the green floral curtains are adequate to keep out any prying eyes.

The hotel is not that far from the site of one of Kuta's most well-known spots — the two nightclubs in Jalan Legian where murderous terrorist bombs in October 2002 killed 200 innocent people, including 88 Australians. Almost 70 per cent of the Kuta Lagoon's guests are Australians — or were, before 1 October 2005, when three suicide bombers chose Bali restaurants in which to end their lives and the lives of so many others. After that the numbers dropped off dramatically, as wary Australians retreated from Bali in fear.

Guests at the Kuta Lagoon are treated to a Saturday night performance of the famed Balinese *Barong* dance, and Friday nights are happy hour at the hotel's Lagoon Café — buy three large Bintangs (the cheap local beer) and get one small Bintang for free.

Lawrence and Stephens kept to the schedule dictated by Chan. According to Lawrence, Chan had told the pair to meet him at the Centre Stage bar at the Hard Rock the same day they arrived in Bali. The instructions had been doled out back in Australia and there was no option but to stick to them. So at 6 p.m. the duo headed for the Hard Rock. So too did Matthew Norman and Si Yi Chen, who had been on the same flight as them earlier in the day. But they were staying in a more salubrious establishment — the White Rose Hotel, just behind the Sari Club bombing memorial in Kuta, where a prayer mounted in gold lettering on a large board at the hotel's entrance bears testimony to the night that will haunt the island for ever.

Rooms at the White Rose begin at US$95 per night, not that this pair was paying either. With an opulent marble foyer area, glass chandeliers and big vases of fresh flowers, the hotel is definitely more upmarket than some of the establishments used by other members of the group.

That evening as they all gathered, Lawrence would later tell police, they talked about the flight and had dinner. Chan gave directions on what assignments would be completed in Bali. Next morning there was no sleep-in for Lawrence, who says she had been ordered by Chan to meet him every day during her stay. So at 9 a.m. she saw him but says now that it was 'normal' and that there was no special talk.

It was now 8 April 2005. Another bunch of the conspirators was due to fly in. They were the Brisbane connection, along with a 'dark-skinned man'. Scott Rush, Michael Czugaj, Tan Duc Thanh Nguyen and Myuran Sukumaran — whose identity, almost until the time of his arrest, would remain unknown to the police and who was known variously to the police as the 'negro' and 'dark-skinned man' — arrived to the smell of incense at around 2.30 p.m.

Rush and Czugaj headed to the Aneka Beach Hotel in Kuta, just a couple of doors down from the Hard Rock on Kuta's beachfront. It seemed there was a pecking order almost, in terms of the hotels chosen for the different members of the group. Those in charge appeared to want to keep a watchful eye on the Brisbane rookies, making sure they were within easy reach. The two boys were young, still teenagers, and this was the first time they had ventured away from home. So Rush and Czugaj were kept very close to Chan, Sukumaran and Nguyen.

Meanwhile, the Sydney mules, Lawrence and Stephens, were kept further away. Not so far as the crow flies, but far enough given the maze of Bali's one-way streets, often jam-packed with cars crawling at little faster than walking speed. Sometimes you might only want to go across the block, but it could take half an hour to get there by car because the main street running along Kuta's beachfront is one way, so getting to your destination involves going all the way around.

Part of the plan was to ensure that the Sydney and Brisbane mules did not meet up — they were not to know each other. While this was Stephens's first trip, Lawrence had done it before and could be relied upon to keep Stephens on track. And the White Rose where Chen and Norman were staying was not all that far from the Hard Rock. Again, Norman had done this before and could be on hand to guide Chen. A hierarchy, based on the rookies and the old hands, and on the Brisbane and Sydney connections, had clearly been established.

Rush and Czugaj's lodgings for the next eight days would be room 404 at the Aneka, booked from Australia as part of their flight and accommodation package. The 5- by 4-metre bedroom with two single beds sporting white bed coverings and maroon cushions, and a bedside table in the middle, was more than adequate for these two teenagers who had never been outside of Australia before. A carved and colourful wooden Balinese wedding couple drew the eye to the wall above the television. Luscious green palm trees framed the balcony of the second-floor room, and the bathroom, while dated, had everything Rush and Czugaj needed. They seemed to be happy there, making good use of the Aneka's 20-metre swimming pool and sunken bar.

Room 404 is a standard room, with a published rate of US$60 per night; however, their room rate was less given that it had been booked from Australia as part of a package. Sukumaran, who would later be elevated from being the unknown 'dark man' to one of the kingpins of this enterprise, along with Nguyen, was also ensconced at the Hard Rock, headquarters of the big bosses.

In keeping with their orders, the latest arrivals — Rush, Czugaj and Nguyen — headed to their meeting with Chan. It was 6 p.m. and the designated meeting place was far more downmarket than that for the group who had arrived two days earlier: the international drug conspirators convened at the KFC outlet in nearby Kuta Square. Sukumaran was also there.

KFC was as good a place as any — no one would have taken any notice of this group there. Tourists wanting a cheap meal duck in there for some Indonesian-style KFC (served traditionally with rice like most dishes in this part of the world), mingling with locals who have also developed a taste for the Western fried chicken. Outside, motorbike and car drivers hang around hoping to snare someone who needs a lift. 'Transport, transport, you want transport?' they chime, miming the holding of a steering wheel.

Chan had one more important job to fulfil on 8 April — the most important of his trip. He had to make his way a couple of blocks down the beachfront road, Jalan Pantai Kuta — which, translated, means Kuta Beach Street — from the Hard Rock to Kuta Seaview Cottage. The promotional brochure describes it as 'a place for leisure' and it looks it — some rooms boast ocean views from the balconies. But one of the guests was not there for leisure. Cherry Likit Bannakorn, alias Pina or Paket, was there on business. The twenty-two year old had flown from Thailand to meet with Chan and hand him a specially constructed silver suitcase — built so it would slip easily through Customs without its valuable contents being detected. They hadn't been, and neither had her presence in Bali. No one was even looking for Cherry Likit Bannakorn. At that stage the AFP's letter to their Indonesian counterparts was still being written and sent to Bali police, but her name wouldn't appear on it. Chan's name was on it, but when he made the journey to the Seaview Cottage, no one was watching him. He collected the suitcase, which contained up to 5 kilograms of heroin, without a hitch. And Likit Bannakorn went home.

XVII

A Week in Bali

To Michael Czugaj, it must have almost seemed too good to be true. An all-expenses-paid eight-day vacation in one of the world's best holiday spots. For any nineteen year old, it would be an exciting adventure. But to the nineteen-year-old Queensland glazier with no international air miles notched up, it would have been almost unbelievable: the white-water rafting and surfing, swimming and jet-ski riding; the busy sidewalks packed with good deals; the nightlife that gives Kuta a buzz from dusk to dawn, and then the loud, chaotic din of city living that revolves around making tourists feel special. And the beer — really cheap beer. Bali's diversity has always been its drawcard — it offers everything for everyone. And that's how it must have seemed for the Oxley teenager, who was in a Brisbane nightclub one week and on the holiday to Bali the next.

On the day Czugaj arrived in Bali on board an Australian Airlines flight with his Brisbane mate Scott Rush, one Australian dollar converted to about 7500 Indonesian rupiah — one can only imagine how many beers that exchange rate allowed. And the good deals didn't stop at the bar: a seafood barbecue meal, the likes of which Czugaj might never have tried back home, could cost as little as $10, and a plate of *nasi goreng* (fried rice) or *mie goreng* (fried noodles), a staple for the locals, only cost a few dollars, if that.

In comparison, a night out in Brisbane's Fortitude Valley could cost Czugaj or Rush more than $100 by the time they paid for parking, nightclub entry, a bite to eat and a few rounds of drinks. But here that kind of money could keep you going for night after night. People flocked to have dinner at one of the hundreds of cheap-as-chips restaurants. The low-budget accommodation, which looked pretty upmarket to the Brisbane boys, seemed to attract hundreds of Australians just like them. They didn't care for the ritzy joints along the beach, but those places were filled with Westerners too, all helped by the lucrative exchange rate.

However, this holiday was going to be lucrative in another way, even if Michael Czugaj didn't really understand all the consequences of that. He was along for the ride.

Within one day of Czugaj's arrival, though, the picture postcard of Bali started to lose its gloss. His buddy and roommate, Scott Rush, answered his telephone, taking a call from Tan Nguyen. Nguyen had been responsible for getting Rush and Czugaj to Bali, providing the connection which allowed their stay to be financed. Now he was inviting the pair to the Centre Stage bar at the Hard Rock Hotel. It was 9 April. Saturday — the beginning of the weekend.

Rush and Czugaj went to the Centre Stage, which seemed to target people just like themselves: young, toned and single. It was already busy on this Saturday afternoon, and the real entertainment was still hours away. That's when the Hard Rock Hotel's Centre Stage bar would come alive with anything and everything: body-painting competitions; bar-top dancing; a good live band. It all happened here on a Saturday night. But now, at this afternoon meeting, Nguyen was sounding more like a businessman than a tourist.

Nguyen told the two Brisbane teenagers that they would be required to carry a 'package' back to Australia in seven days' time. It was all part of the deal. And, if they were successful, they would pocket A$5000 each, according to information provided early to police. If they were suspicious at that time about what kind of package it was, or if they asked anyone about it, they didn't let on to the police who questioned them later.

In the meantime, the youths could kick up their heels. They had a week, Sunday through to Saturday, and a hell of a lot to try. Parasailing, jet-skiing, banana-boat riding and rafting could all fit their adventurous spirits. And those things could be interspersed with more serene activities like regular dips in the big hotel pool, along with drinks from the sunken bar. That was all the man-made stuff — but right at their doorstep sat Kuta Beach, where the sunsets were surreal. Tourists flock there for a dip in the ocean or a ride on its waves, or a walk on its sands. Czugaj didn't miss the chance to have a surf. He loved taking on the waves on Queensland's Gold Coast, and now here was an opportunity in Bali, renowned for its surfing.

Each day, hundreds take off their shoes and walk down to the trendy district of Seminyak. Rentals dot the strip. Not just for surfboards, but for whatever one may need. Licensed vendors and hagglers sell their wares there too: sarongs, T-shirts, board shorts and all manner of Bali souvenirs. The sound of tourists haggling over the hire of a deckchair and umbrella, asking about the price of a beachside massage or manicure, or to have their young daughters' hair braided in dozens of tiny plaits, provides the background music. And the smell is of toned bodies and food: suntan lotion and the Indonesian fare — mostly noodles and snacks cooked on gas burners with big woks — that tourists down between their morning and afternoon beach visits.

Two doors down from the Sari Club bombing memorial, in Jalan Legian, is a different kind of place, one of those trendy new bars and restaurants that have sprung up in recent years to challenge the traditional venues in Bali. Some people love it; others loathe it, remembering the less commercial 1970s and '80s in Jalan Legian and places like it, and believing that the new type of place changes the heart and soul of Bali.

The Mbargo Bar is one of those places. It was built and opened in the wake of the 2002 bombings, on the opposite side of the road and just one or two shops up from where the Sari Club once stood. The site's former building was destroyed in the bombing and Mbargo is a world away from the Sari Club. Members of the Bali Nine spent a bit of time there in the week leading up to 17 April, indulging in drinks and dancing. Some would later claim to police that it was there that they met other members of the gang for the first time, although some of those claims are disingenuous.

Open from 8 p.m. to 3 a.m., the Mbargo doesn't serve food, and its décor mirrors that of trendy bars and clubs the world over. It has big open spaces and two rooms, one graced with leather lounges which are scattered throughout. In the other room, a series of red squares dominates one wall and a huge fresh flower arrangement sits atop a table smack-bang in the room's centre. This room is more decadent than the other but one can't help wondering how, on a busy night, the flower arrangement doesn't fall victim to the rowdy talk and jostling banter of the club's patrons.

Everyone fits in at the Mbargo club — the well dressed, well manicured and well suntanned mingle with the casually dressed tourists who have just lobbed into Bali searching for the same tan. Beers sell for the equivalent of A$2, and A$4 will fetch a gin and tonic. With those prices it's not the cheapest joint in town, but it has its pluses — it's upmarket and large and open, and still cheap if you compare it to Sydney or Brisbane.

Sukumaran later told police that this is where he first met Andrew Chan and Matthew Norman — a claim later shown to be untrue. And it was also the club where he planned to celebrate his twenty-fourth birthday, had he not been arrested that evening. Lawrence and Stephens also visited Mbargo once, but never when Rush or Czugaj were present. Chan and Sukumaran's insistence that the two groups of mules not meet took care of that.

The Brisbane crew of Rush and Czugaj were making the most of their time in Bali. They were acting for all the world like a couple of true tourists. One day they tripped up to Ubud, just over an hour's drive northeast of Kuta. It too has become gentrified in recent years, with boutiques and swish restaurants nestled alongside market stalls. Described as a cultural centre where artists and painters like to make both their homes and their livings, it's known for its art. The famed Monkey Forest is also nearby, and here hundreds of monkeys run around trying to steal tourists' bags while baring their teeth. Most tourists buy little bags of food at the front gate to feed them, their cameras at the ready to ensure no opportunities are lost. A Hindu temple has been built just inside the forest grounds.

Rush and Czugaj also visited the mountains of Kintamani, to see Mount Batur, a semi-active volcano which last erupted in 1994. Its crater, Lake Batur, is the biggest lake in Bali and on a clear day the view is spectacular. On a cloudy day, however, you can feel a bit ripped off.

The Brisbane lads were like the thousands of other visitors to Bali each year who take note of the guidebooks and hotel brochures, which invariably recommend a trip to Ubud and Kintamani. Shopping, too, is highly recommended, partly because it allows an extra bag of gifts for those at home without breaking the bank. Clothes are on sale everywhere, but wood carvings are popular too (especially of male genitals) and planeloads of them — as stand-alone ornaments of all sizes or as key rings — have become a popular, if not comical, souvenir of many Bali holidays.

Some of the nine young Australians in Bali that week also wanted them as keepsakes. Mana Hanang, a handicraft shop in Jalan Legian, sells them along with a variety of other wooden objects, not all of them aimed at foreigners' senses of humour. Indeed, when Stephens and Lawrence went there during their week in Bali, Stephens chose a medium-sized replica penis as a keepsake of his Bali holiday. The pair was not alone on that shopping trip, however — they had a companion who was helpfully suggesting which souvenirs they might like to take home with them. It was Andrew Chan. And their choices were not strictly souvenirs they would cherish for ever — they were pragmatic purchases which would later be used to divert attention to their luggage and away from themselves when they were arriving home in Australia.

In addition to shopping with others, Andrew Chan was out and about inspecting the local wares on his own, but his shopping was strictly business. On his second Monday in Kuta, he wandered the streets inspecting the market stalls that lined the roads. Here, he put his mind to shopping for shirts — brightly coloured ones like those tourists the length and breadth of Bali were donning. But he was specific: he wanted blue shirts with white, yellow or other coloured flowers as motifs. And they needed to be big-sized. The skimpy little versions, also popular, were useless to him. They had to be loose.

Chan found that the shirts he wanted were a dime a dozen and he had no trouble sourcing them. Every second place offers them for next to nothing, just a couple of dollars — depending, of course, on your bargaining skills. And reductions are always offered for bulk purchases. That helps when it comes to haggling, a sport enjoyed by both the locals and the tourists. You can tell those who aren't on their first trip to the markets

— they start bargaining at half the asking price and secure a deal quickly. Others don't know what to do, which disappoints the stallholders, who are genuinely let down if they get a tourist who won't bargain.

Chan was in a good position to bargain. He didn't want one or two of the shirts, but at least four and all in different sizes. They were gifts to others in the Bali Nine, whether they welcomed them or not — Renae Lawrence and Martin Stephens, who were both stocky, and Scott Rush and Michael Czugaj, who were a bit smaller. Chan didn't need to buy the smallest size, though — he wanted the shirts to swim on the wearers. They were a uniform, needed to keep secret the kilograms of drugs that would be strapped to the waists of the four young Australian mules.

Scott Rush and Michael Czugaj were having a swell holiday, tripping off around the tourist sites. But sometimes they were forced to remain in town, as on 12 April, when they were summoned to a meeting, again at the Hard Rock Hotel. Chan was there; so was Sukumaran. And, of course, their Brisbane connection, Tan Nguyen. It was a crucial meeting, one that reminded all present that it was business at the heart of this trip, not pleasure.

It was Nguyen who delivered the news to the nineteen year olds: that they would be returning home on an Australian Airlines flight with packages strapped to their bodies. The packages would contain heroin, although evidence varies on whether they were aware of that. That's why the boys were brought to Bali, and that was the catch. If Czugaj had had any secret doubts about the true nature of their 'free' holiday, they would have hit him now with spectacular clarity. Heroin. On his body. A game of life and death — literally. But certainly lucrative too, they were told. If they made good with the task, a cool A$5000 would be handed to them as a reward.

Chan, Sukumaran and Nguyen seemed organised — SIM cards were handed out with an instruction for the boys to install them in their phones. One number programmed into the cards was particularly important — that of the person they needed to call on touchdown in Sydney.

Then the meeting was over, and Czugaj and Rush had two days before their scheduled return flight on 14 April. Two whole days.

Rush and Czugaj might have been given their instructions on this day, 12 April, but it was also the day that Bali intelligence squad officer Nyoman Gatra was taking possession of the AFP's letter. The next day at 8.30 p.m., Officer Gatra, who was in charge of the investigation, convened a meeting with other members of the surveillance crew to dish out the tasks and work out who would monitor which Australians. Like a net cast into the ocean amid a school of unsuspecting fish, it was being thrown wide over the group.

Their tasks assigned, officers set about their work; by 10 p.m. the surveillance crew knew that Rush and Czugaj were in room 404 at the Hotel Aneka, Chen and Norman were at the White Rose, and room 5314 in the Pop section of the Hard Rock was inhabited by Chan. It was a good start. But they still had to locate Stephens and Lawrence.

In a covert operation, officers moved into the room opposite Chen and Norman so they could better monitor their movements. As things turned out, the surveillance crew — many of whom had never done an operation quite like this before, would have more time than they originally thought for their task. Had things gone the way they were first planned, the group of Australians would have been departing for Sydney with their heroin the next day. But there had been a hitch: Cherry Likit Bannakorn, who was to supply the drugs to the Bali Nine, had not brought enough of it with her on her first trip to Bali, and Chan wanted to wait for another shipment before the mules set off home. So, with the decision made, the mules' return flights were changed.

If Rush and Czugaj were perturbed by the mission they were set to undertake, it wasn't immediately obvious. They certainly didn't stay locked in their rooms. The next day, 14 April, they left their hotel at 8 a.m. to try their hands at white-water rafting at Teras Ayung in Ubud, on the Ayung River, Bali's longest river. Six hours later they were back at the hotel, resting for five or so hours before venturing out for a fifteen-minute stroll. It was about 7 p.m., and they were totally unaware that they were being followed. The two surveillance officers assigned to them, Nyoman Suastika and Wayan Warsa, were watching closely and following from a distance. Later that evening, at about 10 p.m., Rush and Czugaj were peckish so they ventured out for a walk, down the beachfront road a few blocks to the Circle K, a 24-hour convenience store. They returned with a few snacks before settling for the night.

Chan was busy — he had to make sure the other two mules were up with the plan too. He told Lawrence and Stephens that their return had been delayed and that they needed to move hotels — to the Adhi Dharma in Jalan Benesari, one street behind Jalan Legian. Room 124 had already been booked for them by Chan and Sukumaran. Lawrence and Stephens would have liked the room — it was right next to the swimming pool. Chen and Norman's room was close by, too. They had also checked into the Adhi Dharma on that day, at about 2.30 p.m. They were in room 118; Nguyen was in room 105.

The Adhi Dharma was to be the new headquarters for the Bali Nine. It wasn't a bad place from which to run a heroin-smuggling operation. It wasn't on a busy road but, rather, secluded at the end of a laneway, and many of the blocks along the laneway leading up to it were vacant, reducing the number of eyes that could record the group's comings and goings. But it wasn't quite secluded enough — the surveillance squad was onto them, watching their every move. They monitored which rooms were booked in the group's names, how and what time they came and went, with whom and in which taxis.

Chan and Sukumaran, who were still lodging at the Hard Rock, had fixed up the bills at the previous hotels and spent the day bouncing backwards and forwards between the Hard Rock and the Adhi Dharma. They were checking things, organising things, and then re-checking things. The surveillance team was watching it all, but still had no idea who Sukumaran was. His name had not been included in the original list sent by the AFP; indeed, the AFP had never heard of him. Officers thought he was possibly Chan's bodyguard, because they seemed to travel everywhere together.

Friday, 15 April turned out to be a busy day for all of the Bali Nine, starting with an early morning meeting all the way over at Sanur. A 25-minute taxi ride to the east of Kuta, Sanur is a beachside resort area favoured by families and Europeans. At 7.15 a.m., Lawrence, Stephens, Chen and Norman hopped into a taxi to the Grand Bali Beach Hotel in Sanur; a surveillance crew watched them. They stayed only an hour and by 8.50 a.m. were back in the Adhi Dharma. They had gone to delay their flights. At 10.35 a.m. another unlikely trip took place, this time to the State Hinduism Academy in Denpasar. Again it was only for an hour, then they returned to the Adhi Dharma.

Meanwhile, over in Rush and Czugaj's room, things weren't looking rosy. A day rafting had taken its toll and the hotel worker who provided them room service at 9 a.m. reported back to police that one of them was sick with the flu. They needed ice cream to cheer themselves up, and set off a couple of hours later to the Circle K store to get some. Later that day they ventured out again, this time to a local laundry where they got their clothes washed and pressed for a fraction of the price it would have cost at their hotel.

From a safe distance, surveillance crews watched. And watched. It was a slow process, waiting for someone else to make the move, but it was paying dividends. For example, at 1.30 p.m. the Brisbane pair walked from their hotel, past the Hard Rock Hotel, where they met up with Chan, Chen and Sukumaran, who joined them on the walk to the laundry. Washing dropped off, the groups went back to their respective hotels.

Andrew Chan's next job for the day was the most important of the lot — a 9 p.m. meeting with Cherry Likit Bannakorn at Seaview Cottage. She had arrived in Bali that afternoon at 5.30 p.m. with the second shipment of heroin, which Chan had been waiting on. The operation could now proceed. Taxi driver Dewa Gede Risdana Mesi remembers picking up Bannakorn from the international terminal at the airport. She had a black suitcase and he took her to the Seaview Cottage.

Surveillance crews watched as Chan walked from the Hard Rock Hotel down the road to the Seaview Cottage, where he spent ten minutes inside before leaving. They had no idea what he was doing there or who he was meeting. They had no way of knowing that the woman he met inside for those ten minutes was someone they would turn out to be very interested in indeed. That wouldn't become obvious for a few days yet. But the countdown was on.

XVIII

A Woman Called Cherry

Police called Cherry Likit Bannakorn, born in Thailand on 12 June 1983, their master key, and a very lucky one at that. At least twice she had travelled to Bali carrying special X-ray-proof suitcases full of heroin. Flying from Bangkok to Singapore, Java and Bali, twice she had escaped the police net. Twice she met with Andrew Chan and twice she stayed at the same Kuta hotel. But, despite a surveillance operation, she managed to evade those officers employed to keep a sneaky eye on the Bali Nine. The first time wasn't hard — her initial meeting with Chan was held before the surveillance even started. But the second meeting was right in the middle of it. Except no one knew who she was.

About 160 centimetres tall with brown, shoulder-length hair, Bannakorn was a pretty good master of disguise, often wearing wigs to make herself look different. But the one thing she couldn't disguise was the blue braces on her teeth. Eventually she was caught, but even then, like a cat with nine lives, she managed to slip away. Bali's former drug squad chief, Lieutenant Colonel Bambang Sugiarto — who left Bali soon after the arrests, promoted to a new position — says the failure to nab her was one of his regrets. They needed her, he said, to unlock the bigger picture of the heroin trade in Indonesia, and to find out who was supplying the drugs and easing their path from Burma to Bali. It wasn't to be.

Cherry's brush with capture came on 30 May 2005, about six weeks after the Bali Nine were apprehended. She had been placed on an immigration watch, and on this day, on the Thai–Malaysian border as she tried to re-enter Thailand, officers stopped her. Thai Immigration authorities confiscated her passport and held her, pending questioning. An Interpol 'wanted' poster for her had also been circulated after authorities had managed to glean her identity from members of the Bali Nine. Police intelligence reports described her as strongly suspected of being a member or messenger of an international drug syndicate spanning half a dozen countries, including Australia, Nepal, Nigeria, Thailand and Indonesia.

The Thais told Indonesia about Cherry being nabbed, and by 2 June a team of officers from Indonesia and the AFP were in Bangkok. But Cherry was not happy. She had no intention of dobbing herself or anyone else in; instead, she was evasive. She said she was not a drug syndicate courier or messenger, but a prostitute. While she admitted that she did know Andrew Chan, she said it was only in her capacity as a prostitute. Shown Chan's picture, Cherry exclaimed to the officers, 'Oh yes! True, I know this person. His name is Tony.' She went on to say that she had had sex twice with the man she knew as Tony, whom police knew as Andrew Chan. Given time and evidence, though, they felt confident that they could wear her down.

The Indonesian police wanted Cherry brought back to Indonesia for further interrogation. But there was a hitch: under Thai law, an individual could not be arrested or detained unless evidence of narcotics was found on their person. In addition, the Indonesian police quickly needed an extradition application, which they didn't have, to provide a basis for keeping Cherry detained in Thailand. They tried another way: perhaps Cherry would volunteer, freely, to come to Indonesia as a witness in the case?

Amazingly and miraculously, she agreed. As a sign of the sincerity of her pledge, she handed her passport to the female Indonesian officer. And she further promised, with all the sincerity she could muster, that the next day she would turn up to the Banyan Tree Hotel, where the Indonesian team was staying, and would spend the night there with them, getting reading to fly the next day to Jakarta.

Of course, it was too good to be true. What criminal, of any calibre, would agree to come back for punishment if the choice was to run away, freedom beckoning, or put your own head on the chopping block? Cherry never intended to spend the night in a nice hotel and wing her way to Jakarta to answer some questions that could put her before the firing squad. She intended to disappear with great haste, and could not get out of the Thai police office quickly enough that day. It had been a close call — too close for comfort — and she turned her phone off. She didn't want the pesky Indonesian police tracking her down through the mobile phone records. She moved out of her home as well, an apartment in a Bangkok block inhabited by a large number of Nigerians.

Police intelligence reports describe Cherry as working as a freelance employee at two import and export companies owned by a Thai entrepreneur. She had received transfers of US$1000 into her Bank Asia account and had travelled to Cambodia and other neighbouring countries. Intelligence suggested that her livelihood was funded by a Canadian journalist boyfriend, and that she also had a Nigerian boyfriend.

It was, however, too late. Cherry, the disguise queen, had slipped the net, more through luck than anything else.

* * *

Not so for the recipients of the heroin she had brought over from Thailand. Mobile phones were their constant companions, and it's often the case that too much talk on phones brings people doing the wrong thing unstuck, especially when it comes to police connecting the dots in a criminal investigation. Connecting the dots here provided police with a further fascinating insight into the hierarchy of the nine. The most junior — and first-timers — Czugaj, Chen and Stephens didn't even have a mobile phone supplied to them. Instead, their partners in the crime and roommates — respectively — Rush, Norman and Lawrence did all the communicating with the bosses and simply relayed the orders. They had been provided with phones, but those calling the shots did all the talking. Police charts showed that Chan spoke mostly with Norman, Lawrence and Nguyen, and most of his conversations were with Norman. And Nguyen and Rush spoke often with each other as well. At the top of the ladder, Sukumaran had no telephone contact with any of them, except a few calls with Chan. He was staying in the same hotel as Chan and obviously left the rest of the communication to those lower down the pecking order.

The members of the group were not unaware of the dangers phone talk could post to that plan. Chan, especially, knew this, and Lawrence would later tell police that Chan instructed them to speak only in code when using the mobile phones, all of which had pre-paid Indonesian SIM cards in them. Lawrence said that she was forced to fulfil all of Chan's instructions to her every day, and that the deal was that if he called her, she was not allowed to ask any questions of him.

'During the conversations via telephone we were not allowed to ask or talk about our hotels where we stayed. In our conversations we used code,' Lawrence told police during one interrogation session.

The codes went something like this: 'Are you at home?' was code for 'Are you in the hotel?'. If they were not in the hotel they would say, 'I am shopping'. Matthew Norman's code name was, apparently, 'John' and some members knew Sukumaran as 'Mark'. Lawrence said she had been instructed to remain together with Stephens at all times, and she was told not to hang out with Chen or Norman.

Prosecutors would later describe it as a neat and tidy organisation, the separation of the two groups a deliberate strategy to guarantee the secrecy of the operation. Only Andrew Chan ever met with Cherry — and police investigators couldn't get her to answer her phone.

XIX

A Last Supper

Words are not always what they seem. Sometimes they say one thing but mean something entirely different. Renae Lawrence knew that. On 16 April, Andrew Chan sent an SMS to her mobile phone: *Later, might take you out for a great dinner. Pray you don't get Bali belly*. But Chan never had any intention of taking Lawrence out for any kind of dinner: the message was a code, not an invitation.

Chan had ordered all the mobile phone holders to speak and communicate only in code and never talk about anything important over the phone lines. They obeyed him, but he had stupidly overlooked the fact that as long as they were all using the phones, the devices would end up providing investigators with a golden opportunity to link members of the group to each other. This person called that person fifty-nine times; another person called eighty times; this one made thirty-three calls out and received twelve calls in. Too easy, really, once all the phones were seized. All senior members of the group had bought local SIM cards once they arrived in Bali. Pre-paid SIM cards are a huge market in Indonesia, and they can be bought on any street corner anywhere for just 25 000 rupiah, or a few dollars. All you need then do is buy phone credit in vouchers of 50 000 or 100 000 rupiah. It made it very difficult for members of the Nine to claim, as some later would, that they didn't know other members of the group. The amount of phone chatter between some of them spoke volumes.

While Andrew Chan was probably planning to have a good dinner that night, Renae Lawrence actually wasn't invited. Neither was Martin Stephens. It was the Brisbane crew, along with the chieftains, who would sit down at the same table for what would become their last supper.

Lawrence knew, though, that the SMS from Chan had nothing to do with food. Instead, it meant that the drugs were ready and the group would soon be leaving Bali. Had Michael Czugaj known it would be the last time he would sit down and order dinner in a real restaurant — and a nice one at that — from a menu, he might well have ordered something far more substantial than a plate of hot chips with sauce. Or he might not. Perhaps it was the nerves, knowing that the next day he would be doing his first-ever drug run, that forced him to pass up the extensive menu of pasta, pizza, steaks, lamb, fish and Asian dishes. Or perhaps he just wasn't into fancy cuisine at all.

There were five people at dinner that night. Chan, Sukumaran and Nguyen arrived first, at 9.40 p.m. They had just been at the Adhi Dharma visiting those of the Nine who would not be dining with them. Chan must have been looking forward to the dinner — he had been out and about all afternoon, to and from the Adhi Dharma and the Hard Rock, finalising arrangements for the return to Australia. The trio was joined almost one hour later by Rush and Czugaj. Sitting around a table, Rush and Czugaj were on one side and the bosses were opposite them.

They were at The Maccaroni Club in Kuta. In Jalan Legian, and almost opposite where Paddy's Bar stood before it was destroyed in 2002, the Club was another one of those trendy bars and restaurants that have sprung up in the area.

And it offers an extra incentive — free wireless internet terminals in the upstairs section. First opened in 1996, it was refurbished after the 2002 bombings which destroyed large parts of the building. It wasn't a bad place for a last supper, even if the prices were a bit on the steep side compared to other less upmarket places.

Candles surrounded by traditional banana trunk burnt on the table where the five Aussie lads sat. Some had ordered full meals with the works. Others, like Czugaj, had something simple. Chatting, the younger guys appeared relatively relaxed, at least outwardly, and looked like regular tourists.

Chan and Sukumaran were less at ease. Their furtive eyes constantly darted around, looking upwards to the club's second floor. But they weren't sharp enough — sitting upstairs, pretending to be yet another regular tourist with a handycam, was a man called Herry Pribadi. Had the Australians known about Herry, they would have made themselves very scarce indeed, for Herry was one of the surveillance officers charged with filming and taking photos of this group, and on this night he captured them sitting down to supper. It was dark, and the ambient lighting didn't help matters, but Herry didn't dare turn on the video camera's light or try to use the night-vision mode which would have projected a red beam and alerted the group to his interest in them. It didn't really matter, though — he got what he needed: five of the nine sitting down together, chatting like old friends.

At one stage Sukumaran, who appeared suspicious, looked up and around. But Herry was out of sight and nonchalantly doing his best disinterested-diner impersonation. Earlier, he had walked into the Maccaroni minutes after the group and passed right by them as he went upstairs. He had also filmed Chan and Sukumaran as they left the Adhi Dharma and got into the taxi that took them to the restaurant. The evidence was growing.

Much earlier in the day, around 11 a.m., Rush and Czugaj were captured both on video and in still photographs frolicking in the swimming pool at their hotel; they were told that day to change their departure date to 17 April.

Perched on the other side of the wall, near the reception area, Herry held his breath. He was desperately worried that he would be spied and caught out. It was the first time he had ever done a surveillance job like this and he was operating more on instinct than on training. Unlike his counterparts in Australia, or those portrayed in television dramas, Herry had not received any special training, and this kind of surveillance was new to the officer.

Aside from some contemplative moments, when Rush held on to the side of the 20-metre-long pool, lost in his own thoughts, the pair looked pretty calm and relaxed, like they didn't have too many problems in the world. There was, however, no laughing and tomfoolery. They were having a gentle swim, playing with a float and having a drink or two from the sunken pool bar. They stayed in the pool for two hours, until about 1 p.m., before resting up and getting ready for the last supper.

While the Brisbane recruits swam and relaxed, Chan and Sukumaran were busy, starting from the early hours of that morning. Only the evening before, Chan had met Cherry Likit Bannakorn to collect the rest of the heroin. Police surveillance crews watched them; everything was documented.

2.45 a.m. The target [Chan] and his black-skinned friend went out riding Bluebird taxi 002 carrying two suitcases to Plamboyan Hotel in Dewi Sartika Street.

3.15 a.m. They arrived back at Hard Rock Hotel riding Komotro Taxi 056 without the two suitcases.

7.40 a.m. The target left Hard Rock Hotel, went to Plamboyan Hotel and returned with two big suitcases.

The surveillance records went on.

4.50 p.m. Arriving by taxi, Andrew Chan together with a black-skinned man entered Adhi Dharma and went to room 105, where Nguyen stayed.
6.50 p.m. Andrew Chan with a black-skinned man leave Adhi Dharma hotel on foot.
7.40 p.m. Arrived on foot, Andrew Chan together with the black-skinned man entering back to the hotel.
9.40 p.m. Andrew Chan together with Nguyen and the black man leave the Adhi Dharma hotel using Bali Taxi number 422 towards Maccaroni restaurant in Legian Street, Kuta. At that place they met Scott Anthony Rush and Michael William Czugaj.

The same day, 16 April, Lawrence and Stephens were watching DVDs in their room at the Adhi Dharma. They had rented a DVD player from a tiny shop just down the road, and it had cost them less than A$10 for two days. Wayan Sudiarta and his wife remember the pair coming to their small convenience store, called Amka. They looked innocent enough and certainly no different to the other tourists who drop by to stock up on the cigarettes, bottled water and beer the couple sell. Wayan Sudiarta likes a chat, but he remembers that this pair never hung around to shoot the breeze with him. In and out, they got what they wanted and left again. Ever the diplomat whose business relies on tourists, it worried Wayan. He thought he must have done something wrong or somehow offended Stephens, hence his reluctance to even engage in small talk whenever he came into the shop. Wayan also remembers that some days, while Stephens was inside the shop, a black man would be waiting outside, silent as a tomb, he never returned greetings. Wayan thought it was rude and again wondered what he had done to offend these guys, and why the black man never,

ever ventured inside his shop. He would always wait sullenly on the sidewalk.

Departure day was fast approaching: 17 April 2005. Rush and Czugaj ate breakfast in their room at the Hotel Aneka. It really would have been far more pleasant and relaxing to head down to the hotel's restaurant area, next to the pool, to choose from the extensive buffet, but they were more content to order room service. They had done it the previous day as well.

Nguyen then called to tell them it was time to check out, and at about 11.20 a.m. they met Nguyen in the lobby. It was Nguyen who paid the bill for their extra days before the trio headed off to the Adhi Dharma Hotel and into room 105. The point of no return was beckoning.

Later that day, between 2 and 3 p.m., Stephens was blissfully unaware of an encounter with one of his pursuers. He was returning the rented DVD player to Wayan's shop when he almost ran straight into Herry Pribadi, who was waiting outside the Adhi Dharma for his next order when he glanced up and standing right there, within arm's reach, was Stephens. Herry didn't actually know what Stephens looked like, as he had not yet been called upon to film him, but something told Herry the man walking towards him was one of the nine targets. He adopted his best 'I'm just hangin' around with nothing to do' poses; Stephens didn't seem to be the least bit suspicious and kept walking, barely even glancing in the officer's direction. Herry breathed a sigh of relief. It would not do for the team to be sprung at this late stage of the operation.

Chan was up and about early on 17 April. He had to be — it was time for action. The mules needed to be ready, both physically and mentally. Everything else was almost in place.

At 7.40 a.m. Chan caught a taxi from the Hard Rock to the Adhi Dharma, where he met with Stephens, giving him a wooden statue that he was to put into his luggage. He also gave him a bag. By 8.30 a.m. Chan was at the tiny reception desk of Yan's Beach Bungalow in Kuta. Yan's is not a flash establishment, but it does have one thing on its side: location, location, location. It is on Jalan Dewi Sartika, within easy walking distance of the Kuta markets and Kuta Square shopping area, and directly across the street from the Melasti bungalows, where Sukumaran and the other three would check in later that evening. In terms of price and plushness, Yan's is not a bit like the Hard Rock. It is a budget place, designed and priced for backpackers or those with little cash who still want a Bali holiday.

It didn't much matter anyway, because Chan had absolutely no intention of staying there. He wanted to use the room for storage.

The rooms at Yan's are cramped, with simple single beds, dark interiors and very few extras, but cost a meagre 150 000 rupiah or A$21 per night for air conditioning or 100 000 rupiah (A$14) for ceiling fans only. Chan chose fans: he didn't need cool air, because he intended spending no more than a few minutes inside before heading back to the Adhi Dharma.

Using the fictitious name of David Yu, Chan checked into room C5. It was straight up the stairs behind reception. With him he took two suitcases — a silver one and a dark blue one. By 9 a.m. Chan was out of there again and on his way to the Adhi Dharma. Three hours later, he and Sukumaran left the Adhi Dharma and went back to the Hard Rock; within one hour they were back at the Adhi Dharma, entering room 105. And now, to load up the mules.

XX

The $24 Million Gift Wrap

It was Scott Rush's turn. He stood up and turned so his young, toned body was facing the bed. Ahead of him, a big piece of Balinese art featuring three ducks hung on the wall. Rush put one hand on the bar of the bed and lifted his right leg, balancing on his left, just as Sukumaran ordered. He had his eyes closed tightly, but every now and again he would sneak a look — just a little one — careful to ensure that Nguyen and his friends, Sukumaran and Chan, didn't catch him out. Rush's friend, Michael Czugaj, had just been through the same ritual, and now, for the next hour or so, Rush could expect that they would be making demands of him. *Move this way, bend that way, come closer*. The two Brisbane youths were scared witless: they had been informed that their families would be killed if they didn't do what they were told, if they did not obey every little instruction.

Rush closed his eyes again. His right leg rested on the bed as Sukumaran bent down and carefully attached a clear plastic package to his right thigh, then Chan wrapped a bandage around it. Chan then sprinkled pepper over the bandage before wrapping it another time, using a light-brown binding. Working in relay, Sukumaran and Chan continued. Rush put his left leg on the bed, Sukumaran attached a second clear plastic package to it, Chan wrapped another clear bandage around it, sprinkled it with pepper and wrapped it some more. And so it went on.

A third plastic package appeared, just as it had for Czugaj. This one required Rush to bend over slightly so it could be attached to the back of his waist. Again, Sukumaran and Chan worked as part of a polished two-man team: Sukumaran meticulously placing the package on Rush's back before his former school friend wrapped it up like a Christmas present. First, a clear bandage, then a small sprinkling of pepper before the same light-brown bandage was wrapped around that. Around Rush's waist they bound an extra bandage, again light brown in colour, but lined with a blue cloth this time.

Rush stood tall, now almost 1.7 kilograms heavier, his young body carrying a stash of heroin that could reap $500 000 on the streets of Sydney and beyond. But first he had to smuggle it through Indonesia's Ngurah Rai airport, out of the country that delivers death to drug traffickers and onto his flight to Australia. The gamble didn't pay dividends at that point, either: he would then have to sit uncomfortably for hours knowing that his body was laden with heroin, without raising suspicions. After the flight landed at Sydney's international airport, Rush and his friend, Czugaj, had to navigate their way past sniffer dogs, Customs officials and other staff, before being free to collect their promised booty.

Sukumaran and Chan began packing up what was left of their tools: a pair of scissors, adhesive tapes, cloth waist-belt and pepper powder. It had taken about an hour, but Rush and Czugaj were now ready. Rush was told to put on his shorts and shirt.

Their job complete, Sukumaran and Chan left the room.

* * *

It had only been a matter of hours earlier that Tan Duc Thanh Nguyen had swung by the Hotel Aneka to pick them up. Their friend from the southern suburbs of Brisbane paid for their room and the three young men grabbed a taxi, travelling to the Adhi Dharma Hotel, where they went straight to room 105. It was a nice hotel, quintessentially Balinese, two-storied and filled with Balinese architecture. The room was a deluxe one, demanding US$70 each night, and had been booked by Nguyen. He'd paid the higher rate for the three-star accommodation because it was the only room available.

When the Brisbane contingent arrived, Matthew Norman was already in the room; the grand four-poster bed with the crisp white and cream bedspread seemed at odds with the operation soon to get under way. Chan and Sukumaran, carrying a dark-blue suitcase, arrived soon after, and Norman was told to leave. That was only the beginning of the orders. Chan pulled out a wooden figurine and handed it to Rush and Czugaj, directing them to stuff it into their suitcase. And then the two older men left, promising to be back shortly.

True to their word, they returned at about 4 p.m., this time with a black and grey striped backpack, a black carrying case and a meticulous plan to evade investigators in two countries by using four young drug mules to deliver big chunks of heroin to the Australian market. And Rush and Czugaj were working for them, being paid to help them do that. They told them to have a shower.

When Czugaj wandered out, his body covered only by a pair of cycling shorts, Chan and Sukumaran set about the task at hand. They started on Czugaj. Using gloves, they took a big, clear plastic bag of heroin and placed it on the back of the nineteen year old. Using a brown and blue cloth bandage they fastened it, ensuring that it would not move in the hours between now and touchdown at Sydney airport. Next Chan told Czugaj to put his right leg on the bed before another

400 grams of heroin was plastered to his thigh, this time with clear adhesive tape. A similar amount was then taped to his left thigh with bandages. Chan knew that with one slip all the punctilious planning would be undone. It was critical that none of the packages could be seen — their lives could depend on it.

Czugaj was told to walk around inside the hotel room, an opportunity for Chan and Sukumaran to inspect their workmanship. Seemingly satisfied, Czugaj was told to dress, and Chan and Sukumaran left the room. Nguyen remained. He sat with his two Brisbane colleagues for almost an hour in a small Bali hotel room, where almost 3.5 kilograms of heroin was fastened to the bodies of the two nineteen year olds. It is doubtful whether any of them would have ever owned anything quite as valuable.

Barely 50 metres away in room 124, just down the walkway bordered by a fish pond on one side and the hotel pool on the other, another two young Australians were preparing for their own dice with death. Room 124 was popular, often booked out, because of its proximity to the pool and its sunken bar. The pair had booked into that room a couple of days earlier, on orders, and had never heard of Scott Rush or Michael Czugaj, despite all four of them being bound together in a risky operation where they could all face the same fate. But that was part of the detailed plan: Rush and Czugaj, the two teenagers from Brisbane, and Stephens and Lawrence, the workmates and friends from New South Wales, didn't need to meet each other now. Or ever, if things worked out the way Chan and Sukumaran had planned. The mules had been in Bali for days and not even sighted each other. They were there to do a job, and it was safer if each group of mules was unaware of the other's existence. That was the plan.

Matthew Norman walked through the door, a big black and grey backpack making little dent on his large frame. 'I feel rich carrying this bag,' some remembered him saying. He dumped the bag under the table and looked towards Stephens and Lawrence, two of his co-workers from Sydney. 'Don't touch it,' he commanded. He wasn't their boss at the Sydney Cricket Ground, but on this day he seemed to be giving the orders.

Norman left the room. Within minutes, Chan strode through the door, again with his friend Sukumaran, who was celebrating his twenty-fourth birthday. Chan had a bag slung over his shoulder and another one in his hand. Few pleasantries were exchanged before Chan ordered Stephens to open the bag Norman had just placed under the table, and take its contents into the bathroom. Chan and Sukumaran donned gloves and prepared for the operation ahead. They knew exactly what to do.

Lawrence was ordered to remove the shorts she was wearing and replace them with the blue adidas short leggings packed in her luggage at the Formule 1 hotel in Sydney more than a week earlier. Lawrence did as she was told and then stood in front of the bed, lifted her right leg and let it rest on the bed in front of her. She had done this once before, about six months ago, and she knew the drill, even if her friend Martin Stephens, also in the room, did not.

Sukumaran started this time, on Lawrence's right leg. He arranged two packs of heroin carefully, ensuring that the 668 grams remained intact. After wrapping the packs together in a white bandage and pepper, Chan secured them again, this time with a further two bandages. Then Chan attached the next two plastic wraps of heroin onto Lawrence's left leg. Combined, they weighed slightly heavier, but it was almost impossible to tell that with the naked eye. The wrapping ritual was repeated by the two young men who had gone to school together: a white bandage, ground pepper, followed by a tighter white bandage and finished off with a brown bind.

Lawrence's legs were now 1.2 kilograms heavier. But Chan was not finished yet. He had a large plastic bag of white powder next to him, and ordered Lawrence to bend over on the bed. When she did, he wrapped almost another kilogram of the powder to her waist. This one was secured with a fourth wrap made of red fabric.

Bandages secured, Lawrence stood up. She was told to turn around — once, twice, three times. Chan checked his work, then told her to put on her clothes, and, before moving on, he taught her how to pick up her luggage without bending over. Every movement mattered, and this was yet another detail not to be overlooked.

Martin Stephens had to take off his shirt, too, before the packages of heroin were stuck to his body: a red body pack on his back and on each of his thighs, held in place with brown sticky-tape and layers of binding. With his body playing host to 2.3 kilograms of heroin, Stephens's stash was bigger than those of his co-worker and roommate Lawrence and of the two young Brisbane drug mules he was unaware of in the room just across from the hotel pool.

Chan knew that in just a few hours the four drug mules would join him on the long flight back to Australia. They would leave in three separate taxis and walk through the airport without acknowledging each other, but with a total of about 8 kilograms of heroin attached to their bodies. Their flight home had already been delayed after a hiccup to the plan — the heroin had taken longer to source — but any hiccups at this late, crucial stage could create a real drama. Nothing could go wrong.

Already, though, this trip was proving vastly more successful than their last one, just four months earlier. A few of them had come to Bali then, but left empty-handed; that certainly wasn't the case this time. Chan's Sydney co-worker Renae Lawrence was carrying 2168.97 grams of heroin and Martin Stephens, whom he had also met through his casual catering job at the SCG, was transporting a bulk of 2341 grams. And the two

Brisbane youths introduced to him by Nguyen were carrying their share too, Czugaj with 1754 grams and Rush with 1692 grams. Four mules. Eight kilograms of heroin. One flight. And just a couple of hours to fill.

Sukumaran and Chan strode purposefully back to room 105, where Nguyen, Rush and Czugaj waited. They doled out 150 000 rupiah, giving clear instructions as to what it was to be used for: the taxi fare to Ngurah Rai airport and the departure tax they would need. Nguyen then made a final promise to the two youths who had been enticed into the Bali plan in a Brisbane karaoke club only weeks earlier: A$5000 would be swapped with the packages that clung to their body, if they managed to get them to Australia.

They had hours of work ahead of them now — the most important part of the trip — but had the telephone number to call on arrival at Sydney airport programmed into their mobile phones. With the clock ticking, Chan provided a few final orders: Rush was to call him when they were in the taxi on the way to the airport, and again when they stepped out of the cab and into the international terminal. And with those final orders made clear, Chan called reception to order a taxi. A few minutes later Czugaj and Rush's free ride to Ngurah Rai pulled up at the hotel. Lawrence and Stephens were heading in the same direction in another cab, their luggage now home to two wooden statues and a wooden jewellery box. Those items, chosen by neither Lawrence nor Stephens, were a final insurance policy by organisers who were banking on the items diverting the attention of Customs officers away from the young people and their bodies.

With every detail of his plan taken care of and his work done, Chan called a taxi for himself, and soon climbed into Komotro Taxi No 099, giving the driver orders to go directly to Ngurah Rai airport.

Nguyen and Sukumaran headed back to the Melasti Bungalows to meet up with Si Yi Chen and Matthew Norman. It was Sukumaran's birthday, and there needed to be some celebrations.

Chan's taxi pulled out from the Adhi Dharma Hotel and headed in the same direction as the taxis carrying Lawrence and Stephens, and Czugaj and Rush. Three taxis delivering five young Australians to a date with destiny. And none of them knew that surveillance teams were onto them, recording their every move.

XXI

Ride and Risk

The passenger in Komotro Taxi No 099, taking the journey from the Adhi Dharma Hotel to Bali's Ngurah Rai airport, exuded confidence. He talked big, like a rich man, and walked the walk. He was as smooth as silk. He laughed and joked with the driver, the short journey punctuated by the easy-going banter between driver Muhammad Zakaria and his lone passenger. In contrast, the atmosphere inside Bluebird Taxi No 081, which was making the same journey from the Adhi Dharma hotel to the airport, just slightly ahead of Zakaria's car, was one of deathly silence. Driver Komang Surat Nata was struck by how solemn his two young, male passengers were for the entire journey. Barely a word was spoken, between the pair or with the driver. There was no banter, no laughing and no joking, just a funereal pall. Nata wondered what was up with these two young fellows. He would never have guessed the truth, even if he had tried.

The journey from that particular Kuta hotel to the airport takes about ten to fifteen minutes, depending on the traffic. About 4.5 kilometres in length, it begins by weaving through side streets and laneways with dodgy surfacing, potholes and ragged edges. Then there is one last drive down Jalan Legian, past the haunts of the Bali Nine — the Mbargo Bar and Maccaroni Club, meeting places for their secret plan, which was now nearing completion — and the bustling myriad streetside stalls where some of the nine had shopped and whiled away some time.

On this Sunday evening, the taxi drivers ferrying the five young Australians from the hotel to the airport were unaware of the million-dollar merchandise they were carrying. With no speed limits, the shops flashed by quickly before they were in the business end of Kuta, with its mobile phone shops, motorbike service centres and food stalls offering the local Balinese delicacy of *babi guling* or suckling pig, cooked pig heads displayed grimly in the windows. The trip costs only a few dollars in Australian terms and the drivers are always keen to impress in the hope that departing passengers will throw them the remnants of their rupiah as a tip.

Bali taxis are not always known for their cleanliness, and often the air conditioners don't work. Some drivers talk incessantly with their passengers, giving them a last-minute guided tour of their homeland and handing over business cards with their mobile phone numbers, urging tourists to pass them on to their friends who might also visit.

The drive that evening wasn't particularly comfortable for Martin Stephens. The heroin strapped tightly around his waist was pinching, but it was only a small dress rehearsal for the six-hour flight to come. His taxi colleague, Renae Lawrence, wasn't bound as tightly. Within thirty minutes she would need to detour to the toilet to rescue hundreds of thousands of dollars of merchandise that was threatening to slip down her right thigh.

Just before the airport is one last and lasting memorial of Bali: the huge, imposing stone statue of Gatot Kaca, a mythical character. It is near the airport because legend has it that Gatot Kaca can fly. Legend also has it that Gatot Kaca is immortal. Did Lawrence and Stephens and those following behind, in two other taxis, think they were immortal as they passed by the gleaming white statue?

Scott Rush and Michael Czugaj were not far behind the taxi carrying Stephens and Lawrence. As the final stages of their mission approached, their nerves betrayed them. They were as silent as tombs. Aussie tourists — especially young fellows like these two — were not generally like this on their final ride to the airport; after two years of driving taxis, Komang Nata's experience told him this. Normally they were boisterous, friendly and happy, cracking jokes after having imbibed their last few Bintang beers before heading home.

To Nata, glancing in the rear-vision mirror at his two back-seat passengers, it seemed that the pair's thoughts were a million miles away. They looked solemn and confused; clearly, something was irking them. Nata wondered why they didn't speak at all, not even to each other — it was not normal for passengers to be like this. The only sound in the taxi that evening was from the base radio, delivering instructions to drivers around the island. And the only time either of the passengers spoke was as they neared the Gatot Kaca statue, when one of them made a very quick phone call.

Rush was calling Andrew Chan, as instructed, to tell him they were approaching the airport, just as Lawrence had done moments earlier. There probably was no need, as Chan was only minutes away from the airport himself, destined for the same check-in queue and the same flight to Sydney. But none of the four in the first two cabs dared deviate from their instructions. They would later be asked why they didn't perhaps ask the cab driver to take them to a police station to report the crime, instead of continuing with it. Their answers were the same: they feared for themselves and their families, and they feared that Chan's men were watching them to ensure they carried out their mission.

In contrast to the atmosphere in Nata's taxi, the driver of Komotro Taxi No 99, Muhammad Zakaria, was having a ball with his passenger, Andrew Chan, who was displaying none of the nerves of his younger cohorts. Chan told Zakaria that he worked for Pioneer, the electronics company, and that his time in Bali had been part work, part holiday — he had been working to begin with and then tacked some time on the end for a break. Chan even named the shopping centre — Centro in Jalan Kartika Plaza — where he had gone in his duties as an electronics technician. As part of the banter about his job, a confident and boastful Chan volunteered to Zakaria that he earned a whopping 9 million rupiah (A$1260) per day. Zakaria could only marvel at the handsome salary — it took him a whole month of driving his taxi to earn only one-third that amount, and he told Chan so. Chan responded by telling him, 'Don't worry, I will give you a big tip." A tip would have come in handy, but Zakaria wasn't bothered either way. He was used to tourists — some tipped and some were stingy, treating every rupiah like it was their last.

The pair talked all the way to the airport, Chan showing no signs of the nerves that were plaguing the others. And he was talking himself up. His style was that of a rich man who was sure of himself. Zakaria thought he had the swagger and demeanour of a 'big boss' and remembered Chan fielding a couple of mobile phone calls as he drove.

At the airport, Chan made good his promise to give Zakaria a big tip. The meter read 16 000 rupiah but Chan handed over 50 000 rupiah, telling Zakaria to pocket the change. It was a good tip and Zakaria bade his passenger farewell, not thinking another thing about him until much later, when Chan's face appeared on the TV news and in the local newspapers.

* * *

The taxi carrying Lawrence and Stephens arrived at the airport first. Each had a backpack and a suitcase, along with their bodily cargo. Rush and Czugaj were next with just their suitcases. Chan had the most luggage, but it was nowhere near as valuable as the cargo he had helped strap to the other four. He knew how they felt, though — he had carried the same kind of valuable cargo once before on his own body.

In addition to his bags, Chan had two Bali souvenirs: a big wooden fish and an odd-looking voodoo stick contraption with a hairy face at one end. No one took much notice — Aussie tourists cart home all manner of odd and strange-looking souvenirs from Bali, giving Customs officers in Australia something to check and to laugh about.

Even though this group had arrived at the entrance to Ngurah Rai airport only minutes apart, the two pairs with heroin strapped to their bodies didn't know each other, so there was no chance of an awkward meeting. Within moments they would all be walking through their first test — hoping to shake hands — their date with destiny a success.

XXII

The Blame Game

Andrew Chan might have thought he was being clever. One thing was for sure, though: in the stickiest situation of his life, he was squirming. And he was about to start squirming even more.

Since his arrest, Chan had been less than forthcoming with investigators about anything to do with the drugs found on the four mules. Had he known that in nearby rooms his underlings were singing like birds and pointing the finger directly at him, he might have been more honest. Or perhaps he did know and decided to point the finger right back. Certainly, over the next few weeks he would shift the blame — away from himself and towards other people. He had no compunction in doing so. Everything that was done had been done by other people, not him, he said. In fact, all he had been doing was following orders. At least, that was his claim.

Painting a picture of innocence, Chan was shocked when police told him that they thought he was the 'Godfather' of a drug-smuggling operation. It couldn't be, he protested — he had come to Bali for a holiday.

It was 21 April, four days after his arrest, and Chan was in a police interrogation room under heavy fire. Sure, he knew some of the people who had been arrested. He worked with some, had gone to school with others and met some of them in a Kuta bar. No big deal. Yeah, sure, on the day he was due to leave for Sydney he had gone to see Lawrence and Stephens in their hotel room, but he didn't remember where that was. He took Sukumaran along for the ride. When he got there he did nothing more interesting than lie down on the bed and watch a 'silly' program on television. Stephens and Lawrence were in a hurry to go to the airport and didn't want to wait for him to take a shower, so they left.

What about that other matter of Chan booking into Yan's Bungalow in Kuta under a false name and leaving some suitcases there? Chan had the answer ready — evidently he had been thinking about this issue ever since police had discovered that he had checked in there under the name of David Yu and left two suitcases there. Those cases contained traces of heroin, which would later be linked forensically to the heroin strapped to the mules.

Chan was no dummy — he knew he needed a reasonable explanation for why he had been seen and identified checking into the low-budget hotel. And he knew that the explanation must be clever enough to implicate someone else and exculpate himself — he was a novice when it came to police interviews but he was intelligent and canny. He couldn't remember the name of the hotel, he told officers, but it was Renae Lawrence who told him to check in there, and gave him 1 million rupiah to pay for it.

He was warming up now: 'Renae Lawrence asked me to use another name, namely David, and false passport number," he said, the words rolling off his tongue. He hadn't actually stayed there, and the officers wanted to know why not. 'Because Renae Lawrence asked me to bring a suitcase into the room, then because I was anxious to find out the contents of the suitcase because it sounded like a bomb, I opened it. Unfortunately it was empty. After that I went to the hotel where Renae Lawrence stayed and asked her, "Why did you ask me to bring an empty and broken suitcase?" She replied, "Later I will explain when we arrive in Sydney". That's the reason why I did not stay in the hotel.' But he was admitting to nothing else — he had, he said, never asked anyone to deliver any drugs to Australia. He was doing enough to throw investigators off his trail and just a bit to point police in another direction — that of his work colleague, Renae Lawrence.

Meanwhile, Lawrence herself was being more than helpful during her sessions in the interrogation room. She was a font of knowledge and she wasn't holding back. She was in no doubt just how much trouble she was in, and something had happened since the night she was caught on tape at the airport tearfully exhorting Martin Stephens not to dob anyone in. The sobering thought of the fate that might await her — a firing squad — had something to do with it.

Lawrence had been to Bali twice before for the same kind of venture and both times Chan had also been in it up to his neck. She told police that he had been threatening her the entire time and that she feared for herself and her family. In October 2004 she had been in Bali with Chan and Sukumaran, and both she and Chan had taken drugs back to Australia; Sukumaran had strapped them on. That trip had lasted six days. On that occasion Chan had also used the Hard Rock Hotel as his base and the modus operandi had been the same as the April 2005 run, except Chan had used his own hotel room to have the drugs attached. Lawrence told police that when she got to Chan's room on that earlier run, Sukumaran was there, and she was instructed to change into tight shorts. She told police that Sukumaran strapped packages to her body but she did not know, and was not told, what the contents were. With packages strapped on her left thigh, then the right thigh and her waist, she said she went to the airport for her flight to Australia with Chan and his girlfriend, Grace. At the airport in Sydney she was picked up by a friend of Chan's and in the car told to remove the packages with scissors, and warned not to split the plastic. Lawrence had named other people who were there too and gone on to explain how, after getting back to Australia, Chan had called her to his house and handed her an envelope stuffed with $10 000 in cash. Lawrence said she gave it back to Chan, telling police she hadn't known what it was for. Chan told her it was money to keep her mouth shut, that she was not to put it in the bank and not to tell anybody. Lawrence took the money home.

There was more, though, and Lawrence was proving to be a Pandora's box. She said she had also come to Bali several months later, in December 2004. With her were Tan Duc Thanh Nguyen, Matthew Norman and several others known by aliases. Chan had paid for the trip. But while awaiting instructions, Lawrence was told by one of the group that because of financial problems the mission was to be aborted.

Things were moving along but, frustrated by the inability to crack some members of the group and the fear that the four mules had of the ringleaders, police decided to start using some psychological pressure. Chan and Sukumaran were shifted to jails in other police stations on their own. Chan was in jail at the Sanur station, where he at least had the company of some local prisoners, including one mobile phone thief who helped him avert the media. In contrast, Sukumaran was completely on his own at the Benoa Harbour water police station. Tan Duc Thanh Nguyen was moved too — into a cell with an undercover police operative posing as a drug dealer. He tried to get Nguyen talking, offering up the details of his own arrest, but he didn't get far. Nguyen was not talking, even to a supposed kindred spirit in the drug game.

The four mules were left together in the Polda cells. They had been extraordinarily cooperative with the police, and what they were telling officers was yielding results. The officers just had to crack Chan. His persistent denials were beginning to grate.

Enter Gories Mere, a charismatic Indonesian detective, crack interrogator and the man famed for hunting down and arresting the smiling terrorist Amrozi in the crucial first breakthrough of the 2002 Bali nightclub bombing investigation. Mere had a feared reputation. The Bali Nine bust was momentous and the National Narcotics Bureau (known as the BNN) was involved in trying to track down the big end of the story to find out where the drugs came from and who else in Indonesia was involved.

With other BNN members, Mere flew down to Bali for a chat with the Godfather. Speaking perfect English, Mere was more than capable of interacting with Chan, offering him cigarettes and drinks. The question was, did Chan, the 21-year-old school dropout, have the intellect to outwit him? One thing Mere did have was police intelligence — the surveillance report and the phone records of the Nine. And he had smarts. Chan was about to squirm.

It was 7 May, sixteen days after Chan had told police that he knew nothing about the heroin, and that it was Lawrence who had told him to check in to a hotel using a false name, that miraculously Chan's memory seemed to be improving. Confronted by the imposing Mere, he started remembering more and more. In fact, it wasn't Lawrence alone who had instructed him to book into Yan's Bungalows — the instructions had come via Myuran Sukumaran.

Chan also remembered that, after he checked in there, a hotel officer had come to the room to get a copy of his passport.

Knowing he had used a false name, Chan decided to bypass requests to drop down to the office with his passport when he got a chance. Chan said he abandoned the empty suitcases at the hotel, locked the door and slid the key under it before grabbing breakfast at a nearby McDonald's. After this he caught a taxi to the Adhi Dharma Hotel, where he met Sukumaran in the room of Matthew Norman. By this time it was about 10.30 a.m. on 17 April. Confronted with the mobile phone records which showed who had called who and how many times, Chan's memory about this began to improve as well.

At the Adhi Dharma he spent a couple of hours lying on the bed and watching DVDs with Sukumaran, before the pair adjourned to the Hard Rock Hotel for a spot of lunch — at least, that's what he said. After lunch they came back to the Adhi Dharma and watched some more DVDs, this time with Norman, Chen and Nguyen. He admitted later going to the room of Lawrence and Stephens, but this was where Chan's version deviated from that given by the mules themselves.

In the room, Sukumaran had instructed him to stand guard at the door and monitor anything suspicious. Why, he was asked, was he told to monitor anything suspicious? 'Because Myuran Sukumaran would like to stripe [strap] something wrapped in brown plastic tape,' Chan said, adding that he had seen these goods earlier in a silver suitcase at the Hard Rock Hotel when he was together with Sukumaran and Nguyen. But as to how the strapping was done, he didn't know because he didn't see. All he remembered was hearing Lawrence and Stephens laughing while the strapping was occurring. Sukumaran, Chan said, had asked him to help out with strapping something to the bodies of Lawrence and Stephens but he had declined.

Chan said they then went to the room of Rush and Czugaj, but he didn't see much of what went on in that room because he was in the bathroom taking a shower. Nguyen had been there too. He hadn't joined in with any of this business of strapping stuff to people's bodies.

There was one other thing investigators wanted to know: where did that silver suitcase which he had seen at the Hard Rock Hotel, and which contained the packages, come from? Chan was obliging. While having dinner with Sukumaran and Nguyen on 8 April, Sukumaran had asked Chan for a favour — could he possibly duck over to the Kuta Seaview Cottage later that night and see a woman called Packet in room 114?

'At that time Myuran Sukumaran told me, "Just say 'package' and she will understand what you want",' Chan said.

Chan insisted that there had been no other conversation with the mystery woman except to ask her to call him a taxi. When he got back to the Hard Rock Hotel he took the suitcase to his room and called Sukumaran. For some reason that night Sukumaran couldn't open it, but by the next day he had figured out how. Chan said he saw only brown packages but he was clueless as to their contents. Chan then drew a rough sketch of what the mystery woman in room 114 had looked like.

Finally investigators were getting somewhere. Chan's story differed from what the others were saying but at least he was giving a version. But it wasn't to last: by 23 May, when he was again questioned, Chan was in no mood for talking. To every question he answered that he did not know or he did not remember. He was reminded that on 7 May he had told police that he collected the suitcase from Packet. *When did you do that?* 'I don't know.' *Was she in her room, what was her room number and who was with her at the time?* 'I don't know.' *When you booked Yan's Bungalow on 17 April under the name of David Yu and brought with you two suitcases, where did they come from?* 'I did not know who is the owner of the suitcases and I am not sure where I got the suitcases.' *If you didn't know about the suitcases, who brought them to your room at the Hard Rock Hotel?* 'I don't remember.' *If you did not remember about the suitcases, where did you get them? Why did you leave the suitcases in such a way at Yan's Beach Bungalow in Kuta and put the key under the door?* 'I don't know.' *Have you ever gone to Kuta Seaview Cottages to collect something from Packet?* 'I don't know.' *Is the statement just given to the investigator true?* 'Yes, it is.'

Police were getting nowhere. Chan was quite obviously in no mood to cooperate this time and had no intention of confirming or elaborating on what he had said two weeks earlier. They had reached an impasse. It was the same story with those arrested in the Melasti bust — Chen, Norman and Nguyen — who quite simply refused to admit much at all — even the obvious, like knowing some of the other nine, even those who had worked with them.

XXIII

Kerobokan Jail

The man at the front wearing the guard's uniform says it costs 5000 rupiah to get in. No one asks why. That's just the way it is at Kerobokan Jail, and the way it's always been. And it doesn't end there — hire a mat to sit on during your visit in preference to the ground, that's another 10 000 rupiah or so, and more if you want to sit in the preferred visiting places. Then there's the enterprising prisoner offering cold drinks: red or orange Fanta, iced tea, Coca-Cola. There would be table service if there were tables; there aren't. Sitting on the ground is the only option, although there are one or two plastic umbrellas.

A couple canoodles in a secluded corner. No one takes any notice as the passion hots up and hands slide under clothes. The rules posted at the front door say that visits must last only fifteen minutes each, but no one takes any notice of that either. Stay for hours if you want. Visiting your loved one separated by bars or glass partitions like you see on television, armed guards patrolling nearby with eagle eyes? Forget it. These are full-contact visits, and while the guards are there, they are pretty relaxed — within limits, of course.

A kind of ad hoc rules system has evolved. Those inside know and understand it, and appreciate the limits. It doesn't help to put anyone offside by trying to overstep the mark or be a little bit too clever. It's far easier to operate within the boundaries of the established system, however unorthodox or intriguing it may appear from the outside.

The *warung* or small café outside the main gate — which has since closed, after the proprietors became drunk on *arak* — sold what could be rated one of the tastiest serves of *mie goreng* (fried noodles) on the island. The chefs were both prisoners, small-time druggies who were trusted to spend most of their days outside the walls, giving them unfettered human interaction. Better than sitting in their cell all day. Business had soared exponentially for them since a whole bunch of Australians started residing inside the jail, because with them has come a press corps that spends hours sitting outside, waiting for visitors to come and go. The *warung* boys had a captive market. When business started booming they even spruced up the area, putting a poster on the wall, a rickety plastic ceiling fan on a beam and a cloth on the lone table. The fan did nothing, really, to ward off the humidity, but it was the thought that counts.

A recent security and drugs crackdown ended the freedom of another man who would spend a lot of time going in and out of the wooden doors at will, looking for all intents and purposes like a free man. He is serving thirteen years for drugs and hand-grenade possession, but the guards paid no heed to his comings and goings before the crackdown. Another man, supposedly serving time, was found in a nightclub. Most people thought he was inside and he was — except when he was allowed out. Welcome to Lembaga Permasyarajatan Kerobokan, or LP Kerobokan for short. Translated it means — aptly or oddly — 'socialisation institution', but most people just call it LP, and it is Bali's main and most well-known penitentiary.

Kerobokan is actually the name of the suburb where the jail is located, nestled next to the super-trendy district of Seminyak and not all that far from Kuta. In recent years some of Seminyak's spunk has rubbed off on the village of Kerobokan, which now boasts its own chic cafés and shops, and a series of sleek furniture shops. The jail is almost shabby in comparison, its whitewashed walls looking as though they could do with a good coat of paint.

There is little to distinguish the jail as one drives past on Jalan Tangekuban Prahu. Until recently, and around the time of the Bali Nine's arrival there, one could almost pass by without any idea that it was even a jail. There are no armed guards outside; no tall guard towers with officers, rifles at the ready to deter would-be escapees; and no surveillance cameras recording everything and everyone that moves on the perimeter. It's an ordinary, nondescript building in the middle of what is turning into a tourist shopping district. What is gleaming new is the razor wire and new security entrance which went up around the top walls of the complex — the main sign that this is, in fact, a high-security prison.

Until October 2005, LP Kerobokan was home to the three Bali bombers, on death row for their roles in the murderous 2002 nightclub attacks. So-called smiling assassin Amrozi, his older brother Mukhlas and Imam Samudra had been there since their arrests and convictions, and were destined to remain there until the executioner came calling, except that security was an issue and they were bundled off to the Alcatraz of Indonesia — an island jail off Java called Nusa Kambangan — on the eve of a protest rally calling for their immediate executions. They had been Kerobokan's most infamous inmates.

For security reasons, mainly, and for their own safety, they were kept in their own cell block and never allowed to socialise with the other prisoners, save for religious festivals, when they were allowed out to pray with the rest of the Islamic prisoners. But in recent times they had banned themselves from even that brief respite, declaring that the prayer area was spiritually dirty because it had also been used by Christians for their religious services.

The three men were housed in a circular series of cells with a fence around the outside, known as the tower block. Their only contact with the rest of the prison population was through a barred window. It was from here that Imam Samudra, on the days the media were allowed inside the jail, took the opportunity to shout a homily to the waiting cameras. More than twenty other people, convicted of more minor roles in the Bali bombing, are also serving their terms at Kerobokan, mixing with the rest of the population.

As jails go, and when compared with the overcrowded penitentiaries in neighbouring Southeast Asian nations like the Philippines or Thailand, Kerobokan is not so bad. That doesn't mean it's good, but it could be a lot worse. Compared with the number of prisoners it was originally built to house, Kerobokan is hopelessly overcrowded, with almost 800 prisoners in 2005; but the cells bear no resemblance to jails in the Philippines, where places built for 80 prisoners have more than 500 inmates, up to 50 crammed into one cell, and the cells regularly flood in the rainy season.

At various times during her stay in Kerobokan, Gold Coast woman Schapelle Corby, jailed for twenty years for trying to bring 4.1 kilograms of marijuana to Bali, has shared her cell with eight or nine other women. When Adelaide model Michelle Leslie first arrived following her arrest for possession of two ecstasy tablets, she was sharing with only a handful of women, including a Mexican woman also serving time for drug offences. The women's cells are less than 10 metres in length and within them the inmates work out their own pecking order — those there for the longest tend to get the best sleeping position, determined through a kind of natural attrition. As one person leaves, the next in the hierarchy moves into their spot.

Each cell has its own bathroom, known as *kamar kecil.* Literally translated, it means 'small room', and they are certainly that. The *kamar kecil* has an Asian-style squat toilet and a *mandi* — an Indonesian-style bath which really is a big, square-shaped tub filled with cold water which you ladle over yourself. Inmates also wash their clothes here. It sounds pretty awful to those used to Western facilities, and hot and cold running water, but most homes in Indonesia, especially those of the lower and poorer classes, are no different. In those classes whole families sleep in one room of a house and mattresses are rolled up each day to allow a thoroughfare.

When Westerners recently complained about ants in their cell, authorities treated the complaint with more than mild amusement, and then sarcasm: 'Ants, I have ants in my house. What's the problem? This is a jail, not a hotel.' The letter of complaint was promptly filed in the rubbish bin. It doesn't help, in a place like Kerobokan, to complain too much, especially to people who live the same way in the their own homes as the prisoners do in their cells.

Inmates at Kerobokan learn quickly not to whinge too often or too loudly, and that many advantages come one's way if one keeps one's own counsel and learns how to work the system, not to buck it.

Kerobokan mirrors the rest of Indonesia's jails in that about half its prison population is doing time for drug offences. And, as in many jails, drugs are not hard to come by inside. Some people believe that drugs are easier to get inside the dull walls than outside. Authorities do regular drug sweeps of prisoners' cells, and the odd guard has been caught acting as the dealer.

Often the jail's drug dealers think that if you're inside for drugs you must be an addict. The Bali Nine members learnt that very quickly when, not long after their arrival, some were offered a range of narcotics. Some of the prisoners thought that this bunch, caught with so much of the gear strapped to them, must surely be users and hanging out for a hit.

Everyone knows the drugs are a problem in Kerobokan but it seems there are not too many solutions for fixing it. Prison psychiatrists are confronted with it every day and joke that people who go in for minor larceny offences often emerge drug addicts. Then there's alcohol, which is also available to those in the know and those who can pay. Because that's the thing about Kerobokan and jails like it — if you've got the money and the know-how, anything is possible and life can be much more comfortable. Ready cash can buy many privileges in a country where corruption has historically flourished and where people like jail guards earn a small salary, but can make up for it by taking some cash on the side to make a prisoner's life more comfortable, for things like turning a blind eye to alcohol and drugs, or charging a 'fine' to those caught with illegal mobile phones in order to ensure that the phone is returned and not confiscated. One well-known lawyer with a number of clients in Kerobokan says that some people run their businesses entirely from behind bars, a practice facilitated by the advent of mobile phones with email and internet capability.

In short, the more money you have, the more comfortable life inside can be. In the men's section of the jail, money buys quite a lot, like wood to make proper wooden beds to sleep on rather than a dingy mattress on the floor; Michael Czugaj got a bed made not long after moving there. And it's said that, for the right amount of money, inmates can even purchase the right to have a blind eye turned to conjugal visits in a special room.

LP Kerobokan is not the most attractive place; inside it has a dullness that makes it look like it has no personality. The visiting area is a concrete courtyard, with the odd shade tree but not much else going for it. A pond in the middle was, for a time, full of stagnating green water in which some inmates even washed their clothes. Fortunately someone decided it was better empty, and now prisoners and their visitors sit in the area. Given the calibre of prisoners inside — murderers, drug dealers on death row and the Bali bombers — the front doors are almost disappointing: two thin, brown wooden affairs, with a little peephole in one.

Official visiting hours are Mondays to Fridays from 9 a.m. to 12 p.m. and 1 p.m. to 3 p.m., with weekend visits allowed between 9 a.m. and 12.30 p.m. Inmates and their visitors can sit in a visiting room — although this is not always recommended, given that it is often used by passionate couples who have spread mats on the floor — or they can choose the area around the pond.

Once inside the wooden doors, Kerobokan looks more like a prison, with a locked and caged area. To get past here one must surrender 5000 rupiah (less than A$1) and ID. Then it's around the corner to be searched and have all bags searched as well, before finally being allowed in to visit. Someone will then go and tell the prisoner that they have a visitor. The saving grace for many prisoners, especially Westerners, is that their visitors can bring any kind of food they want — pizzas, sandwiches, sushi (one of Schapelle Corby's favourites), whatever they like.

In the jail's common area is a grassed rectangular space, adjacent to the Bali bombers' tower block, which is used for ceremonies on special days and so those who aren't in their cells can wander around.

The women's and men's blocks are segregated — jail authorities are very sensitive to the issue of pregnancies between inmates, which can be difficult to explain to those in higher authority. The women are kept in their block, a row of cells, and allowed out only to receive visitors in the common visiting area or if they pay a special sum to be allowed to go to the visiting area. This means that the only interaction between Renae Lawrence and the other members of the Bali Nine occurs when they are receiving a common visitor. Members of the public are banned from going into or anywhere near prisoner cells.

The cuisine on offer at LP Kerobokan is not gourmet. For a Westerner it's well below standard, but for those who don't have friends or family members on the outside, there is no other option. Jail rations come around on a kind of cart; there are big pots or drums of rice and whatever is on the menu to accompany it that day. Some say the food is almost inedible, that the rice is full of dirt, sticks and stones, and the pots are encrusted with dried food from the days and weeks before.

Many prisoners opt to cook for themselves on small gas stoves, like camp stoves, inside their cells. For a fee the guards will even duck to the fruit and vegetable market down the road and pick up some fresh supplies. It pays to keep the guards onside, especially if you want to make life easier for yourself.

For special celebrations like birthdays, no one stops a little party; several of the Nine have had one, and they all joined in a Christmas bash. But it is health and nutrition that suffer most for inmates — especially those in for the long term — unless a family member or someone close is living nearby to bring the things the inmates need to survive but just wouldn't receive otherwise.

For many, twenty-four hours in LP Kerobokan seems like so much longer. Boredom sets in; the hours take for ever to pass and all you are left with sometimes is your own thoughts about the future. Some, like the male inmate from Sierra Leone, don't even have that: he was sentenced to life for drug trafficking and on appeal his sentence was increased to death. A future is something he can only dream about as he waits and wonders how long he has before the execution.

This is not like Western jails, where inmates complete university degrees while serving their sentences and have access to tertiary courses, structured counselling sessions and computers. There is not an abundance of leisure activities in Kerobokan, and even less if you are female. There is a tennis court but it's generally only for male inmates to use; others play badminton, and they can kick a ball around the grassed area.

Prisoners are locked in their cells from about 4 p.m. each afternoon to 8 a.m. the next day. Whether you like the person next to you or not, it's too bad. Christian church services provide respite for some prisoners. Conducted by civilian chaplains and ministers, they are a way of breaking up the day, and they provide the inmates with outside interaction, along with solace from God. Schapelle Corby has turned to her religion since being inside, even being baptised before her verdict. Martin Stephens has also embraced his religion. They attend the weekly services and most have Bibles in their cells. But it still doesn't break the desolate monotony that their lives have become. You can only read so much or study so much language before you wonder what else is going to fill the day — and the next, and next.

When the Bali Nine arrived at LP Kerobokan — the group of mules at the end of July 2005 and the others a few days later — it was after three months spent in the airless cells at Polda and other police stations around Denpasar. With scant chance to see the sunlight, the Australians were looking decidedly pale and pasty. At least at Kerobokan — where they would be able to walk around outside — they would get some sunlight.

Initially all nine had been held in the same small cell blocks in Polda, but, as alliances formed and with police interrogations under way, it quickly became evident that they needed to be separated. Half were then held in one cell area and the others in the cells across the courtyard. In a move as much aimed at appeasing those like Lawrence and the other mules — who said they were scared of Chan and Sukumaran — as at breaking the others, police decided to move some of them to other police holding cells. It was a pragmatic decision: it had become clear that the interrogations would not yield the truth if the nine were all housed together.

The two least willing participants in the interrogation process were Chan and Sukumaran. So police decided it was time for them to taste some solitude. Chan was moved to the cells at the nearby Sanur police station. He was not alone there, as he shared time with other Indonesian prisoners. Meanwhile, Sukumaran was packed off to the water police cells at Benoa Harbour. For at least some of his time there, he was on his lonesome. There were no other prisoners held at Benoa, and most of the officers did not speak English. Sukumaran cut a lonely figure as the police plan to encourage him to start talking was actioned.

The youngest of the group, Matthew Norman, was sent off on his own as well, to the high-security Brimob police station jail, while others were held in the airport police station. It would be several months before the nine would see each other again, in early August, when they were moved to LP Kerobokan.

When the day dawned for the four mules to move, 28 July, it was bittersweet. They were leaving a place they had become accustomed to, heading for a place they had only heard about. They were scared and they looked it — especially Lawrence, who had a quiet cry before she left. She didn't want to go to any jail — she wanted to go home. Her lawyer, Anggia Browne, who had in the past three months become not just her legal advisor but her confidante and friend, put her hand through the bars to give Lawrence a gentle caress, telling her not to worry. But they really didn't know what to expect.

Stephens admitted his fear. 'I'd be lying if I [said] I wasn't frightened. I have never been to jail before. I have never been in trouble before in my life.' Tears brimming in his eyes, he had just finished reading a letter from his parents. All the while, as his eyes scanned the page, he held the silver cross on a chain around his neck. His parents had given him the necklace early on, soon after his arrest.

By the time the four had gathered their possessions, changed out of their prisoner T-shirts and were waiting in the prison van for the 16-kilometre journey to LP Kerobokan, their moods had lifted slightly. They were trying their best to hide the fear that a few minutes earlier had been etched into their faces and radiated from their eyes.

'I love you, Renae', someone shouted from the recesses of the cell block area.

She laughed good-humouredly. 'Maybe we can stop at McDonald's on the way,' she joked, in reference to the fact that McDonald's had now become a delicacy for them.

The journey from the police station to the jail was the group's first look at the outside world for months. Past the business districts of Denpasar — the part not usually frequented by tourists, with its gold jewellery shops, the town square and electronics shops — and past dozens of families squashed onto one motorcycle: Mum, Dad and the kids. Once on the bypass road, the area became less built up, characterised by rice paddies and half-finished buildings, and cows grazing in fields. It would be the mules' last look at the outside world in a long time. Did they see and take in the sights on the slightly circuitous route taken by the van driver? Or were they lost in their own thoughts, overcome by fear?

If they had been looking, the group would have seen that on the thirty-minute drive there were two billboard signs, in blue and not meant to be missed. The first was just around the corner from Polda and the second was about halfway through the journey. Both said the same thing: *Narkoba* [Narcotics]. STOP!!! Warnings such as these were too late for this crew.

Once at the jail, lawyers for the mules made representations to ensure that Chan and Sukumaran were not housed in the same cells as their clients, citing fears for the mules' safety. But no amount of representations could ever ensure they did not cross paths inside the jail, even if they were not in the same cells.

Stephens and the two Brisbane boys made it their business to keep largely out of the way of the others, although Stephens held no great animosity towards Norman, Chen or Nguyen. It was Chan and Sukumaran who frightened them the most.

Anggia Browne, knowing the fragility of Lawrence's condition and having dealt with her through her previous self-harm attempts, asked some of her female Indonesian clients who were already inside to look out for Lawrence, to explain the routine and help her settle in.

This group was going from the known to the unknown and it was not going to be easy. They were not the first Australians to make the journey from Polda to LP Kerobokan, and they would not be the last.

XXIV

Friends and Foes on the Inside

By the time the Bali Nine moved into their cells at LP Kerobokan, Schapelle Corby had already been there for about eight months. Two months earlier she had been found guilty and sentenced to spend twenty years there. She'd had plenty of time to settle in, learn the routine and learn the ropes. In another time and another place, Renae Lawrence and Schapelle Corby probably would not have been friends. It is difficult to see it: they are completely different people, like chalk and cheese. But, thrown together in a Bali jail, both with uncertain fates, it is understandable that the only two Australian women in Kerobokan would end up developing a bond. It was a kinship born out of loneliness, fear and a shared fate along with a shared homeland.

Corby has always maintained her innocence, saying she is a victim of drug traffickers who planted the marijuana in her luggage without her knowledge — loaded up then locked up for something she says she didn't do. Lawrence, too, believes she is a victim, but in a different way. While she admitted to being involved in the drug smuggling, she has long insisted that she was threatened and forced and had no choice but to attempt to carry the heroin to Australia.

It didn't take long for the pair to pal up inside the jail's walls. Corby helped Lawrence with the dos and don'ts of jail life, gave her tips on how best to survive, and of course the pair was able to speak in English together. It is fair to say that Lawrence didn't think she would immediately warm to the well-groomed young Gold Coast woman. And it did take a while, but it happened eventually. Corby and Lawrence were not sharing a cell, but the women's block is small and they had ample opportunity for interaction.

It was Corby who was there to help Lawrence when, not long after the latter's arrival, she punched the wall in her cell in desperation, badly injuring her hand and requiring a plaster cast. Corby came to her aid, helping and trying to console the depressed and highly distressed Lawrence. Strung out, Lawrence was on the edge of losing her battle to cope.

When the time came for Renae Lawrence's first day in court — 14 October 2005 — it was 28-year-old Schapelle Corby who helped her get ready. In Lawrence's cell, Corby applied some make-up to her friend's face. It was just a touch, not overdone — Lawrence is not the kind of woman to get primped and preened to within an inch of her life, but she welcomed her fellow Australian's help.

Lawrence had not been feeling too well, plagued by a bad toothache which eventually saw a dentist pull the tooth out. But it wasn't a smooth extraction and Lawrence was left with an infection, which gave her a pale complexion. For the second court day Corby suggested some Natural Glow to give Lawrence's face some colour. Later, when the media picked up on it and suggested Corby had given her fellow Australian a 'makeover' for court, Lawrence was incredulous. Firstly, she couldn't understand all the fuss about something as small as a bit of make-up, and she scoffed at suggestions that it had been a makeover in the traditional sense of the word. She joked that next time, to excite the media, perhaps she would put clips in her hair.

Corby's family and army of supporters keep her in regular beauty supplies, and she is well known for sharing them around with her cell-mates and other prisoners who are less fortunate than herself. Plus, being a former beauty student, she knows all the tips for make-up and was always immaculately groomed for her own days in court.

Pretty early on, Renae Lawrence also developed allegiances with several female Indonesian prisoners. When she had a visitor, she would often ask that several of the women she was friendly with also be called to the visiting area, thus breaking the monotony of their days in the cell block. These women were similar in personality to Lawrence, upfront and opinionated.

Before long, Lawrence and Corby were joined by a third Australian woman — 24-year-old Adelaide-born model Michelle Leslie, who had been arrested entering a Bali dance party with two ecstasy pills in her handbag. Leslie was not housed in the same cell as either Lawrence or Corby, and from early on she kept to herself. Thus there were to be no lasting allegiances between these three women. And while Corby at times sweltered with thirteen women in her tiny cell and Lawrence had up to ten in hers, Leslie shared with only two other women. You could say it was the luxury cell, although nothing at LP Kerobokan could seriously be described as luxury — but it was generally better than other cells. Like everything else at the jail, money could secure better living conditions.

Leslie's first day in court happened to coincide with one of Lawrence's appearances. Their joint showing created a media crush that chaotically jostled and pushed both women. Being the only two females brought in the prison truck from the jail that day, the pair arrived handcuffed to each other; the media had a field day with the image. But it was an image Leslie and her public relations team were keen to avoid — the slim, young model caught with a few pills handcuffed to the alleged heroin trafficker. As soon as the pair reached the court's holding cell and the handcuffs were removed, it was splitsville — Leslie went to the opposite end of the cell, to sit alone. The two young women were from different backgrounds, poles apart, and it looked for all the world like Leslie wanted to be as far away from Lawrence as humanly possible.

However, all three Australian women were learning that in a Bali prison cell, accused of drug crimes you did or didn't do, you all faced the same treatment. For some, money and the people around you can help to plug some of the holes. Almost from the day of her arrest, 20 August 2005, Leslie not only had an Australian lawyer in Bali overseeing her case, but a public relations spokesman to deal with the omnipresent media. Lawrence and Corby, from modest upbringings and modest means, did not have that luxury. During their time at the Polda jail, most of the pair's visitors were received in the cell visiting area; they and their families had to endure the indignity of visits and kisses through the bars. But for the first period of time after Leslie's arrest, she received her visitors in an air-conditioned room of the police station, away from the prying cameras.

Lawrence was not happy about the way the whole thing had been handled on that first day of Leslie's trial, describing it later as a debacle. She had been pushed and shoved, and the handcuffs had hurt her wrist.

If Corby and Lawrence were different personalities who would never have connected in the real world, then the same could certainly be said of Lawrence and Leslie, and of Leslie and Corby, for that matter. LP Kerobokan is not and never will be the real world, but for Lawrence and Corby it was the closest thing they had and would have for a long time. Leslie's would be a short stay, however, and she didn't need to form the same alliances in order to cope with the long days and nights. By 19 November 2005, she was tasting freedom. The day before she had been sentenced to just three months in jail, backdated to take into account the time already served. It meant she was freed the day after the verdict.

Since their April 2005 arrest, Lawrence has also formed a strong bond with Martin Stephens, who has become something of a protector and confidant to her, looking out for her welfare, especially through her self-harm attempts. Their closeness is evident whenever they are together.

Their friendship really formed during their early days of incarceration at the Polda cells. They had worked together in Sydney but, until their time in Bali and subsequent arrests, had not really known each other very well. Stephens had only worked at the Sydney Cricket Ground for a short time, and during most of it Lawrence had been ill. And there was not a great deal of love lost between them in Bali — Stephens had decided that he didn't really like Lawrence and he intended severing the connection after they got back to Sydney. But after their arrest, bound together by shared circumstances, they became pals.

Stephens and Lawrence initially had the same legal team, and when one of them had a visitor at the jail, they would always ask for the other to share the visit. It meant they could both get out of the cells to the visiting area for some interaction with people other than their cell-mates, and it was the only time the pair could spend together, given the segregation of the male and female cell blocks and prisoners.

The pair also shared a dislike and fear of Andrew Chan and Myuran Sukumaran. This was not such a problem for Lawrence, because she was in the women's block, but it weighed heavily on Stephens's mind. There was no way in the world he wanted to be sharing the same cell as either one of them, his lawyers, as well as those for the Rush and Czugaj, made representations to that effect. But that couldn't stop the men bumping into each other around the common areas.

Unlike the Australian women, who, despite their different personalities, backgrounds and outlooks, had formed an alliance of sorts, the same situation was not to be replicated on the other side of the wall. Too much had happened for Stephens, Rush or Czugaj to suddenly pal up with Chan and Sukumaran, so they tried to stay out of each other's way — which was not always possible when jail authorities sometimes handcuffed Chan or Sukumaran to one of the mules for the ride to court. But Stephens missed out on that as well, insisting that if authorities ever tried it, he would refuse to share the manacles.

The men's block of Kerobokan is much bigger than the women's area. Block C is generally reserved for the *bule*, or foreign male prisoners. And there's never a shortage of them either — mostly from European and African nations, and generally always on drugs charges. Of course, the number of Aussies inside swelled when the eight males from the Bali Nine took up residence.

Anecdotally people say that male prisoners in Kerobokan get far more benefits than the women, and far more leeway — like the three male prisoners who, at 4 a.m. on the day of Michelle Leslie's arrest, were clearly spotted coming 'home' to jail after a night out. Stories abound of how much it costs to spend the night outside — one Indonesian man with a *bule* girlfriend is said to have paid $60 000 to ensure that for his year-long sentence he could spend every night outside the jail walls. In the men's block it is also far easier to secure favours like having a proper bed or bunks, rather than a mattress on the floor. Pay for the wood yourself and no one will stop you building a nice little bed.

The so-called Melasti group — Sukumaran, Norman, Chen and Nguyen, who were arrested at the Melasti Beach Bungalows — shared a cell. When they first moved in, the floor of the cell was concrete and the place was pretty ordinary-looking. By the time the trials started they had jazzed it up, putting cheap tiles on the floor and painting the walls; it made the place much more livable.

The Melasti group liked to play basketball together in the afternoons. Meanwhile Czugaj engaged others in kicking a football around. But the Melasti and airport groups kept their distance from each other — particularly the airport group from Chan and Sukumaran. There was no affection amongst this crew and no amount of lonely jail time or shared homeland was going to heal the rift. Whether it was fatal would be seen when their trials got under way and they all started giving evidence against each other.

POLICE PHOTO

POLICE PHOTO

Police photos of Scott Rush (above) and Michael Czugaj (left) in the pool at the Hotel Aneka in Kuta on 16 April, still enjoying their holiday just one day before their arrest.

BELOW: Andrew Chan and Myuran Sukumaran under surveillance at the Hard Rock Hotel.

POLICE PHOTO

All photographs by Lukman S Bintoro unless stated otherwise.

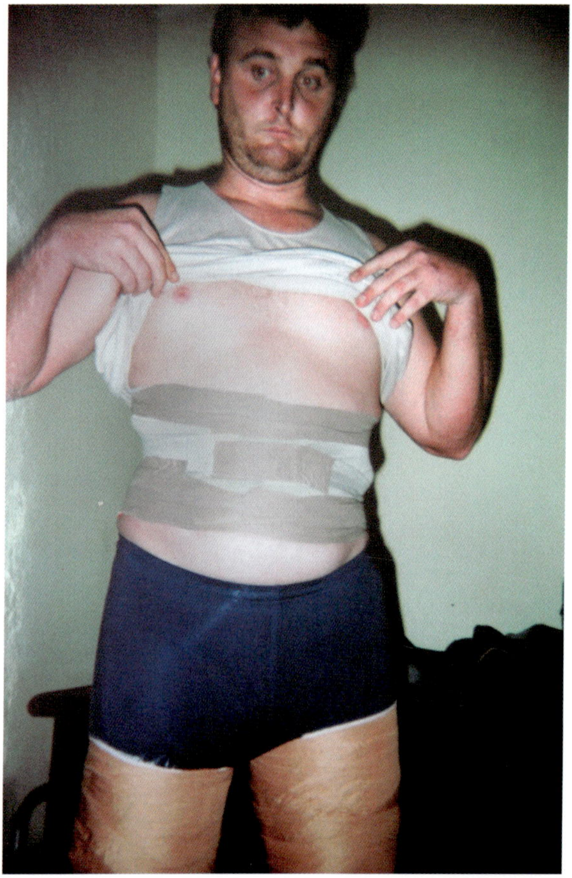

POLICE PHOTO

LEFT: Martin Stephens photographed at the Customs office in Bali with heroin strapped to his torso.

BELOW: Scott Rush at the Customs office as his secret cargo is revealed.

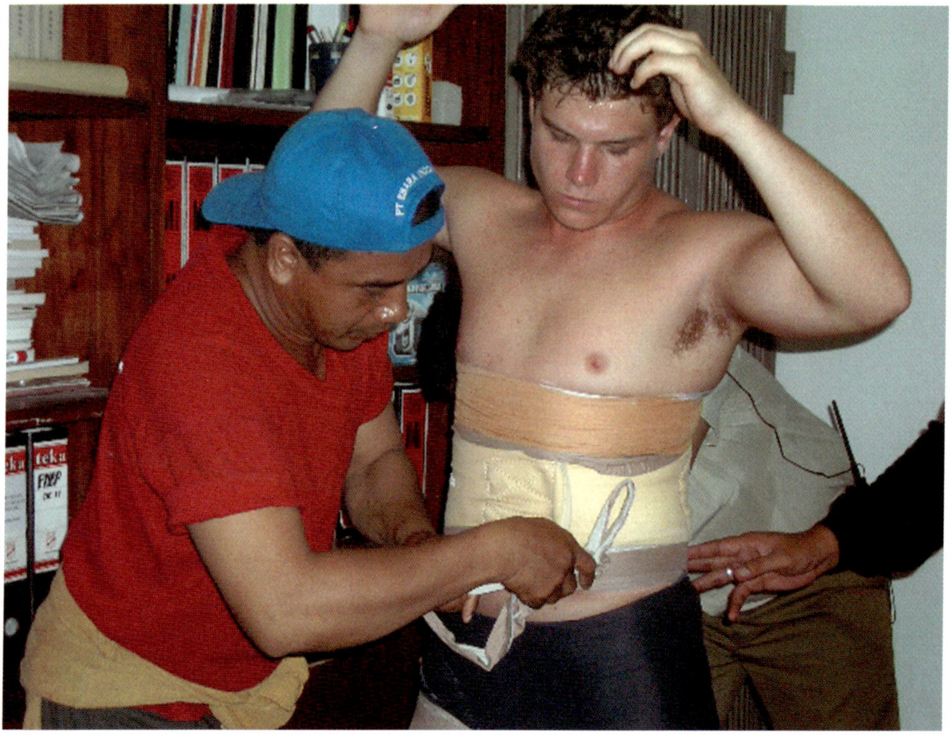

POLICE PHOTO

POLICE PHOTO

RIGHT: (L to R) Scott Rush, Michael Czugaj and Renae Lawrence in custody at Ngurah Rai airport – the first time they had met each other.

POLICE PHOTO

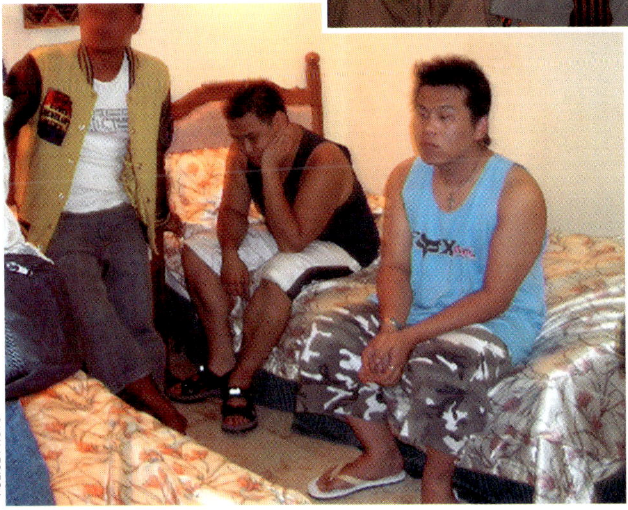

LEFT: Tan Duc Thanh Nguyen (left on bed) and Si Yi Chen, sprung at the Melasti Beach Bungalows.

BELOW: Nguyen, Sukumaran and Matthew Norman cover their faces to avoid being affected by the pepper that was placed on the heroin to deter sniffer dogs.

POLICE PHOTOS

Mug shots of the Bali Nine (L to R):
TOP: Renae Lawrence, Michael Czugaj, Martin Stephens
MIDDLE: Scott Rush, Andrew Chan, Myuran Sukumaran
BOTTOM: Tan Duc Thanh Nguyen, Si Yi Chen, Matthew Norman

LEFT: Renae Lawrence, her hand bandaged after harming herself, in a paddy wagon.

BELOW: Andrew Chan, the alleged ringleader, runs the gauntlet of press and police.

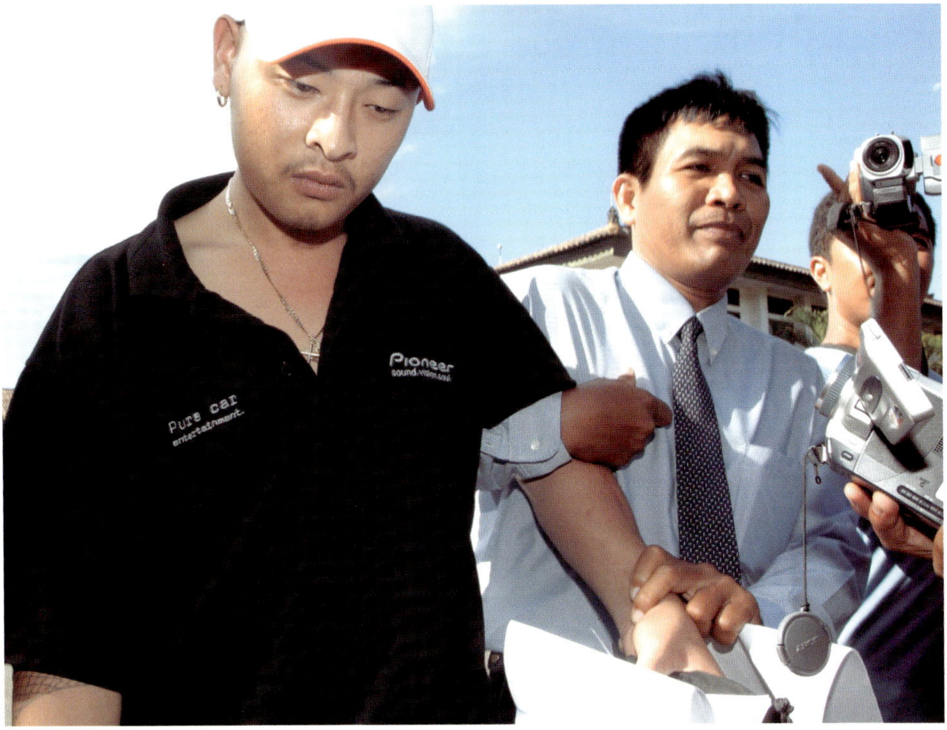

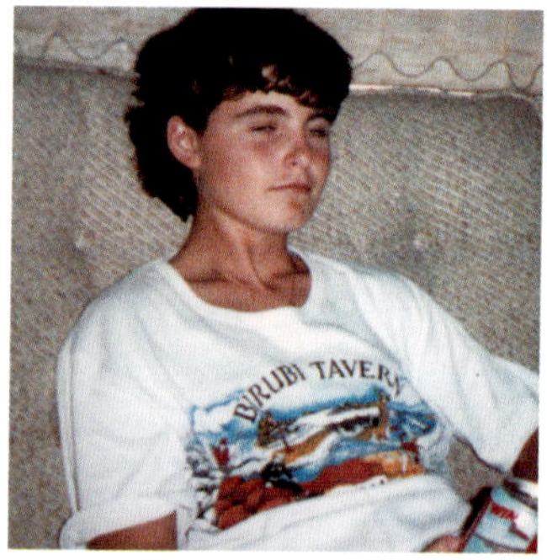

Before it all went wrong — Renae Lawrence as a smiling, outgoing child and teenager.

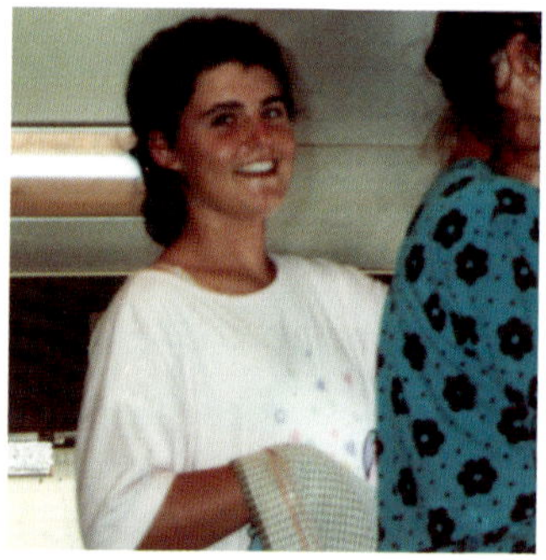

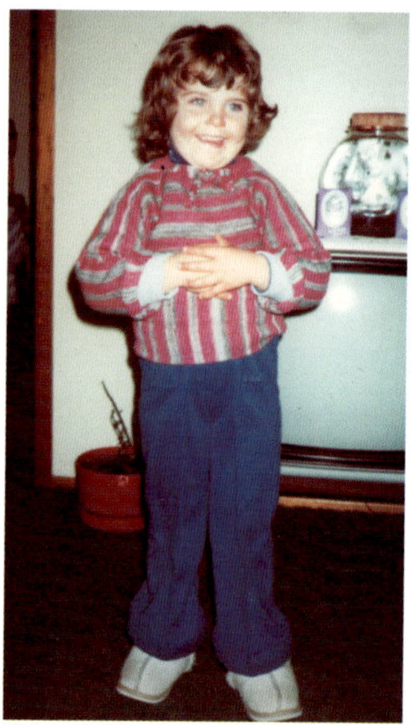

ABOVE: After it all went wrong — Renae's current and future view of the world.

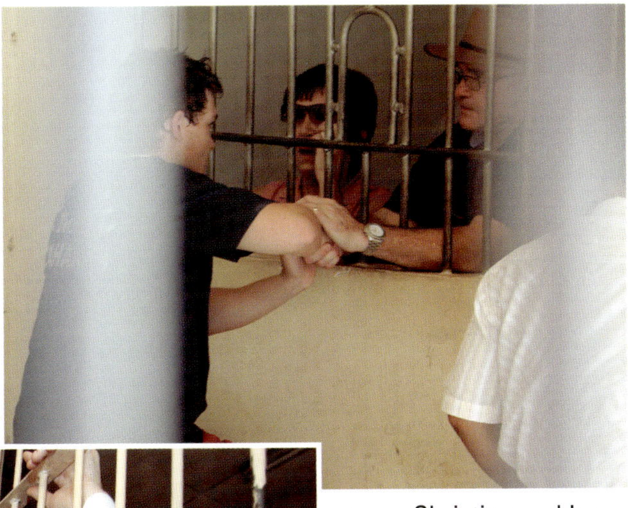

ABOVE: Christine and Lee Rush visit their son Scott.

LEFT: Vicki Czugaj with her son Michael.

CLOCKWISE FROM TOP LEFT: Stephens, Rush, Czugaj and Lawrence behind bars.

XXV

Keeping it in the Family

Vicki Czugaj was desperate to fly over to Bali and see her son Michael on the eve of his court case. He was to be the first of the Bali Nine to face trial and she wanted to boost his spirits, remind him of how much his seven brothers and sisters loved him, and make sure he was looking after himself. She worried about him nonstop and wondered whether the sick feeling in the pit of her stomach would ever subside. Some days it was under control; others, like the day leading up to Michael's birthday, it was insufferable.

Vicki had been driving to Brisbane that day when it all got too much. With tears rolling down her cheeks, she was oblivious to the cars around her, or the traffic lights in front. She didn't know what to do or where to turn. Her son was facing the possibility of the death penalty, and he was not yet out of his teens. She wanted to scream.

Pulling over, Vicki reached for her mobile phone and put in a call to one of her lifelines, a woman who had offered her support. She hadn't had a day like that for a while, but it wasn't getting any easier — for her family, or for Michael.

The Czugaj family liked to split up their visits to Bali, so Michael had someone there on a fairly regular basis. Vicki booked a flight in October 2005, on a Sunday; Bob Lawrence and his wife, Jenny, did the same. They had only been over to visit Renae once — that's all their finances had allowed, despite all the scrimping and saving they could muster. By coincidence, they were flying out on the same day as Vicki, their travel and accommodation this time met by a group of lawyers who had volunteered to help the families of the Bali Nine.

Robyn Davis, Matthew Norman's mother, boarded the plane in Sydney just like the Lawrences — the same flight, to the same destination. Robyn was a sickly woman whose ongoing illness made it difficult to give Matthew all the support she wanted to. But she would do anything for him and she was on the same flight, courtesy of the same group of lawyers, to see her boy. Three parents, all on the same lonely journey to visit their children in Bali's Kerobokan Jail.

It was only six months earlier that those children had boarded another flight, traversing the same skies, but on a very different journey. Renae Lawrence and Matthew Norman had shared a flight to Bali, but never acknowledged each other. The co-workers sat in different rows, avoided eye contact and pretended to be strangers. That was the order given to them, and they obeyed it — to do otherwise could have proved too costly for them and their families.

A couple of days later, Michael Czugaj had to ignore fellow travellers on his flight too. Chatting with his Brisbane school friend Scott Rush, he never spoke to Tan Duc Thanh Nguyen or Myuran Sukumaran. If he knew they were on the plane, he never let on. They'd never been mates, but even if they had been, he wouldn't have acknowledged them.

Friendships had been cast aside and acquaintances forgotten as the group of nine young Australians set off on their Bali odyssey; now their parents were doing the same. Three families whose children were intricately bound together in life or death. And no real bond between them.

The same goes for the other families of the Bali Nine. Each family member felt the terror that gripped the pit of their guts when they were told their child had been arrested; each knows the frustration and, sometimes, anger that comes as their households are pushed from being private property into the realm of public circus. Each family knows that the future has been dimmed for the children they love so dearly. But instead of that creating a bond between the families — in the same way that sharing a tuck-shop roster or working backstage at a school concert might begin lifelong friendships — most of the Bali Nine families are going their own way.

Petty arguments, small jealousies and a desperation to blame someone else have marred the relationships between some of them. Their children are bound together for ever, but they see little reason to befriend each other or to seek support from those who might truly understand their anguish. Each set of parents is searching for an answer to the unfathomable: how their child could have ended up in this mess. And finger-pointing and blame have grown from the tiniest of issues. In a particular instance, one family arrived back in Australia with a birthday card for a member of the family of one of the Bali Nine and a request to pass it on; they posted it, as requested, with a brief letter and to their disappointment did not even receive a 'thank you" in response. One father claims to have been abused by one of the other families for not rushing to his son's side. Another father admits to wanting to punch someone else after they spooked some of the women with their talk of the death penalty. The blame game goes on for many, despite some allegiances being formed.

In the battle to employ lawyers in a country which few of the family members have visited and where few people speak English, things can grow tense. One father claims that some families are trying to lessen the evidence against their children by pointing the finger at others. A split can also be seen between some of the mules' families and those of the Nine caught at the Melasti without drugs strapped to their bodies. One family took great umbrage when a husband and wife showed snapshots of their previous week in Bali, unable to comprehend that they were not spending their time hidden away in a cheap motel room between the fifteen-minute visits they were granted four times a week. They couldn't understand how the pair could enjoy the sights, sounds and smells of the country that would soon decide their son's fate.

One father, a reluctant public figure, scoffs at the idealism of others. Some of them really believe, he says, that they will return to Australia with their child at the next visit; that the whole sordid mess is nothing more than a big mix-up.

At Lee Rush's Brisbane workplace, a friend says mates have kicked in a slice of their pay to help out with his expenses. The offer was unprompted. So was the generosity shown to Bill Stephens one day when he answered the door of his home. The father of a boy Martin Stephens went to school with stood there, bearing a $40 cheque. A group of children told Vicki Czugaj at a fundraiser for Michael that they had raided their piggy banks in order to hand over the small change they'd saved, and a friend of Michael's brother sent a cheque for $500 from his hospital bed. An anonymous businessman funded Bob Lawrence's first trip to Bali, and Australians have contacted media outlets to lend a hand to Matthew Norman's mother, Robyn Davis.

The munificence shown by strangers has astonished many of the families who, without exception, come across as hard-working, law-abiding Australians hoping for the best for their kids. Almost all of them have other children, many of them still at school. And all of them, from the moment they were contacted and told of the arrests in April last year, are struggling to understand how their child could be involved in what authorities painted from day one as a sophisticated, complex, international drug-smuggling ring.

Like parents across Australia, those involved like to think the best of their children. Martin Stephens's parents, Bill and Michele, believe he is too trusting; Michael Czugaj's family wish he wasn't so naive. Bob Lawrence regrets Renae's immaturity; Scott Rush got mixed up with the wrong crowd, and Matthew Norman was deeply affected by his parents' divorce. Even Andrew Chan was, apparently, as loyal as the day was long. The defences come thick and fast, as do the childhood stories of youngsters who would care for their siblings, teenagers who stuck by sick friends and sometimes spent their spare time helping collect for charity. They were normal Australian youths — perhaps reckless in not thinking through the consequences of what they were being offered, but good kids at heart.

It's a double-edged sword for those parents who genuinely still believe their children were threatened with their lives and the lives of those they loved: an odd comfort in knowing that their children didn't, allegedly, do it of their own free will, but scared witless that, despite that, their children will pay a lifelong price for being the clueless victims forced to surrender their bodies to an international crime network.

Bob Lawrence's house in Wallsend, the small western suburb of Newcastle set up in the mid-1850s as a coal-mining town, is not flash. But it's spotless and he concentrates on making sure that not a skerrick of ash from his cigarette drops onto the coffee table. The television drones on in the background.

Renae has inherited his eyes — you notice it immediately — but his have dulled in recent months, and they fill with tears easily as the pensioner blames himself for his 28-year-old daughter's bleak future.

'I was too strict on her," he says. 'I was too overprotective. No one said it to me then, but they have since. I wouldn't let her out of my sight. That's why she left home."

The row they had soon after Renae's eighteenth birthday keeps replaying in Bob's mind. Over and over. If only he had let her come and go as she pleased, then maybe — just maybe — she wouldn't be sitting in a hot, smelly Indonesian jail cell contemplating the most miserable of futures.

In the search for answers, Bob Lawrence is not the only parent pointing the finger towards themselves. Another parent, a mother this time, shakes her head and wonders how her son could have ended up in this mess. Were there warning signs she ignored? Could she have stopped it?

Lee Rush tried to stop his son — he had a family friend call police and tell them that Scott was leaving the country the next day and might be in trouble. He feared for his son and wanted to prevent him coming to harm. And now some people, despite much evidence to the contrary, are wondering whether Lee was to blame for the capture of the Nine. Someone, after all, had to be to blame for all this.

The finger-pointing is made trickier by the fact that, in nearly all instances, the Bali Nine share wonderful and warm relationships with their parents. They don't forget birthdays, or weekly phone calls home, or important anniversaries. None of the parents had lost faith in their child before the arrests and none expected them to make headlines as an accused drug smuggler. Certainly, some of the Nine had struggled as teenagers — a couple even notching up lengthy criminal records — but that mirrored the trials and tribulations of parents nationwide.

This was different. The descriptions of their children now being plastered across the international media could not be true. Were not true. And yet, when foreign affairs officials made the life-changing call to each of the parents on a Sunday in April 2005, none of them even believed their child was in Bali. Scott

Rush was supposed to be elsewhere, Michael Czugaj was in Cairns, Renae Lawrence in Sydney, Martin Stephens in Darwin. Or so some thought. Si Yi Chen's parents believed that their son's disappearance was so out of character, they reported him missing to local police.

That first visit to Bali to see their child remains the hardest single moment for most of the parents. And it's been played and replayed in the photographs that have graced the front pages of newspapers and filled television screens around the world ever since: Christine Rush, a Brisbane schoolteacher, wipes a tear from her eye as her husband, Lee, clutches the arm of his nineteen-year-old son Scott, who looks like he could be in his mother's class — a schoolboy desperately trying to keep it together, to be a man; Michael Czugaj doesn't try as hard — he rests his head in his hands as his mother, Vicki, cradles him like a baby while his heartbroken father, Stephan, looks on. Renae Lawrence's face is pressed hard up against the bars, her eyes willing someone to come and set her free.

The images are of torment: youths looking for reassurance and parents trying to answer the impossible. They all know that words are useless, and a hug under the heat of the world's media cannot turn back the clock. So the younger boys, not long out of school, cling to their mothers desperately, and parents whose faces have aged in hours leave after their allotted visiting time, wondering where it will all end.

Michele and Bill Stephens's first visit to their son Martin coincided with their thirty-second wedding anniversary. What a way to celebrate. Ordinary people, with all the love in the world for the boy behind the bars, had as their anniversary gift the look in their son's eyes when they told him they continued to believe and support him.

Vicki Czugaj couldn't wait to see her son — she held her lad's face in her hands. And as soon as she laid eyes on her boy, she needed an answer: 'Mate, why did you do it?" she asked. Having received the answer, she now shrugs her shoulders in telling the story. Michael said he had no choice — if he didn't follow orders, his mother and the rest of his family would be killed. 'And after that,' says Vicki, 'I started thinking of him as my hero rather than as an easily influenced, silly little boy." Vicki wears her confidence in her son as her armour; it helps on those days when she could scream with sadness.

Parents will do whatever they need to in order to cope. Bob Lawrence handled his first visit to Renae a hell of a lot better than his farewell. That tore at him — the need to say goodbye, not knowing when the anonymous charity of a local benefactor might again allow him and his wife to visit. Now he spends most of his days thinking of how he could make his only child's life a degree or two easier. The invalid pensioner saved up his pennies, bought an MP3 player on sale and prepared a list of his daughter's favourite songs; he shopped for the clothes she wore to one of her court appearances; lined up to get a Harry Potter book thinking it might distract her, and walks in hope to the mailbox every single day. And when there's a letter or card from his only daughter, like the handmade one she sent for his birthday, he feels like a lottery winner. 'To my dearest Daddy, happy birthday, have a beautiful day," his last birthday card read. 'Sorry about the card it was the best I could do. Have a drink (or two) for me. Love you more than words can say. Lots of love Your Daughter Renae."

As hard as it is for the young Australians in jail, it is sometimes even harder for those left behind. Like Michael Czugaj's little brother and sister — delightful children forced to be adults way too soon. They looked up to their big brother, just as he adored them. After news of Michael's arrest broke, his little sister took two days off school — partly to allow her family to take stock and decide on the best way to handle things, and partly to avoid the relentless media glare. By the time she returned, teachers and students had been briefed and told not to raise the issue with her. A confident young girl, she was, however, encouraged to talk about it as much as she liked.

Her brother's school did much the same thing, but Vicki doesn't know if the students were told not to raise the issue of Michael's arrest with her youngest son. Michael's brother tells his family that no one at school has ever mentioned it, but he's quieter, more reserved than his sister, and his family is not quite sure. They're watching him closely. At an age when drugs shouldn't even be in their vocabulary, Michael's younger siblings are living their family's nightmare.

Similarly, for others the arrest of those they cherish has turned their lives upside down. Renae Lawrence thinks the world of her younger stepbrother; Matthew Norman has a twin sister. Tan Duc Thanh Nguyen has younger siblings — so does Myuran Sukumaran. They all have parents. And all family members are dealing with it any way they can.

Scott Rush's parents have become a fixture in Bali, escaping Australia to be by their son's side at every chance, and watching the trials of his co-accused. They seem to be next to Scott whenever possible, attending court cases, taking notes, asking questions and seeking documents. They tried to stop Scott from leaving Australia for Bali, and now they need the best possible outcome for him. The Czugajs, too, are ensuring that Michael has plenty of visitors, rostering family members so that everyone doesn't visit in the same week. Michele Stephens is a daily visitor and Lawrence, the only woman, is receiving visits from Australian supporters as well as both her parents. As is Norman.

They have become part of the story, these parents, spending their holidays and their incomes to be by their children's sides. Some have stayed out of the limelight, still not recognisable to the public. Sukumaran's young brother cuts a lonely figure visiting him, his parents sighted rarely by the local press. Chan receives visits from his brother too, his parents remaining firmly behind the camera.

Nguyen's father and sister have travelled from their Brisbane home to support him, but the shame brought on them by the position he's in has changed their lives irrevocably. In the Vietnamese community, more than most, children can be their parents' greatest pride, or their greatest shame. It's a gamble, raising them in a clash of cultures in which they want them to remain true to their ethnicity but also do well in the world that surrounds them. And when the gamble fails, the family takes a tried and tested route: they remove themselves from their local community, hanging their heads in shame, and never uttering their grief out loud.

The Nguyen family is a deeply private one. And it's a mixture of that and the mores within the Vietnamese community that has prompted them to break off contact with many of those who played a role in their lives. Even Brisbane's community leaders have found it difficult to deliver the message of support they so want heard. The Nguyens cannot countenance that their eldest son, who had a future in the baking business and who seemed to respect their wishes, could be accused of drug smuggling.

Si Yi Chen's parents, too, are a desolate sight, their small frames covered in bulky jackets in Bali's stifling heat the first time they've been captured on camera visiting their son. Si Yi is their only child. To some parents, it almost seems as though they've been delivered their own personal death sentences.

XXVI

Name and Shame

The call came into Neil Mitchell's 3AW studio at 10.19 a.m. on Tuesday, 19 April, less than thirty-six hours after news of the arrests broke. 'These people that got caught over in Bali are a bunch of twits, mate," the caller said. 'Honestly, I reckon they should be lined up and shot."

The Melbourne caller wasn't alone: across the nation, on talkback stations and in the letters-to-the-editor pages of newspapers, Australians vented their anger. Some were cheering for the death sentence to be imposed quickly on the nine young Australians now taking centre stage in Indonesia; others needed to have an old score settled, having lost a loved one to the scourge of drugs provided by someone, somewhere, sometime. Public anger was almost palpable. It spawned whole talkback shows, internet forums and barbecue debates the length and breadth of Australia.

Melanie didn't offer any personal story to Derryn Hinch, also on 3AW, but you couldn't miss her point: 'These people who strap heroin to their body — they deserve the gunfire because they kill a lot of innocent children," she said. One call spurred on another, and another, and another. Few — about one in ten — were supportive of Sukumaran, Chan and their cohorts, but even those people didn't for a moment suggest that any of the group was innocent.

The images that filled television screens after the group's capture were indelibly etched in everyone's minds; images of four young Australians with their bodies caked in kilograms and kilograms of finely packed powder that would be worth a fortune on the streets of Sydney or Brisbane or Melbourne or Adelaide or Perth. Or anywhere in between. We weren't just told about it — we saw it with our own eyes. We saw it sitting on the table beside the confused and scared faces of those who had been wearing it. And when George called 2UE's John Laws and told everyone who was listening how his daughter was a heroin addict and that was why he could not have sympathy for those now looking down the barrel of death, the calls flooded in again.

It wasn't just George. Michael, who lost his son to heroin abuse, called Laws's rival station, 2GB. A father who was bringing up a handful of children after his wife died of an overdose called Brisbane's 4BC. Others called their local radio station with similar tales of tragedy and woe. The talkback chorus was clear in what it wanted: for the punishment to fit the crime and for these young Australians to serve as a deterrent to any others who might follow down the same reckless path. Day after day, the calls continued, with 90 per cent of callers nationwide airing their disgust at the group who quickly became known as the Bali Nine.

While the sentiment was similar, however, the specific points people wanted to express swung wildly. Some callers wanted to discuss the decision to prosecute the nine in Indonesia, which supports a death penalty, over Australia, which opposes death as punishment. Others wanted to express their disgust that heroin was the drug involved in the racket, not something seen as less poisonous. Still others called to discuss the greed and stupidity which must have filled the minds of those at the centre of the unfolding criminal and legal drama. Many wanted it known that no leniency should be granted, no matter what happened.

Dozens also wanted to compare the Bali Nine to Schapelle Corby, who had been arrested six months earlier and who was sitting in the jail that the Bali Nine would eventually learn to call home. Some felt that the Australian Federal Police should have waited until the Bali Nine lobbed back into Australia before arresting them. But probably a greater number, in the aftermath of the arrests, wanted to make sure that our politicians weren't rushing over to bring them home. Like hell they should get to serve their sentences in 'five-star" Australian jails, callers said; they were a disgrace to our nation.

Sometimes the best barometer for what people are thinking is talkback radio and letters-to-the-editor columns of newspapers, and that's where many people turn when an issue arises in their neighbourhood, or when a local politician steps out of line, or even in the event of a national scandal unfolding.

With the Bali Nine, the people-meter was quick and vicious. Internet forums took slightly longer to work up a head of steam, but when they did, they were no more forgiving. People logged on to chatrooms and forums in countries around the globe to have their say about the nine Australians who were at the heart of an international criminal and legal debate. Bloodthirsty online discussions became cheer squads for the death penalty; heroin smugglers were deemed akin to murderers. Australian taxpayers were warned to refuse any move that might help fund appeals or witnesses requesting immunity.

Perhaps it was a response to rising crime levels in our own communities, or a growing intolerance for those who abuse their bodies by taking drugs, but across the nation it seemed that the overriding reaction of the Australian public to the Bali Nine was that they had made their own bed. And, now, most people were eager to watch them squirm in it.

That response could not have been more starkly contrasted with the reaction that erupted over Corby's arrest. She seemed to be the quintessential girl-next-door. Disarmingly polite and neat, with finely chiselled cheekbones and well-sculpted eyebrows, Corby captured people's hearts. She had been arrested six months earlier when she arrived in Bali with 4.1 kilograms of marijuana in one of her bags. But it had to be a set-up, many people thought. She didn't know it was there, others opined. Why would someone take marijuana to Bali when they could source it there, and who would risk taking a bagful into a country that punished drug traffickers so harshly, others asked.

Going on the talkback barometer, the public didn't believe that Corby was a drug carrier — and they could tell that by looking at her. That was the sentiment expressed many times over as Corby became the darling of talkback shows. Indeed, in the weeks after the Bali Nine arrests, as many people called talkback to discuss her case as they did the federal budget. More than twice the number of listeners devoted their call to Corby than they did to Douglas Wood, another Australian who found himself in trouble overseas after being kidnapped in Iraq. And, with Corby, the calls were overwhelmingly supportive, which contrasted sharply to the judgment the public wanted to make over the Bali Nine's arrest.

Overall, almost four in five callers were on Corby's side. Just take popular broadcaster Alan Jones's 2GB program as an example: it recorded its biggest number of calls in one two-week period around the time of the Corby affair, with 93 per cent of those having their say believing that Corby was innocent of the charges. They didn't know her, but they saw her on television and staring out from the front page of their daily newspapers.

They saw the haunted look in her eyes, the way she was dressed, the way she spoke — and it just didn't fit with them.

Suspect baggage handlers became the bogeymen, along with the Indonesian justice system, which was seen as barbaric, primitive and corrupt; the Indonesian judges even being described on one show as 'like monkeys eating bananas". It was the same system that so many callers had supported during the Bali bombing trials and would support for the Bali Nine trials, but that didn't matter when it came to Schapelle. Corby offered us intrigue, even though the court cameras showed off every tear, every nerve, every grimace. Few saw her tears and thought her guilty. It was the same cameras that showed off the heroin haul that had been strapped to the Bali Nine mules. No intrigue here — it was all on camera.

'Free Schapelle' banners were plastered to cars. Community campaigns urged people to wrap ribbons around the front gates of suburban homes. Some people egged on others to discard their Indonesian souvenirs and trinkets. Tourists dropped Bali from their list of dream destinations, and some travel agents followed that lead. Public parties were held to celebrate the birthday of the young woman now in an Indonesian jail cell. At airports, people lined up to have their bags plastic-wrapped. If it happened to Schapelle, many of them thought, it could happen to their daughter. Or their sister. Or their niece. Or them.

As Corby's case progressed, the chorus of public anger at her plight grew. She was innocent; there was no proof, they said. Not like that other lot, the Bali Nine, where we saw the heroin strapped to their bodies. That killed people, that stuff, they'd say. Corby's case just didn't make sense.

'It's like the refrigerator salesman who didn't do too well selling refrigerators in the Antarctic," one caller told the ABC in Melbourne. 'Why would anyone smuggle marijuana to Bali? It's just nonsense."

People demanded that the government intervene in some way — Schapelle *had* to be rescued. Some complained that Foreign Minister Alexander Downer and the federal government had done more to help Douglas Wood, the Australian hostage in Iraq, than Corby. The SAS should be sent in, someone else offered. One caller who had visited Bali twenty-eight times felt so angry that she thought she might never return.

Day after day, week after week, month after month, Corby was the subject of conversation.

On the streets of Indonesia, though, Corby's predicament wasn't seen in the same light as in her homeland. Her bag had been stashed with marijuana, just as four of the Bali Nine had been found with heroin all over them. To many there, she was seen as another Australian flouting the laws of a country that was trying desperately to grapple with a drug-use problem that was killing their young; a country where legislators had decided to pull out all stops to end the scourge that filled street corners and markets and nightclubs and bars; a country where the law was the law, and breaches of it were dealt with harshly.

Tony Fox, who set up the foreign prisoners' support service about a decade ago, says many Indonesians see Corby as no different to the Bali Nine. 'Here in Australia, everyone wants to believe in a fairytale. And the media have eaten this up with a great big soup ladle spoon," he says. Fox says he has been contacted by media outlets around the world asking if there are any other attractive, blue-eyed Australian girls wasting away in foreign jails. When told he can put them in touch with a young Asian-Australian in Cambodia, they are not interested. They all want to find the next Schapelle Corby. But Corby's fresh-faced image didn't wash in Indonesia.

In the month the Bali Nine were arrested, there were 150 arrests for drug-related matters in Jakarta alone. That illustrates crime-fighters' crackdown on drugs, which end the lives of 15 000 Indonesian teenagers each year. And the toll continues to climb, as drug addiction takes hold in communities across the country; experts say that 3.2 million of the nation's 220 million people are now drug users.

The charges laid at the feet of Corby and the Bali Nine meant that ten more Australians were added to the list of 100 or so other Australians on drug charges in foreign prisons. But in the country where they were caught — unlike three-quarters of those others — a death penalty was the ultimate weapon available to be dished out as a deterrent by those in charge.

The debate about, and reaction to, the arrests of the Nine wasn't confined to Australian suburbia. In media columns, in parliament and in universities, others joined in. Dr Tim Lindsey, Professor of Asian Law and director of the Asian Law Centre, says it would be foolish to judge international behaviour by Australian standards. 'If you want to look at the region, then Australia is the odd one out," he says.

Corby would have faced certain death in Singapore, and almost certain death in other places like Malaysia or Vietnam. Lindsey says that within the Southeast Asian region, Indonesia is a 'low executor, both per head of population and overall in numbers", beaten strongly by countries like China, Singapore, Malaysia, Thailand, Vietnam — and the United States. And he blames the media for some of the public perceptions that paint Indonesia as being out of step in relation to the treatment it hands out for serious offences.

'What it comes down to is a fundamental xenophobic attitude to Southeast Asia, whereby we salute and applaud, with bloodthirsty relish, the death sentences meted out to Imam Samudra and Amrozi for their offences and hear people say they're happy to pull the trigger, they should be burnt and tortured and things like that, and our government says it is an appropriate sentence, but hey, white Australians who are involved in what would here be serious drug offences, they shouldn't have to face death."

Lindsey says he does not support the death penalty. However some, he says, would argue that perhaps death should only apply for terrorism and not for drug charges, but that's not a debate being waged in Australia — at least, not officially.

'Australia's official position is we're opposed to the death penalty. Well, how can the government view the death sentence for Imam Samudra and the others as appropriate? It's a double standard. You either oppose the death penalty or you don't, and of course it creates the perception that we support the death penalty for foreign terrorists with dark skin but we won't want it for drug smugglers who are white-skinned."

Do any of the nine young Australians deserve death by gunfire for their role in the aborted drug run? That became the crux of the Australian debate as the Bali Nine raced through their trials. As a nation, Australia has stood strongly and proudly against the death penalty, and yet, as Lindsey points out, we've supported it in the case of some terrorists who have acted against us. Isn't it then hypocritical, some argue, not to support it when our own are in trouble? Indonesians don't hide their warnings against drug smuggling, or the deathly consequences, and several people said that the Bali Nine could not have missed Corby's unfolding saga as they boarded their planes.

The nation is split in two. On one side sit the proponents of death-as-punishment, arguing that if people commit a crime in a country that promises death, they should die. The argument put forward is usually twofold: first, that Australians should respect the laws of those countries they visit, just as Australia requests visitors here to respect what's on our statute books; second, drug smugglers traffic in death — they destroy families and cost communities dearly — there must be a deterrent, some say, and if the death penalty serves as one, so be it. Both are compelling arguments, heard over and over again as the Bali Nine have travelled quickly towards their fate.

In Australia, experts estimate that drug abuse costs billions, and it continues to rise. In a vicious circle that engulfs whole communities, addicts feed off crime to fund their habits — car theft, stealing, break-and-enters, armed robbery, assault, prostitution and even murder are in an addict's desperate armoury to help them get their next hit. Years ago, researchers found that addicts could earn an average of $1175 each from crime in just one week and that property crime losses, as a direct result of drugs, can cost Australia up to $500 million each year. Add to that the cost to ambulance and health services, social security payments costing hundreds of millions of dollars each year, absenteeism, car accidents, needle-stick injuries, and the toll is even higher. Policing experts even have a term for the collateral damage: the drug harm index, which measures the cost to the community of specific amounts of illegal drugs. For heroin, it is $1.06 million for every kilogram.

Dr Ingrid van Beek, from Sydney's medically supervised injecting centre, sees the cost daily. Especially the human cost. 'I see the worst of it. It's not so victimless from where I sit," she says candidly. The likes of Renae Lawrence and Martin Stephens and Scott Rush and Michael Czugaj had the lives of drug users strapped to their bodies, she says, as they tried to board their flight home. An articulate and thoughtful woman, Dr van Beek doubts any of the mules were thinking that, though. 'I don't know what they were thinking — not very much, I suspect, but they should have been thinking that, because it's the reality. X number of drug users will die as a result of that particular batch of heroin." In her centre, which began operating on a trial basis in May 2001, that X figure amounts to seven overdoses for every 1000 hits of heroin. 'We resuscitate those people," she says simply.

Outside such an environment, the estimates of how many lives might have been at risk if the Bali Nine's haul had made it back to Australia vary widely. It depends on who would have mixed what in it before it was sold, where it would have been bought and, sometimes, how long it would have taken an ambulance to turn up.

Van Beek sees the saved lives as only one of the positive effects of the Bali Nine arrests: 'Maybe the next nine kids working at the showground, when they're asked whether they want to have a free trip to Indonesia, might think twice if they know that there are these operations that successfully bust these type of things,' she says. 'I suppose I do see it as a little akin to being an arms dealer and thinking a little about what those arms are going to be used for. If they're users themselves, I suppose I can understand better why you'd get caught up in couriering. But if you're not a user yourself, I am quite hard-lined on that.' Certainly, though, she doesn't go so far as to support the death penalty. 'I don't think they deserve to die,' she says. None of the nine offered any defence that suggested they were caught in a personal drug spiral.

Most opposed to the death penalty don't have van Beek's daily insight into the situation. But they are just as passionate in their arguments. They say that the death penalty does not act as a deterrent to others; this point seems to be supported by the steady stream of young people who continue to put their own lives at risk by joining drug-smuggling rackets. Members of the Bali Nine would have all heard of Schapelle Corby's case, but they still travelled to Bali. Tuong Van Nguyen, the last Australian to go to the gallows after being found with 396 grams of heroin at Singapore's Changi airport in 2002, must have also known the risks. But still they board planes, attempting to outwit multimillion-dollar crime-fighting operations.

A second reason put up by those who oppose the death penalty revolves around the chances of convicting, and putting to death, an innocent person. It's a real risk, given that, both in this country and others, scientific evidence or new information has later been able to clear someone. The debate in Australia was reignited by Van Nguyen's death, the images of his mother prompting heartache in parents everywhere. The death penalty has a big ripple effect, engulfing whole families, and, according to those who oppose it, stands as a permanent reminder of a society unwilling to forgive.

Tony Fox, from the foreign prisoners' support service, says that views change quickly when it is someone you know at the centre of the debate. 'Sit down and imagine it's your son or it's your daughter. Imagine you've just got a call at 2 a.m. Tell me then that you wouldn't do everything possible to have your kid brought home.'

Despite the anger being vented against the Bali Nine, Fox's service is host to a growing number of Australians wanting to support them. Kay Danes, a volunteer advocate with the service, says Corby supporters have directed others to their website, www.foreignprisoners.com, but it has been a slow process. At first, she says, there would be one inquiry relating to the Bali Nine for every 200 emails supportive of Corby. That has now grown to ten or more emails each day, many of them asking specifically about the welfare of Renae Lawrence and Michael Czugaj.

People have seen Lee and Christine Rush sit in court day after day, hoping their son has a future; they've heard the strangled voice of Bob Lawrence, just wishing that his daughter survives the next step; and they've heard how Michele and Bill Stephens — and all the others — would do anything for their children. 'It's no longer black and white in people's minds," Danes says.

Tan Duc Thanh Nguyen's mother, too, was responsible for a turnaround in Australian views. 'It came down to a photo," says Danes. Mrs Nguyen looked as though her heart had been ripped from her chest. 'When you see a mum like that, it dawns on people that he might have done the wrong thing, but oh my god, look at his mother. People see that there are other people attached to it."

Danes says supporters now want to send members of the Bali Nine all sorts of things. The advice list on what they need is long: toothpaste, soap, talcum powder, laundry powder (but they are told soap is cheaper to send because it is lighter), sachets of moisturiser, tinea cream, Dettol, Chapsticks for dry lips, cracked heel balm, Band-Aids, cotton buds, Wet Ones, mosquito coils, oil of cloves for toothache, cold sore cream, dental floss ... The list is seemingly endless.

XXVII

Shame on our Streets

Somewhere in a public toilet right now a teenager is rolling up his sleeves, ready to sink a syringe hard into a vein in his arm. In a ritual practised perhaps a couple of times already today, the addict will slowly unwrap a tiny foil package, the anticipation in his body building. If he is also dealing in big quantities, he might have already tasted a smidgen of the hammer on purchase, just to make sure he wasn't being sold a pup, ensuring that the flowery, bitter taste on his tongue promised the way ahead.

Now he will lay out the ingredients he needs so desperately: a plastic spoon, some water and his needle or syringe, known as his fit. He'll mix the gear, butterflies invading every crevice in the pit of his gut, drawing up twenty or so lines into his used syringe. And then, with a deep breath, he will clench his fist a couple of times to bring the veins to the surface.

At this stage, time stands still. Nothing else matters but the immediate promise of euphoria. It will be the best sex he's ever had, his best friend and his lover, all wrapped into one. He might tease himself a little, popping the fit in before taking it out. It's called jacking, and it's all part of the ritual. But soon he will plunge the needle with urgency born of desperation and little care deep into any vein he can find in his arm. Perhaps he won't be able to find it as quickly as he would like and he will need to poke around a bit, missing the vein at first, before withdrawing the syringe, now coloured pink as his blood mixes with the heroin. Perhaps he'll then share his fit with the young lad next to him, who is so frantic to block out life, to feel the same hit as the heroin rush spreads through his body, that he doesn't care if he is infected with someone else's blood-borne disease.

In public toilets in Cabramatta, parks that dot the Brisbane River and in back alleys in Melbourne's underbelly, many will spend the rest of their lives and their incomes chasing that first heady rush, the subject of songs and musings by creative junkies for decades.

He will feel the whack within seconds as the heroin travels from his arm to the right side of his heart in just a few beats. From there it will hurtle off to the left side, before it is spat out into the arterial system, reaching his brain within seconds. There's a massive explosion of sensation as all connection to reality is lost. His pain disappears before him; life is blocked out. The addict's body is isolated from his mind. Euphoria erupts, and his mind is able to trip wherever it wants. Life becomes poetic — all terror gone, all anxiety erased.

At least, that's how it feels the first few times, even a dozen times. But, after that, things usually change. It takes longer to get there, more and more china white needed to achieve the same effect. But it still becomes a vital escape, a chance to shut out the noise of life. And when that happens, it seems as though the let-down comes faster and steeper. And the next use sooner. With each use, the euphoria seems to become a little bit shorter and a little bit softer, and he knows that he would do anything — even give up his own life — for the next hit, to feel that way again.

To feel dreamy and dippy with no sense of yesterday or tomorrow. Just now. He'll do anything to feel like that and he'll grow more and more cunning, more able to cheat and steal and swindle from those who would do anything to help him. He won't care. Nothing will matter, except his next hit. Life is in the here and now. There are no consequences — just heroin, smack, skag, hammer, H, horse, rock, white, harry cone, china white or anything else it's called on the street.

Crime will become a necessary part of his life, his addiction costing more money than he could ever earn but preventing him from keeping the most basic of full-time jobs. The cycle will become vicious. He might soon be having four or so hits a day. He will no longer worry about the bad batch of low-grade heroin that might have killed those who sat on the park bench just hours before him; he won't care if the syringe he is about to inject into his cubital vein is stained pink with someone else's blood; he won't care if he's misjudged the heroin's purity and the ambulance doesn't make it in time, or that his arms reveal the sad tale of his daily journey, or that his hollow and glassed eyes play cover page to a sorry plot. He won't care that each time he clenches his fist and prepares to inject, he is rolling the dice in a game of life where the odds are stacked terribly against him. Desperation can do that to you.

Only a couple of months earlier, his fix was being harvested in the remote and hilly regions of Burma, adjacent to the Chinese border. The area, along with Laos and Thailand, has earnt the name of 'Golden Triangle' and, along with the Golden Crescent in Afghanistan, and Central and South America, is responsible for the world's opium production. But it is in Burma that most of Australia's heroin originates.

There, late in the year, sometime around September or October, opium is planted by the families involved in opium poppy cultivation. Some put the number of households at 250 000; others at closer to 300 000. Across the region, handfuls of poppy seeds will be dispersed across the top of freshly tended fields. Three or four months later, from late January to March, the plants will have shot up to about a metre high, and boast ten or so stems. Each will have a brightly coloured flower at this stage and, everything going well, a seed pod that experts say is the size of a chicken egg.

To milk as much as they can from the lucrative international trade, villagers will sometimes plant a second crop closer to Christmas, to be harvested slightly later, in April or May. But the appearance of the flower and pod acts as the impetus for Burmese farmers to begin the painstakingly slow and laborious harvest. They cut into the pod, extracting a syrup which quickly turns dark in colour once it's released from its cocoon. The farmers collect it, load it onto donkeys and head off to laboratories, where the process of making heroin from opium begins.

The laboratories are often described as mobile chemical set-ups dotted across the region, their location a poor secret. Here, the substance is soaked in big vats of warm water before other ingredients are added. In forty-eight hours or so, the substance is dried and packed and ready for its next journey, eventually leaving the Golden Triangle as high-grade number four heroin and fanning out across the world. It now weighs significantly less that it did straight after the harvest, and is immeasurably more valuable. It's guarded like gold.

It used to be that the heroin would travel in just one direction — north over the border into China and perhaps then on to Hong Kong and beyond — but that has all changed in recent years. Now it spurts out in all directions, by mule and donkey and any other means possible, to different ports in China, Vietnam, Cambodia, Thailand, Hong Kong, Singapore, India, Pakistan and Malaysia, for example, before being picked up by sea or air and heading further on its journey to the heroin capitals of countries the world over, including Australia. Its journey is an interesting one: traversing the globe on donkeys; in trucks, cars and motorbikes; on ships, in aeroplanes and secreted on passengers desperate to make a buck or feed an addiction.

Indonesia has become one of the primary embarkation points for heroin trafficked to Australia. Indeed, in recent years, it has become a bigger part of the new mix, and an important one too, giving intelligence officers a run for their money. The busy group of islands is a nuisance for those charged with policing the international trade, and once heroin lands in Jakarta and Bali it can be flown directly into Sydney, just as it can from Singapore, Bangkok and other busy international cities.

Sometimes it will be stockpiled, poised for the next rush, but mostly it won't be, the steady demand within our shores and others encouraging its continuous journey. Most of it will escape detection as the ballooning law enforcement agencies in our airports and marine centres are not equipped with the finance, resources or intelligence to kill the trade. Certainly most of it will evade detection in some of the twenty-six countries where the Australian Federal Police have personnel.

The AFP have sixty-five people placed in thirty-one different cities in those countries, and drug trafficking is not their total brief. Their job is to liaise with local authorities about all manner of illegal activities, and in a world of big illegal business, drug smuggling is just one part of it. In any case, the six to ten drug cartels that control the flow of drugs out of the Golden Triangle are well equipped to do battle with authorities. It's not a new trade, and they've learnt over years and years how to diversify, change track quickly, and vary their travel routes and communication tools.

It's a billion-dollar business with profits and freedoms at stake, so they'll do all manner of things to evade capture.

Sometimes the cartels will join forces; other times they'll compete ferociously in burgeoning new markets, anxious for their share. With pragmatism, they've learnt to deal with any losses to law enforcement and move on to ensure they can meet the annual supply of heroin needed so desperately by addicts around the globe.

Their target touchdown in Australia is invariably Sydney and its big, bustling airport that plays host to thousands of international visitors each day. Often it will instead be one of the busy ports where detection might be avoided. Or, sometimes, the point of disembarkation will be less obvious: through the big expanses of coastline that present border authorities with an almost impossible task to police.

From the Asian ports, it's Australian cartels or freelance drug lords who organise the heroin's final trip to Australia. Organised crime groups behind the distribution within Australia, mostly Vietnamese and ethnic Chinese, will pay all sorts of prices, depending on availability, to get the uncut blocks of heroin onto Australian soil. This year they might pay between \$100 000 and \$120 000 for a 700-gram block. Next year it might be wildly more or less, but price isn't the crucial issue at this point. From the moment the heroin lands in one of the Asian ports that form an uneven arc over Australia, the most important job is to transport the heroin safely home. However they can. Without being caught.

It used to be easier; monster importations would slip through big holes in the policing net. But that all changed about the time of the heroin drought in early 2001. Some attribute the cause of the drought to policing being beefed up, closing the loopholes that allowed the trade to flourish in Australia. But its cause was probably influenced by other factors as well, like the severe drought in Burma and the Taliban ban on opium poppy-growing in Afghanistan. Others still attribute the fall in supply to the growing demand for heroin in China — and a massive seizure that put an Australian-based cartel out of business for a while.

Whatever the real reasons, the masses of high-grade white that flooded Australian towns and cities, taking into its clutch addicts from all socioeconomic groups, suddenly stopped. Heroin became harder to source, and awfully expensive to buy. The impact was immediate, not only on the addicts, who turned to other drugs in a bid to feed their habit, but also those running the smuggling operations. They could no longer take the same risks — there was too much at stake. They had to be smarter and faster and spread the risk. They could not afford to have a single bust putting them out of business, so they could no longer afford to gamble on one big, single importation making it through the enhanced border patrols. They had to diversify, change distribution patterns and import smaller amounts more often. And that's the way they continued to operate, even after the low supplies eased a little in the first half of 2002.

Mules were an essential part of the changed importation patterns: young recruits who would use their bodies to ferry drugs on international flights in return for wads of cash. The risk could be immense, but so too could the payment. White Anglo-Saxon backpackers made up a chunk of the mule recruits, rarely raising the suspicions of those employed to keep drugs out. Sometimes the drugs would be sewn into the hems of their clothes, or sandwiched in their toiletries bags or in the heels of their shoes. Other times mules would swallow tightly bound balloons of drugs, carrying them through electronic detectors in the pits of their stomachs — knowing the risk, but counting the cash in their heads. Still others would plaster the heroin on their person, or secrete it inside their genitalia in a bid to escape detection.

Often mules weren't used and instead the drugs were packed tightly in all sorts of paraphernalia sent by mail or included in passengers' luggage: in cooking pastry and fish fillets; stuffed into candlesticks and car parts; even funnelled into the buttons of clothing. It might have been harder this way, with more detailed plans needed, but it was necessary for the cartels to escape increased policing measures, like a renewed Australian Federal Police presence and a front-line Customs service that was boosting enhanced detection technologies, profiling abilities and intelligence networks.

The drought forced changes once the drug had been successfully brought inside Australian borders, too. The six or so big Australian cartels started collaborating more, the shortage of heroin forcing importers to diversify into other drugs. Many dealers were stripped of their livelihood as in-your-face dealing in some areas disappeared, to be replaced by mobile traders, hocking their heroin aboard travelling trains, making home visits and refusing to cater for new customers they could not afford to trust instinctively. Mobile telephones became the dealers' new tool of trade, with low- to middle-ranking heroin traders boasting 200 telephone numbers or more in their cellular address book.

Once the heroin arrives in Australia, it takes a fairly direct route to Cabramatta, about 30 kilometres south of Sydney city. Up to three-quarters of residents here speak a first language other than English, with 40 per cent born in Asian countries like Vietnam, Cambodia, China and Laos. It's a young population, with higher-than-average unemployment levels, but it has been unfairly demonised by public perceptions. Few, however, doubt its role in the national heroin market.

From here, the drug will fan out over the next twenty-four hours, with orders filled across the nation. Between 3 and 8 tonnes of heroin will be used annually, making up between 18 and 78 million street-level heroin sales each year. The secrecy and illegality of the transactions mask any more specific estimates. But as sure as night will follow day, Cabramatta will usually serve as the central distribution point, with organised drug lords and freelance distributors lining up to pay for their share.

Most of the white will remain in Sydney, being sent back towards the CBD, to Kings Cross on the city's eastern fringe and Redfern on the southern fringe. Lesser amounts will travel by road to Melbourne, Canberra and Brisbane, with roadside deals often done in lonely outback stretches between Sydney and those cities. Minor amounts will be sent across to Western Australia, where the street price will be almost double what it is on the east coast. Indeed, it's always cheaper near the source, and dealers in Sydney's southwest will offer better prices than their counterparts in other parts of the city.

Give or take a few bucks, a gram will cost $300 in New South Wales, up about $80 on what it was before the 2001 drought. Demand will dictate that the price won't vary much in Victoria and the Australian Capital Territory, but users can expect to pay inflated prices elsewhere — $380 a gram in Queensland, rising to $500 in Western Australia. The price of a cap — the amount usually needed for a single injection — will rise and fall on availability, but teeter around $50. Caps are often bought in small pieces of foil, taken from inside a cigarette packet before being fastened inside small water balloons.

Apart from the market forces at play, the different price levels in different states is driven partly by the onion effect in distribution: the more layers in the chain, the greater the price. Everyone has to be paid. Cabramatta's strong freelance market means that middle managers are often not part of any big network or organised gang — there are just addicts desperate to feed their own habits; young men and women drawn to supplying so that they can keep using.

As the heroin changes hands, in some areas its purity will fall as dealers attempt to stretch its quantity and its value. It's not common now, but what's added to it, and how much is added, all depends on who you deal with. There's not much trust in this business, and everyone wants to know they are getting what they are paying for.

Payment is not always in cash, either, although it's never in kind. Electrical equipment is part of the currency now, with laptop computers, iPods and portable DVD players, along with jewellery, all considered as valuable as cash. And that, in turn, adds to a vicious crime cycle that impacts on neighbours and communities across the country. The average heroin user can earn $1175 a week on crime. Someone's got to pay for that, and the effect of that chain ripples through our towns and cities. Burglary owes its impetus too often to addiction; so too does armed robbery.

The dealer has to be paid, just as the addict has to have his next fix. And so while assaults and bashings, stand-over tactics and blackmail are all part of the illegal drug operation, property crime stands out. Homes and businesses — and the people in them — fall victim to the heroin scourge dozens of times a day; young men and women so desperate for money to pay for the next fix that they will steal anything and hock it, or hurt anyone who tries to stop them. They will turn on their mothers and fathers and brothers and sisters, stealing from those closest to them, as well as others they have never met. There are no loyalties, just the here and now of finding money for the next hit.

The cost to the community of drug abuse — in crime, especially property crime, but also in health and policing, welfare and absenteeism, as well as the loss of life — adds up to billions of dollars each year. *Billions*. And everyone ends up paying. Not just the addicts — often with their lives — but their families, whose love and trust of those they saw develop an addiction is sorely tested, often destroyed. Just as they are reaching out with one hand, the addict is likely to steal from the other.

Law-abiding citizens in towns and cities across Australia pay dearly too. Their freedoms are stolen when their houses are robbed. Valuables go too, to be hocked for little. Businesses suffer, as do taxpayers, whose contributions to the nation's crime-fighting effort and health system grow and grow. It's a vicious cycle of crime that restarts every time a chunk of heroin arrives on our shores.

None of that, though, was front of mind in April when four young drug mules walked into Indonesia's Ngurah Rai airport with heroin valued at between $2.4 and $4 million on the streets of Australia strapped to their bodies.

XXVIII

The Legal Lobby

Kevin O'Rourke picked up the newspaper over breakfast on Monday, 13 October 1997. The story tore at his heart: two young children, aged just five and seven, had been virtually orphaned after their father died of a suspected drug overdose. The man's name was Ian McKenzie and his children had found him on the bathroom floor on Saturday morning. Unable to wake him, and no doubt with the innocence that only comes with being a child, they ducked off to play with a neighbour. O'Rourke didn't have to wonder what had happened to the children's mother — that was explained too. Jane McKenzie, along with Deborah Spinner and Lyle Doniger, was serving a fifty-year jail term in Thailand after pleading guilty to attempting to smuggle 115 grams of heroin from Bangkok to Sydney. That small amount of heroin equalled fifty years in jail, and a couple of young children were forced to grow up without parents.

It didn't make a lot of sense to O'Rourke. He looked up from the newspaper and across the breakfast table to where his son, Ryan, sat. He smiled at the morning antics of a child fresh from a big sleep. Ryan was loud and alive with laughter that filled the dining room, just like kids across Sydney. But not Jane McKenzie's. O'Rourke's son was young, as were Jane McKenzie's kids, but he seemed so much more fortunate. Jane McKenzie's children, just across Sydney in the suburb of West Ryde, had lost their father to a drug overdose and their mother to a Bangkok prison. O'Rourke left for work, unable to shut that out of his mind.

A year later, O'Rourke was visiting McKenzie, Spinner and Doniger in jail, desperate to secure a prisoner exchange treaty between Thailand and Australia which would allow McKenzie and Spinner to serve out the rest of their time in their homeland. That would mean they could be near their children, while still being punished for their crime. O'Rourke was the NSW Council for Civil Liberties president and that treaty had become his campaign, one he waged until 2002, when it was ratified by Australia and Thailand. It was Australia's first such scheme and it allowed prisoners to apply to serve out their term in Australia, after the completion of four years in Bangkok. Two years later, in 2004, McKenzie and Spinner flew into Australia to be united with their children for the first time since their arrests.

By 2005 O'Rourke was the chief executive officer of PricewaterhouseCoopers Legal, and this time he turned on the television to catch the nightly news. His children were a few years older, but so too were the ones that filled his television screen. He stood transfixed as close-up images of Schapelle Corby and some of the Bali Nine appeared. The cameras panned across their faces, recording every raw emotion. The lens seemed to be within centimetres of the youths as they looked out, lost, from their jail cells, pressed hard up against the windows of the vans transporting them from one centre to another. O'Rourke found it distressing to watch, and he wondered about the young Australians at the centre of it all.

Did they understand what was happening to them? Did their parents understand the full ramifications of their arrests?

The next morning, still with those questions in mind, O'Rourke decided to do something about it. Arriving early at work, he sent out an email to colleagues at PricewaterhouseCoopers Legal, asking if anyone else wanted to donate their time and offer assistance to the families of the nine young people facing the possibility of execution. Any help, everyone was told, was unrelated to their current workplace and needed to be conducted in their own time.

One hour passed ... and O'Rourke was overwhelmed by the response. More than thirty colleagues, almost all lawyers, had popped into his office, picked up the telephone or sent him an email volunteering their time and their expertise. A legal lobby was formed, and behind closed doors — without any media fanfare — work began to 'save" the lives of the nine youths in Bali.

No members of the public knew about the group. It wasn't that the group was hiding its activities, they just considered that their best chance of making a difference was to close the door and get on with it; find out what needed to be done, and do it.

A letter was hand delivered to each of the Bali Nine, explaining the role of the top-notch team. It was made very clear that the group would not provide legal assistance for their court cases — that was the responsibility of their individual lawyers. But the Sydney-based legal eagles would be there as back-up, as a behind-the-scenes maintenance crew to ensure that the road ahead was as smooth as possible for both the Nine and their families. Not that anyone thought it would be too smooth — it was going to be an uphill battle no matter how anyone looked at it: for the lawyers working behind the scenes; for the families thrown into the public eye through their children's involvement; and for the Nine themselves, most of them with no knowledge of what the months ahead would bring.

Some of the Bali Nine, once handed the letter, tossed it away, probably not understanding it. They'd become minor celebrities of sorts, with everyone wanting to interview them, people passing them notes and seeking their views. To some of them, this might have been just another request. But others passed it — along with other notes they had received from strangers — to their parents the next time they visited.

For Matthew Norman's mother, Robyn Davis, it was the helping hand she so desperately needed. Her boy was in trouble, and she had to both understand his predicament and raise the funds to travel to Bali to see him. And by herself she couldn't do either. She was the first to put in a call.

Renae Lawrence's father, Bob, and his wife, Jenny, asked for help too. Wallsend is a world away from Bali, and Bob felt frustrated that he had no involvement in his daughter's future. He couldn't turn back the clock and change things, but he didn't know how he could help her either.

Then one of the Brisbane families put in a call, wanting guidance over whether a petition might help their son's predicament. Another of the families from New South Wales was interested in the likelihood of a treaty being set up between the two countries.

Other families stayed clear of the couple of dozen lawyers giving up their free time, worried it had to be a trick. Why would they volunteer to fund flights to Bali when talkback radio was filled with the ire of other Australians? Why would they try to force the Australian Government to adopt a prisoner exchange program when they didn't personally know their son or any of the others mixed up in the whole ordeal? Did they really side with the families over the role played by the AFP?

A couple of families felt they had been tricked into talking to the media once their children had been charged, one removing a reporter from his home at 1.40 a.m. and another furious that their young son was interviewed and quoted without permission. They had learnt to be wary and to trust no one. But some — Robyn Davis and Bob Lawrence, in particular — couldn't afford to think like that right now.

Kevin O'Rourke's operation ran along two lines: specific help for the youths and their families, and big legal issues on the home front that needed investigation. The latter element involved setting up two teams, the first looking at the controversial involvement in the case of the Australian Federal Police. Like many of the parents, O'Rourke wondered why the AFP might tip off a country to a possible crime, knowing it could end in the execution of a group of young Australians. O'Rourke needed an answer to that question and so did many of the lawyers working for him. They started asking questions, seeking the guidelines under which the AFP acted in such cases, lodging freedom of information requests in their search.

That was O'Rourke's first band of lawyers. A second team would explore a prisoner exchange program, drawing on the treaty between Australia and Thailand in the hope that the Australian Government would adopt it. O'Rourke's loud lobby for the Thai treaty had proved fruitful and he saw no reason why a similar program could not exist between Australia and Indonesia.

A third team was entrusted with less legal and more human endeavours; its job was to liaise with those families who had sought help, find out what assistance they needed and provide it. Did any of the Bali Nine have medical conditions, for example, that required treatment? Was proper bedding needed for the young asthmatic among the nine? Did their families — most of whom had thought their children were off on holidays around Australia — need either emotional or financial support to cope with what would happen next? These were the more important issues for the families, rather than the behind-the-scenes legal manoeuvrings that did not change the here and now. What they wanted was a regular — in one case, daily — phone call to explain the latest twists and turns in the drama. Phonecards helped too, with the one presented by O'Rourke's volunteers to Bob and Jenny Lawrence proving of great benefit. Before that, the Lawrences had relied on the odd weekly facsimile that would only sometimes arrive. The phonecard allowed them to check up on their daughter and offer her, through her lawyer, important words of encouragement on the eve of her court appearances.

The charity didn't stop there, either. Families who sought financial help were also offered trips and accommodation in Bali so that they could visit their children. Volunteers kicked in to fund the trips, and all bureaucratic liaisons — an onerous task for the families involved — were handled by the lawyers based in Sydney. For two of the families, that support seemed crucial for their own survival.

Behind the scenes, O'Rourke's team was knee deep in legalese. His team involved a cross-section of young professionals, almost all lawyers, chewing up their spare time in the hope of making a difference. O'Rourke had also picked up the phone and called his mates at his old stomping ground, the NSW Council for Civil Liberties. The Council had been planning to mount a similar operation, so they joined forces, reconvening a council subcommittee to look at Australian prisoners abroad.

The lobby of lawyers received the AFP guidelines for acting in death penalty cases after submitting a freedom of information request, and they were shocked by what they considered to be the inadequacies of the guidelines. The rules allowed wide latitude for the AFP to provide information in cases that could end in the death penalty. The lawyers understood the value of intelligence swapping, even citing the example of terrorist organisation Jemaah Islamiah as an example of why Indonesia and Australia need to share information. But they wanted to lobby for a brake on the exchange; they wanted transparent checks and balances factored into any intelligence-sharing agreement.

The team charged with looking at the AFP's role soon went back to O'Rourke recommending that our law enforcement agencies be able to provide the information to other countries, on the proviso that their actions did not indirectly result in the death penalty. This would stop the willy-nilly trade in which other countries are provided with masses of raw intelligence without reference to the possible effect.

O'Rourke thought that the recommendation was a good idea, and decided to lobby our politicians to force the AFP to adopt it. To him, it's simply a matter of Indonesia respecting the Australian culture, in which both political parties abhor capital punishment, just as Australians are sometimes asked to be tolerant of the Indonesian way.

The treaty team's task would also lead to a request to the government. Its optimism climbed in October 2005 after talks between the Australian and Indonesian governments. It didn't take long to filter back to the team that the go-ahead for two crucial matters had been given. First, any treaty between the two countries could proceed despite an accord between Indonesia and France still being worked out. To the lawyers donating their time and energy to the issue, this was good news — it was like jumping the queue, promising the chance that a treaty was a real possibility — in the short term. Second, it seemed that any agreement reached would not have to be ratified by every Indonesian politician on the block; if it was suitable to the Indonesian authorities, it could be signed off quickly.

With a new spring in its step, O'Rourke's treaty team decided on a minimalist approach — there was no need to reinvent the wheel. The aim was to provide a legal framework under which both countries could exchange prisoners, and the Bali Nine, along with Schapelle Corby and any other

Australians, could be brought home to serve the remainder of any sentences. So the letter drafted to the Australian Government was simple, with three requests. One, that the prisoner exchange treaty provide for the death penalty to be taken off the table when it involved an Australian citizen — this would essentially mean commuting such a penalty to life in jail. Two, the lawyers wanted special consideration to be provided to minors. It didn't matter in the Bali Nine case, because none of those charged was under eighteen years of age, but it did matter in some other cases. When a treaty is enacted, regular stipulations mean that the prisoner must serve a set time in the foreign jail before being eligible to return, a requirement, the Australian Government was told, that should be waived for minors. The letter's final point encouraged the government to enter into treaties with other countries to reduce the chance of being back-footed next time round. O'Rourke believes it is a priority the government needs to consider.

'A lot more effort and resources need to go into working out what we do with 150 other countries and how we prioritise those countries — who should be the top ten — and commence negotiations,' he says. And the Bali Nine offered the immediate impetus to launch such a debate.

Under the volunteer lawyers' exchange plan, prisoners already in jail would be eligible for transfer under the treaty. Prisoners would be required to serve a minimum amount of time in the country in which they were convicted — between two and four years — before being transported to their homeland. Once home, they would be eligible for earlier releases if that fitted under the original terms and conditions handed down by the foreign court. They would also be eligible for other sentence reductions, taking into account a range of issues like whether the prisoner had an aggravated medical condition or whether a disparity existed in the sentences between the two countries.

Once O'Rourke had his argument ready for the Federal Government, he knew that, in the whole Bali Nine debate, four people mattered more than anyone else. It was those people who could help decide the eventual fate of nine young Australians locked in Indonesian jail cells: Prime Ministe, John Howard, Foreign Minister Alexander Downer, Justice Minister Chris Ellison and Attorney General Phillip Ruddock. Four federal government ministers with enormous sway. And without their support, O'Rourke knew, it would be virtually impossible to bring the Bali Nine home.

XXIX

The Role of the AFP

Mike Phelan, the Australian Federal Police's border and international network national manager, is unapologetic about the strife caused by his officers in tipping off their Indonesian counterparts to what was being planned by members of the Bali Nine.

'If these same set of circumstances would happen tomorrow, we would make exactly the same decision," he says.

Phelan is not trying to defend the AFP's decision, one that has not only divided dinner parties but also prompted four of the Bali Nine's families to take the matter to court. He just sees that decision as part of the job. The AFP's role was to fight drugs, and to take the fight as far up the ladder as it could, and it wasn't able to do that without the vital information swaps that occur between Australia and countries across the globe.

The AFP has sixty-five officers in thirty-one cities in twenty-six countries. Fighting drug smuggling, and people smuggling and terrorism and all sorts of other transnational crime, is big business, and without intercountry cooperation, few networks could be closed down.

'We are putting a lot of our efforts into forward engagement and stopping the crime at its source before it reaches Australia," Phelan says.

That means dealing with all sorts of different cultures, intelligence levels and criminal justice systems. And many of the other countries which act as drug transit hubs on the way to Australia spell out the death penalty for those found flouting the law.

The AFP's work in dealing with other countries to combat criminals arriving at our shoreline has rarely been seen as controversial — not, at least, until it was publicly revealed that the AFP had dobbed in the Bali Nine to their Indonesian counterparts. Many saw the move as distinctly un-Australian, as a return favour for a close political relationship, and as a betrayal of nine young Australians who would be forced to face the possibility of a death sentence. And proponents of that view — from high-ranking lawyers and civil libertarians to media commentators and the families of those involved — use the information the AFP provided to the Indonesian National Police (INP) to support their argument.

That information shows that the AFP wasn't just offering a tip-off. The letter penned and sent on 8 April 2005 by Paul Hunniford, the AFP's senior liaison officer in Bali, was bloated with detail. Translated into Indonesian, and sent to the INP in Denpasar, it revealed that an attempt to smuggle heroin from Bali to Australia would soon be made, involving eight people 'carrying body packs strapped to their legs and back".

That was just the start. The letter went on to explain that the group had planned to smuggle the drugs months earlier but had to abort the attempt because 'there was not enough money to buy the stuff". It even contained such details as the couriers not being allowed to smoke for two weeks prior to travel, because they would not be allowed to smoke on the return flight, and might begin to look nervous. It said that expenses had been handed out to the group, and they were told to change the money into the local currency, and buy oversized clothes and thongs.

'The clothes and thongs were not to have any metal on them to avoid the metal detectors at the airports,' Hunniford wrote.

The couriers had been given pre-paid mobile phones and were told to carry wooden carvings needing quarantine declaration through the airport, so they could bypass Customs back in Australia.

The letter listed the names of eight of the Bali Nine, and included Andrew Chan's travel plans. It was fat with intelligence and the AFP were not backwards in asking for help. They wanted the INP to gather evidence or intelligence to track down the organisers of the operation in Australia and the source of the narcotics in Indonesia; they wanted photographs of meetings, telephone records and any surveillance the INP could provide.

Hunniford sent off the letter more than a week before the Bali Nine were arrested with the heroin taped to their bodies. But his correspondence didn't end there — on 12 April he sent a second letter to the INP providing more information, including some of their planned return dates.

So what did the AFP hope to achieve by handing over details of the Bali Nine to their Indonesian counterparts? And should they now wear the blame for the death sentences handed out?

Mike Phelan's tone doesn't change: 'What people need to realise is that, had the couriers been allowed to run ... we may have picked them up at the airport and that may have been the end of it. We wouldn't have known the length and breadth of the syndicate, we wouldn't have been able to track down the upstream ...'

His point is backed up by the fact that the AFP had never heard of Myuran Sukumaran, a bigwig in the Australian network. Sukumaran remained under the radar for weeks and weeks as the AFP progressed its investigation, and his name was the only one missing from both of Hunniford's letters. Officers had homed in on Andrew Chan, whom they believed to be the organiser, and on the two groups of mules from Sydney and Brisbane. Sukumaran remained anonymous until the INP was able to tie him in to meetings with the other members.

Phelan says that the sting operation proved successful because of the role played by Indonesian police, not only in pinpointing Sukumaran, but also in providing the crucial evidence that linked all nine members. It is a valid point. It was the Indonesian police, through surveillance, who were able to link the two groups of mules, provide evidence of meetings and bring the whole operation to a chilling end, with the arrests of the Bali Nine on 17 April 2005. If the four mules had been allowed to travel to Australia, who is to say that they would not have slipped through the net, or gotten rid of their haul, or tipped off the others back in a Bali hotel room preparing for a night out on the town?

However, Phelan is still prepared for those questions being asked by parents of the Bali Nine, academics, civil libertarians and ordinary folk sceptical of the role played by the AFP. Why couldn't the AFP have asked the Indonesian police to let the four mules board the plane, so that they could be arrested in Australia, without the spectre of the death penalty?

'For a start," Phelan says, 'we wouldn't ask that of the Indonesians. We'd never tell them what to do in their own country."

He offers the reverse scenario, where the Indonesian police ask us to allow four couriers to board a flight from Sydney to Jakarta, knowing full well that their bodies were packed with kilograms of heroin.

'Under no circumstances would I allow that to occur," Phelan says. Many, many Australians would agree with that course of action.

The nature of the transnational crime-fighting effort also demands cooperation between countries. 'It's very much a two-way street," Phelan says. And not just with Indonesia. While that country has become a pathway for drugs into Australia, other transit hubs continue to play a big role: Bangkok, Singapore, Hong Kong, Ho Chi Minh City. They are all transit points, and all targets of major efforts to curb the spread of drugs across the globe.

'We operate exactly the same way no matter which country it is,' says Phelan. 'Had this occurred in Thailand, Cambodia, Vietnam, we'd potentially do exactly the same thing given the same set of circumstances.' AFP crime fighters do not have the 'luxury of being able to discern" between countries, he says. 'We respect the rights and responsibilities of other countries and their laws, and we will operate within that. We do not have the ability, nor the desire, to pick and choose which countries we will deal with, depending on the laws of those countries and how they will deal with offenders for offences that occurred in their own country.'

It's a valid point. Just imagine Australia only dealing with those countries that forbid capital punishment — it would mean no assistance for our crime bodies from several countries now known to act as transit centres for drugs destined for Australia.

Supporters of the AFP also point to the statistics which show that in the past decade there has been a fourfold increase in the amount of heroin pulled up on its way to Australia, and this has caused a big drop in the number of people dying as a result of using heroin.

Regardless, the accusations thrown at the AFP over its role in tipping off the INP have certainly hurt its national image in the hearts and minds of many, including senior academics, lawyers and those families at the centre of the Bali Nine drama.

Phelan says that the guidelines adopted by the AFP in making decisions like that made on 8 April 2005 are simple, a point disputed by those who believe that they still need an overhaul. He says that the AFP is entitled to provide intelligence and information right up to the point a suspect is charged — and that is simply what they did in this case.

'The level of involvement and information supplied by the AFP in relation to the Bali Nine . . . is minimal compared to what the Indonesians have developed themselves in Indonesia,' he says. And Australia's close relationship with Indonesia played absolutely no role in the information exchange. 'The level of cooperation that we get from Indonesian authorities and transnational crime investigations has, no doubt, improved significantly over the last number of years, but that certainly has not driven our decision as to whether or not we would share the intelligence with the Indonesian authorities.'

Phelan's message to the parents of the Bali Nine — including the four who ended up taking their case against the AFP to the Federal Court — is simple: 'We have got a responsibility to the wider Australian community to protect Australia from drugs and we will do whatever is necessary, within the law and within the guidelines and the policies, to be able to protect those interests. Being involved in drugs is extremely dangerous. It's extremely dangerous for couriers involved. It has a disastrous effect on Australian communities. And that's what the AFP is mandated to do, is to protect the country from drugs, and we will continue to do that and we'll continue to take the fight offshore."

The AFP, says Phelan, had no influence over whether the Bali Nine would be arrested on their way out of Bali. Having provided the information to Indonesian authorities, it was then up to the INP to decide how to handle the matter, just as it would be up to Australian authorities if any crime was committed here. With the four mules boarding a plane in Bali, it had to be the INP, not the AFP, who were responsible.

'What's been lost a little bit in this is that there's been a perception that we actually asked the Indonesians to go and arrest these people because they're going to bring in heroin," Phelan says. 'What we actually did was request surveillance of the Indonesian authorities on known targets to establish the network."

In other words, the AFP wanted the INP to help them find out where the heroin was being sourced and how the disparate group of Bali visitors fitted together. But in handing over the information they did, they were also not ignorant to the possible consequences: that young Australians would face charges in Bali, and potentially face a death penalty.

The AFP argument doesn't wash with everyone. Some academics have accused the AFP of delivering to slaughter the proverbial young Australian lambs. Civil libertarians, too, have expressed disgust at the AFP playing ball with those countries that boast capital punishment amongst their armour. Kevin O'Rourke has spent sleepless nights pondering the role played by the AFP, which he describes as 'appalling".

'I'm concerned about decisions that are being made by Australian government officials who are representing all Australians,' O'Rourke says, 'where those decisions and judgments have the effect of leaving Australian citizens exposed to the death penalty."

He's not alone. Take the families of those involved, like Lee and Christine Rush, who tried to have their son warned before leaving. As far as they're concerned, and for Renae Lawrence's father, Bob, and hundreds of others, the AFP had no right to hand their children over to Indonesian authorities. Renae Lawrence's 85-year-old grandfather fought for Australia in World War II and he cannot countenance that the AFP would do this to his only granddaughter. 'He just doesn't understand," Bob says now, 'why the AFP did not allow them back into the country" before arresting them.

The Federal Court has another view, with Justice Paul Finn ruling that the AFP had acted lawfully in handing over information to the INP. His ruling was in response to an application by all four of the Bali mules to access AFP documents relating to the arrests. The four Australians — Scott Rush, Martin Stephens, Michael Czugaj and Renae Lawrence — wanted access to documents and records relating to their arrests. But it wasn't to be. They lost that argument in a decision announced as the Nine were beginning to find out their fate. But that was in the Federal Court of Australia — the *real* decisions were being made thousands of miles away, in a courtroom in Bali.

XXX

In Court: Michael Czugaj

Michael William Czugaj walked — or, more precisely, shuffled — the few brief steps to his mother, put his arms around her and whispered nervously into her ear. 'It's okay, Mum, I love you.' As Vicki Czugaj instinctively gathered the sixth of her eight children into her arms and the flashbulbs clicked within centimetres of the pair's private embrace, she could feel the tears welling up within. It was the first time Vicki had ever set foot inside a courtroom and she was a mess. She had been sitting there quietly for the past hour pondering and panicking about this very moment. Now it was upon her and she did the thing that came naturally — she hugged her baby. She felt relief flood through her as she realised that he at least looked okay.

'This is my child and God only knows what the outcome is going to be,' she thought as she extracted herself from the embrace she wanted to never end. 'I just want to take my baby home.'

On that day his mother's reference was apt: Czugaj looked, for all the world, like a boy in a man's clothes. As if he had woken up that day and, instead of going out to muck about with his teenage mates, decided to dress up in the garb of a man. His cream-coloured shirt seemed to envelop his hunched shoulders and skinny frame — he seemed lost inside it. Pimples — those telltale signs of adolescence — shone like beacons on his pale and drawn face, the paleness of his skin making them even more noticeable. But the pimples could not disguise the fact that on the morning of 11 October 2005 he was well and truly in a man's predicament. He had been for five months already, but today the consequences of his actions were very real.

It was day one of the Denpasar District Court trial which would decide Michael Czugaj's fate — of the nine, his was the first to start. Waiting for him inside the courtroom were the two men and one woman who would decide if he lived or died, if he was guilty or not guilty of attempting to export heroin as part of what prosecutors would say was an organised, secretive, militant and international drug network.

At that moment, though, with his mother's protective arms wrapped around him, Czugaj looked anything but a drug boss or even a drug lackey. He looked more like a scared, pimply, pasty-faced kid from next door who had been escorted, in handcuffs, to the courthouse by mistake. In fact, he had always looked like that — from the day of his arrest, when he had cried, to this day. He was not the baby of the Nine — Matthew Norman was the youngest — but he had always appeared so much younger than his years. He would not have looked out of place in a school uniform.

At the time of his arrest Czugaj was a mere nineteen years of age; by the time he appeared in court he was twenty: too young to be in such a dire situation but old enough to have known better. He would soon give the judges his own reasons for doing what he had done, attempting to abrogate and distance himself from some of the responsibility for his own actions. They would be the same reasons articulated by three more of the Nine as their trials progressed, delivered almost by rote. Whether the judges and prosecutors would believe them or think of their stories as fantastical tales dreamt up to save their own miserable skins remained to be seen. It was only the beginning of the trials of their lives.

Czugaj arrived at court at 10 a.m. in a prison truck shared with thieves, drug dealers, pimps and the other Indonesian prisoners also due to face the judges that day. He was barrelled through a throng of waiting media, wearing sunglasses and a baseball cap pulled down low over his eyes, the first of the Bali Nine to experience the media scrum at court. Not far behind him was Myuran Sukumaran whose trial was scheduled to start the same day. They were so different, the comparison was stark. Czugaj was shrinking, trying to hide his face, while Sukumaran was anything but, striding purposefully through, his freshly shaven bald head held high. He was no shrinking violet — not today, and not once since this process began.

It was the first day of the long-awaited trials and prosecutors had chosen to begin them with one of the airport mules and, in another court, one of the ringleaders. Prosecutors had decided to bring the same primary charge against all nine regardless of their roles: exporting narcotics as part of an organisation. It was this charge — carrying the death penalty as its maximum sentence — which gave all nine good reason to fear for their lives. Their fate was now up to the courts, and to the Nine themselves, depending on the strategies they chose to use during the trials.

The stage for this act of the drama was a rather nondescript court complex in the centre of Denpasar — unremarkable from the street and even more average from the inside. It was the same court where, in May 2005, Schapelle Corby had been convicted and so dramatically sentenced to twenty years in jail.

Those expecting a pristine and immaculately manicured and painted court complex, akin to those of Australian capital cities, would have been sorely disappointed. And, for that matter, those expecting courthouse rules like those observed in Australia would also get a shock.

Here no one bothers too much with strict court rules, and that great sin in an Australian court — to accidentally leave your mobile phone turned on and have it ring during a court session — barely causes a ripple. In fact, phones ring and people answer them, carrying on full conversations in the court — even the officials. Admonishments are rare.

There are five courtrooms with no air conditioning, just a couple of sometimes rickety ceiling fans, so the windows — those which aren't already broken — are always left open in the hope of catching a rare passing breeze. Through these windows hang the media cameras and curious onlookers from all walks of life. *Bules* — Westerners — on trial are always an attraction for the locals, who break the boredom of the wait for their own cases by leaning lazily through to peer at the latest example of a white-skinned defendant.

When the defendants were Corby or Michelle Leslie, the locals loved it and packed the place to the rafters. The local press always referred to the women in their stories as *cantik* (beautiful), and locals wanted to check them out to see if it was true. Then you would hear them, gossiping amongst themselves, that whoever it was really was as beautiful as her picture; some said they were *more* beautiful than the photos or the TV images.

There was, however, less public fascination for Perth yachtsman Christopher Packer, accused of weapons charges relating to guns he kept on his boat and which he hadn't reported to authorities. It was the *cantik* women the locals cared about.

* * *

Published court lists? Forget it. Strict adherence to court starting times? Again, forget it. Court starts when it starts and the only people who ever raise a stir about such a relaxed system are the Western media, whose deadlines are often missed because the prison truck didn't arrive on time when bringing the day's court attendees from Kerobokan Jail. Locals call it 'rubber time'.

Official court transcripts or court stenographers? Once more, forget it. The judges take notes for themselves and a court official who sits off to one side also takes handwritten notes of proceedings. This, combined with memory, is what is used to consider the evidence.

Indonesian courts are based on the Dutch system of law, inherited from the days of Dutch colonialism. Unlike the system in countries such as Australia, Indonesian law follows European legal systems and is inquisitorial rather than adversarial. As such there are no juries; rather, a panel of three to five judges decide on guilt or innocence. Trials are run more like inquiries and investigations, whereby the judges lead the questioning of witnesses and suspects. All in all, life at Denpasar District Court is pretty relaxed and people rarely complain. But that's also life in Bali — laid-back and as stress-free as possible.

The Denpasar District Court complex is a community. The families who run the *warungs*, or small cafés, at the back of the court complex live behind their modest shops in modest homes. They make their meagre living from the business of the court, selling breakfast, lunch, coffees and snacks to those whose business is inside the court. A great deal of court business is done in the *warungs* over bowls of *mie goreng*, cups of thick black coffee or tea laden with sugar, and *pisang goreng* (fried banana).

The women who run the *warungs*, like Ibu Slamet, spend their day ferrying trays of food and drink to those working in the court offices. Her husband works for the court, cleaning the buildings and keeping things as neat and tidy as possible, and they have lived in the tiny room at the back of the café for ten years. For the past year Ibu Slamet has run the *warung* from the front of their home, selling freshly squeezed fruit juices like the locally popular avocado juice with chocolate, noodles, rice and assorted meats and vegetables. But whatever juicy titbits Ibu Slamet hears during her days serving judges, lawyers and prosecutors, she keeps to herself. Discretion is paramount in a business like hers. Ask her about what deals she has overheard being sorted out in her *warung* and she just laughs — it's a secret.

A similar response is given by her neighbour and fellow *warung* proprietor, Ibu Abas, who, together with her husband, has been there even longer. The couple, with their toddler daughter Nanda, work, live and sleep in the cramped shop — nothing is sacred as they try to eke out a living and a future. Their bed is right next to the serving area and the fridge where customers wander in and help themselves to cold drinks. People say Ibu Abas's *pisang goreng* is among the best around. Customers help themselves to that too and somehow, in between juggling the serving of customers, the desk deliveries and the cooking, she manages to keep a tally of just how many pieces each person had that day or how many coffees.

The Bali Nine trials and, before them, the trial of Schapelle Corby, saw a swag of foreign journalists and their staff land in town, along with family members of the accused, which gave the women's businesses a big boost. The chief judge who heard Corby's case, Linton Sirait, actually lived in one of the small flats behind the court complex, alongside Ibu Slamet's *warung*. It was here, with her cups of sweet tea and coffee and bowls of *mie goreng*, that he spent many hours pondering the judgment. Judge Sirait has since moved to Medan and his flat is vacant.

However, the cockfighting roosters which used to keep him company are still there. Jago, the shiny black one, and Barak, the multicoloured one with shiny green tail feathers, belong to Edy, a relative of Ibu Slamet. They live in wicker baskets right next to the fifth courtroom, the one in which Czugaj's trial first started. For those who think roosters only crow at dawn — think again. Jago and Barak, like their kin in *kampung* (villages) all over Bali, crow night and day. Their cock-a-doodle-dooing is a backdrop to the business inside the fifth courtroom.

This pair are Edy's pets — prized cockfighters he takes to cockfights around the island. The attraction to cockfighting is not so much the macabre spectacle of watching two proud roosters, sharp spurs attached to their feet, go hammer and tongs at each other to the death, but the money that is won and lost during the gambling that is a central feature of cockfights. It seems odd in the extreme that Jago and Barak are living on the grounds of a court complex in whose courtrooms people appear, charged with the crime of illegal gambling at cockfights. The fight between two cocks, known as *Tajen*, originated because it forms an important part of the Balinese Hindu religious ceremony. It still does, but gambling at organised cockfights is also part of life in Bali, illegal though it is.

Each afternoon, after the prisoners and judges have gone, Edy gets the pair out of their wicker baskets for training, letting them have a mock spar each day to keep them practised for the real game of life and death.

This day, as Czugaj appeared in court, Jago and Barak were crowing outside. It was now life and death for Czugaj too. Czugaj's strategy was clear from early on, when his locally based lawyer, Fransiskus Passar, decided to waive the right to deliver a defence rebuttal to the prosecution's indictment or opening address. He wanted to go straight to the witnesses. Outside court, Frans — as he is known locally — said his client was an 'innocent victim'. He didn't want to say too much more at that stage but he didn't need to: they were going to claim that Czugaj was not a key player or ringleader in this whole sorry saga but, rather, a naive teenager who had got roped into it, and then, when he found himself in too deep, couldn't make his way out — too scared for himself and the safety of his family to do anything about it.

Would the judges believe it? And would they believe that Czugaj really was threatened with death, or that he honestly didn't know what was inside the packages strapped to his body? Or, for that matter, that he truly thought he was on a free holiday to Bali and nothing more sinister? That he honestly never suspected that a free vacation, with no strings attached, was just too good to be true? Time would tell.

Czugaj's trial was almost a template for how each of the Bali Nine trials would run — there were police and Customs witnesses involved in arresting the Nine on 17 April, hotel staff who recognised them from their stays at the various places and the taxi drivers who ferried them around Bali. The aim was to prove where they had stayed, what they did, where they went and with whom — all seemingly innocuous stuff. Most interesting was the evidence of police about the letter that had been sent on 8 April from the Australian Federal Police to the Bali police, along with testimony from Nyoman Gatra, the officer in charge of the surveillance operation. What people really wanted to hear, though, was the Nine themselves, telling their own stories.

Under Indonesian law, in trials where there are joint offenders, prosecutors can call the co-accused to give evidence against each other. So in each trial the other eight were called as witnesses against whoever was actually on trial.

All four mules had told, from the day of their arrest, a pretty similar story of having no idea of the true reason for being in Bali until it was too late; of thinking it was a holiday and finding out, in the Adhi Dharma Hotel, that they were to carry something on their bodies back to Australia; and, significantly, they told similar tales of being threatened with death. For the mules, this evidence from their fellow mules was potentially helpful, a corroboration of their own story. And they were willing witnesses.

Not so the ringleaders, like Chan and Sukumaran. Both men — along with Matthew Norman, Si Yi Chen and Tan Duc Thanh Nguyen — shared the same legal counsel. Their strategy from day one had been denial — denial of any knowledge of the drugs, denial of any involvement. They saw no evil, heard no evil and had nothing to do with anything — in the wrong place at the wrong time, apparently, victims of the malevolence of the mules. It was stonewalling on any interpretation of the word. And there was no reason to believe it wouldn't be the same come the trials and their turn to testify against the others.

That's how it played out: the other three mules were willing witnesses at other trials and readily agreed to tell their stories, which didn't vary much at all really — the offers of a free holiday for some, their protests of not having a clue, of being innocent victims, and details of the menacing threats that forced them into this predicament.

Scott Rush was in the witness box for ninety minutes at Michael Czugaj's trial, during which time the judges gave a good indication that they were not completely buying this story of innocent mules and threats. Female judge Made Sudani wanted to know why, after the heroin was strapped to him, Rush didn't try to report it to the police. 'I don't know why, we were scared at the time,' he said. She was not going to be thrown off the track, though: did he ask Nguyen, when he offered Rush a free holiday to Bali, what the reason was? 'I asked, he said, "Don't worry about it, I'm doing you a favour".' *But didn't you suspect?* 'Yes.' *So what did you suspect?* 'My suspicion was, why is he paying for a trip for us.' *So you didn't ask Nguyen why?* 'Yes and basically we got the response that he didn't have anyone to go to Bali with . . . he also had friends to meet in Bali.'

Didn't Rush discuss the issue with Czugaj? And was he ready for any risk? No, Rush replied. In that case then, if he wasn't ready to take a risk, why did he agree to go to Bali? 'Because he [Nguyen] promised me it was just a good trip, there was nothing.' By the end of the interrogation Judge Sudani looked less than convinced.

When the other five — apart from the mules — were called to testify, they all had the same answer ready for the judges: they did not wish to give evidence because they were also suspects in the same crime. No amount of urging from the clearly annoyed judges could make them change their minds, even when the judges reminded them that if they agreed to give evidence and were cooperative, it would help them later when the question of leniency came to be considered. It didn't matter.

Sukumaran and Chan were slated to give evidence at Czugaj's trial on the same day, but unhappily Chan couldn't come — apparently he was sick. Sukumaran was there, though, and he wasted no time in telling the judges, 'I don't want to make a statement because I am the same suspect.' One judge reminded him that he made a statement to police during his interrogation. 'But I don't want to make a statement today,' he shot back to the translator, whose job it was to then translate the English into Indonesian for the judges. (All of the trials were conducted in Indonesian, meaning that each of the Nine needed a translator to tell them what was going on, and to translate the questions and answers from one language to another. Unfortunately for the defendants, some translators were better than others, and some of the Nine, it has to be said, were not served too well at all in that regard.)

His patience tested, the judge told the translator to tell a defiant Sukumaran this piece of sobering news: 'If you are cooperative and later you are proven to be guilty, the judge will consider leniency.' Sukumaran repeated his earlier mantra that he didn't want to give evidence because he was a suspect in the same case. The judges wanted to know if anyone had told him to say that but Sukumaran assured them that no one had.

In cases where witnesses refuse to testify, their original police statement — taken during the interrogation phase — is then read to the court in lieu of the spoken evidence and is considered as part of the case. It was a frustrating process for all involved as the judges pointed out that Sukumaran's police statement, in which he had been much more forthcoming than he was being in the court, was signed by him.

He was then told to give the judges an example of his signature to ensure that he had, in fact, signed the statement. Up he strode to the bench where, keeping up his obstructive attitude, Sukumaran scribbled a signature that bore little resemblance to the one on his statement. He was ordered to do it again and again and again. It took four tries before he signed his name in the same way he had on the police document. It was not a good start to his interaction with the court, and his insolence threatened to dog him through to his own verdict.

Sukumaran's statement was a series of denials of what Czugaj had said about him — he said he didn't know Czugaj, never gave Czugaj $500, never met him in Kuta, never invited him for a drink at the Hard Rock Hotel bar, never strapped heroin to his body and never threatened to kill Czugaj and his family. Throughout his recitation Czugaj was stony-faced, uttering to the translator 'not true'. At the end of the statement, Czugaj was asked to respond. He was angry and it showed: 'I want to swear that this guy threatened me and my family and strapped the heroin to my body.' Sukumaran looked like he couldn't have cared less and that was that.

There was a similar situation when Tan Duc Thanh Nguyen was called — he too didn't want to testify for the same reason given by Sukumaran.

* * *

With the prosecution's case closed, Czugaj's team called one character witness — Czugaj's old boss at a Brisbane glass and aluminium firm. Trevor Thomas Hennessy told how Czugaj had first come to his firm as a fresh-faced fourteen year old to do school work experience. It was the same place where his father, Stephan, had worked for twenty-odd years, and three of Czugaj's brothers and a sister worked there too.

Mr Hennessy's reference was glowing. 'When Michael went through work experience with my company he was very small, he was very well mannered, he did very good work, so much so that my factory foreman — who has been with me for twenty-five years — said he was one of the best young boys that had gone through our factory for work experience,' he told the court. (One of the judges was slightly confused — in Australia, were people allowed to work at fourteen years of age? It was one of the problems associated with the need to translate everything — sometimes not all parties were on the same wavelength.)

In November 2004, having said goodbye to school, Czugaj was back at the firm, this time as a full-time employee. By this time he had started to develop physically but he was still a 'timid sort of person and did not like confrontation', said Hennessy, but was 'well disciplined, very obedient and very diligent'.

Then it was time for Czugaj himself to take the stand. Clearly nervous about what was to come, and no doubt knowing just how important this moment was, he asked for a toilet break. When he returned, his evidence differed little from Rush's, with judges reminding him sternly at the beginning that he had to tell the truth, and that if his evidence was complicated or convoluted 'it will cause difficulty for yourself'.

At first it was gentle questions. Czugaj told how, before coming to Bali, he'd spent several nights in Sydney at a hotel with Rush and Nguyen, and that Sukumaran had paid for this but there'd been no discussion about the real reason he was going to Bali — he still thought it was a free, no-strings-attached holiday. He also said when there were meetings in Bali with others, like Sukumaran and Chan, there'd been no talk of illegality or drugs, just general stuff like how the holiday was going and what they were doing.

Eventually it got down to the important stuff, like Chan intimating to Czugaj and Rush that he had a gun and telling them that if they refused to take the packages to Australia, 'I'll kill you and your family, I know where they live'. Czugaj said that when he tried to ask what was in the white packages strapped to his body, he was told, 'You don't need to know'. And the questioning continued:

> Q. *Didn't you ask to Myuran [Sukumaran] or Tan [Nguyen] or Andrew [Chan] why the packages were not put in my suitcase? Why is [it] on my body?*
>
> A. *No, at that time I was frightened ... at that time there was a threat made to myself and my family.*
>
> Q. *Did you have any instinct that the package strapped to your body must be a dangerous package?*
>
> A. *At the time nothing like that crossed my mind because, as I said, there was a threat delivered.*
>
> Q. *Didn't you feel any suspicion, didn't you suspect the things strapped to your body were dangerous things, that's why it was strapped not put in the luggage?*
>
> A. *It could have been anything — like I said, it wasn't on my mind at the time. I had asked what the package was and I was told I didn't need to know, and my mind was thinking about other things apart from what was in that package.*

...

Q. Didn't you suspect or feel something strange about the package strapped to your body?

A. Yeah, it felt very strange. There wasn't much I could do about it after there had been a threat to my family. I was intimidated.

Q. Did you suspect something illegal was strapped to your body?

A. It didn't really cross my mind at the time.

Q. Did you feel afraid the authorities will find out?

A. Yeah, at the time and there's also concern for my family.

It seems hard to reconcile Czugaj's last two answers. On one hand he said it hadn't crossed his mind that something illegal was strapped to his body, but he admitted to feeling fear that the authorities would find out. What had he to fear from the authorities, especially if he didn't even suspect he was doing anything wrong? The question was never asked.

With the witness questioning over, the serious end of the trial was quickly approaching — that is, just what sentence prosecutors would seek for Czugaj, and how they assessed his and others' evidence. Was he truly the innocent victim and did they believe the evidence of threats to the point of no return? By the time the prosecutor's sentence request for Czugaj was delivered, he had already heard prosecutors ask that his mate Rush be sent to jail for life, and he was expecting the same treatment. He was right: they asked for his life.

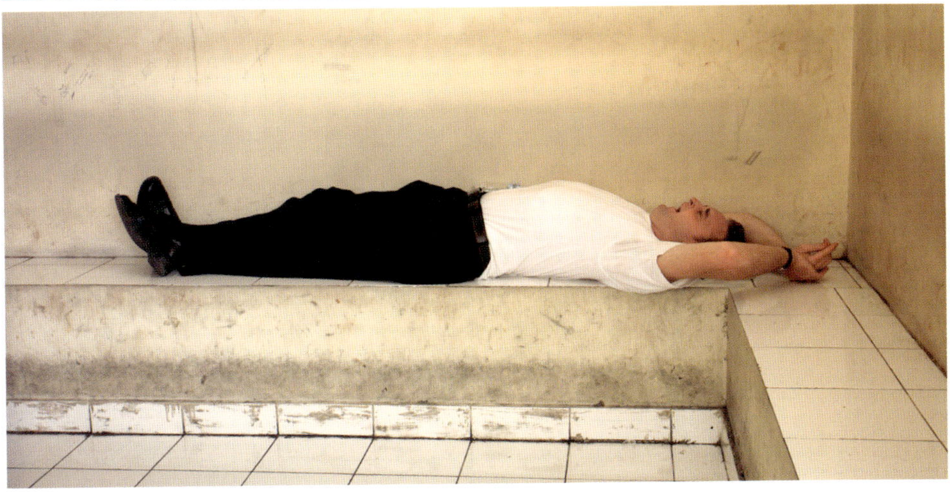

ABOVE: Reading mail, doing the washing and lots of waiting around – the tedium of life behind bars for Martin Stephens.

LEFT: Stephens kisses his mother, Michele, goodbye.

All photographs by Lukman S Bintoro

ABOVE: Lawrence and Stephens, now great mates inside jail — Stephens acts as Lawrence's confidant and 'big brother' inside.

BELOW: The pair has also appeared in court together.

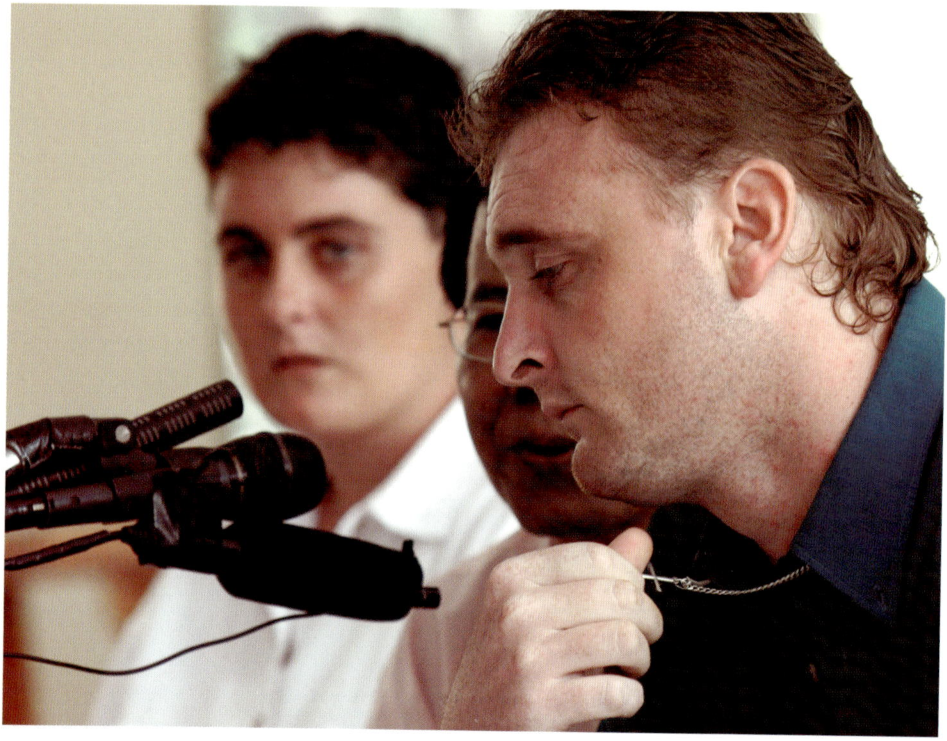

ABOVE LEFT AND RIGHT: Michelle Leslie and Renae Lawrence, shackled together for a trip to court, are pounced upon by waiting media.

LEFT AND BELOW: Renae Lawrence in court

RIGHT: Myuran Sukumaran and Andrew Chan handcuffed together for a trip to court.

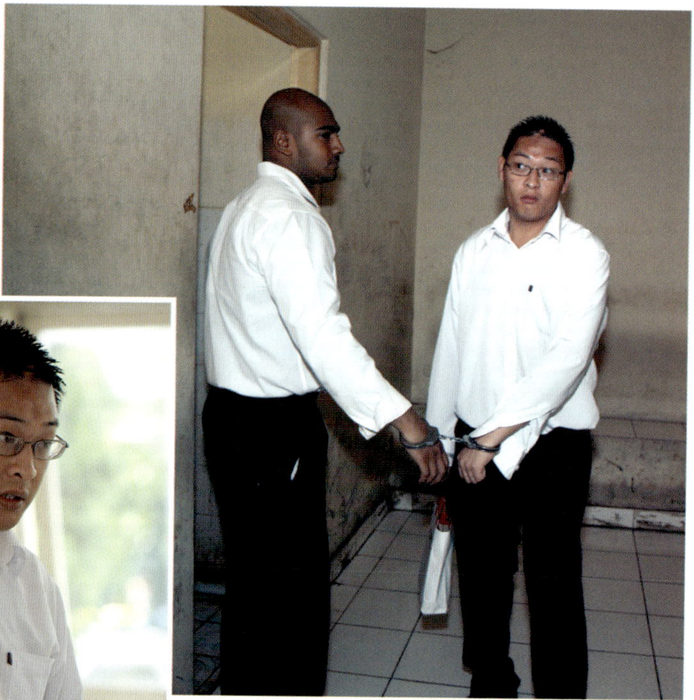

LEFT: Chan delivering a statement to the judges.

BELOW: Myuran Sukumaran and his translator.

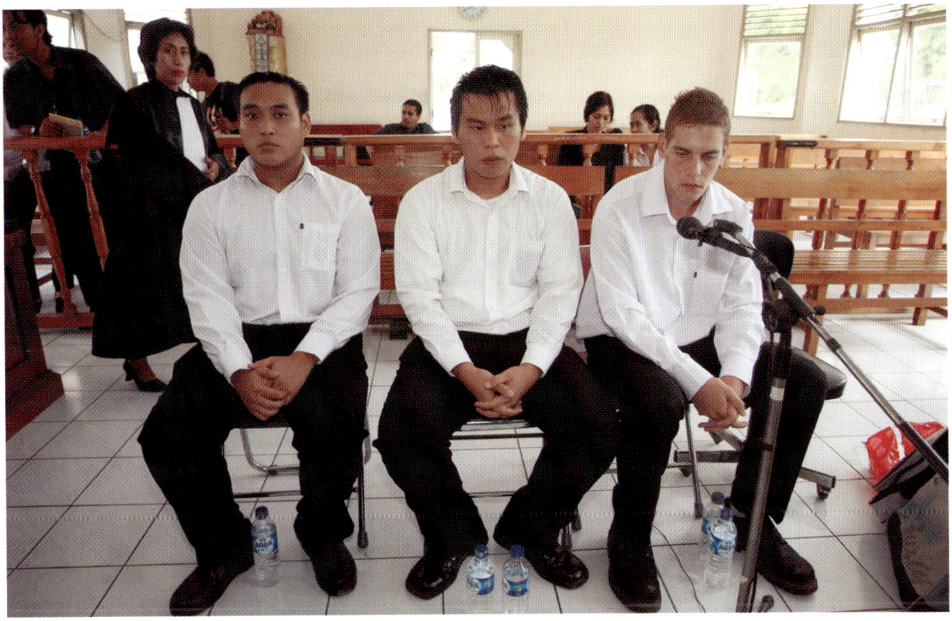

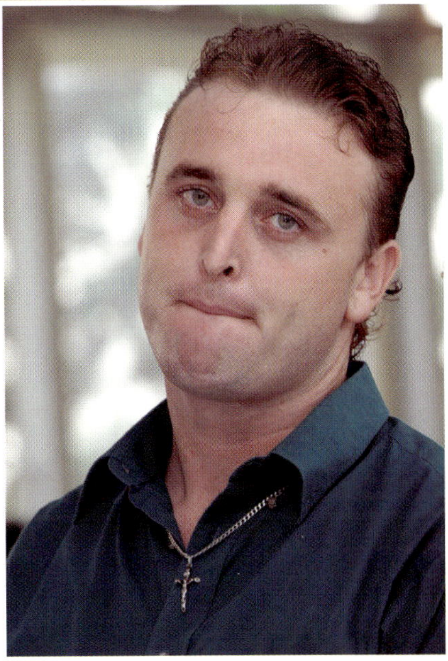

TOP: (L to R) Nguyen, Chen and Norman in court.

ABOVE: (L to R) Rush, Sukumaran, Nguyen, Chan, Norman and Chen in a cell prior to their court hearings.

RIGHT: Stephens at a different court appearance.

LEFT: Sukumaran in court the day his death sentence was handed down.

BELOW: Sukumaran and Chan arrive at court to hear their verdicts and sentences.

BOTTOM: Sukumaran's anger at the press pack threatens to boil over; Chan would calm him down.

RIGHT: Stephens in court to hear his sentence.

BELOW: Czugaj manages a smile for his father, Stephan, after hearing his sentence.

ABOVE AND RIGHT: An angry Renae Lawrence after her expected 20-year sentence was instead announced as life.

On the day his life sentence was handed down, the face of Matthew Norman, the youngest of the Bali Nine, says it all.

XXXI

In Court: Renae Lawrence

Renae Lawrence was bemused. So much fuss about a little dab of make-up — Natural Glow, to be exact. She couldn't understand why anyone would care less that she was wearing make-up. She was, after all, a woman, and women wear the stuff. She didn't think it was a big deal. In fact, she thought it funny that, after all she had been through and was going through, on this particular day, the only thing anyone cared about was her make-up. Never mind the gravely serious charges she was facing or the detail of the solemn court proceedings that would seal her fate — the important thing was the make-up.

Actually, not so much the make-up itself but the person who applied it. When someone on the defence team let slip that a fellow Kerobokan Jail inmate called Schapelle Corby had lent her beautician services to Lawrence that morning, the media was whipped into a frenzy. Corby, a former beauty school student, was well known for her immaculate grooming and make-up at her own trial, and she had been more than happy to help Lawrence with some of the finer points of cosmetics. The image of Corby dabbing and preening the usually rugged Lawrence was too juicy to ignore. Within hours the story had taken on monolithic proportions — Corby, so the story went, had given Lawrence a complete 'makeover'. Radio couldn't get enough of it.

Back in her cell, Lawrence just shook her head. There was nothing to do but laugh at why anyone cared less. It was almost a brief respite from the stressful court appearances. The truth was that Lawrence, suffering the painful effects of a gum infection after having a tooth removed in jail, was pale and Corby had offered her some 'Natural Glow' bronzer to give her face some colour. It could hardly have been called a makeover in the true sense of the word, but it provided a diversion for a while.

It wouldn't take long before the famed Corby makeover paled into insignificance. There was an even more juicy image for the cameras to savour and it came in the form of a waif-thin, poised and immaculately attired model wearing an elegant white Muslim headscarf. Enter Michelle Leslie, the Adelaide-born model arrested in Bali with two ecstasy pills in her handbag. By some quirk of fate, Leslie's first appearance in court happened to fall on the same day as Lawrence's third court appearance. It meant the pair might well arrive handcuffed together in the same prison truck, and the media had their cameras poised. Not since the days of Corby's trial had such a big media contingent converged on the courthouse all at once.

There had been a big crush of cameras for the first week of the Bali Nine trials, but day one of Leslie's case was going to eclipse that. As the prison truck backed into the narrow gate through which the prisoners walk, cameramen jostled for position and locals crowded around. They all wanted to see the model for themselves. They'd seen plenty of her in the local newspapers which ran spreads of the twenty-four year old on the catwalk in underwear, body paint and exotic creations, but this was the real thing. She had morphed into a celebrity.

Lawrence was the first to step from the truck; not far behind her was Leslie. Both wore crisp white blouses and black pants. And they were sharing the same set of handcuffs. *Magic.* It was like a photographer's dream and a PR agent's nightmare. And to the disdain of photographers and news cameramen, Leslie's Australian minders were onto that, doing their best to ensure that images of the two women together were kept to a bare minimum.

Pushing, shoving and shouting ensued as Leslie's minders tried to clear a path and block the cameras. Leslie was dragged in one direction by her people while Lawrence was dragged the opposite way by the guard. The object was to keep the two women, from vastly different worlds, as far apart as possible. The problem was that they were handcuffed together and Lawrence was feeling pain radiating through her wrist. She was understandably furious: none of this had been her doing; she had just been born into the wrong world to end up sharing a camera frame with someone like Leslie. She had been caught with heroin, and a lot of it; Leslie just had a couple of ecstasy pills. As soon as the two women got into the court holding cell and the handcuffs were removed, the pair split, retreating posthaste to opposite ends of the cell. No words passed between them.

They were the only two prisoners there that day and the air separating them was almost thick. Leslie hid her face with her headscarf, and kept her back to the cameras and her legs elegantly crossed. An angry Lawrence massaged her wrist. It had been a debacle, a joke, Lawrence said later. But what could she do? Nothing. She knew that and shrugged her shoulders.

Earlier Leslie's media and legal minders had been at the jail, arguing with authorities that their client should be spared the ignominy of having to wear handcuffs to the court. It was to no avail — prisoners wear handcuffs, end of story. On this day, Leslie might have been wearing a vastly more expensive white blouse than Lawrence, but they were both wearing the same set of worn handcuffs. Leslie just wore them for less time: sentenced to just three months in prison, she was long gone from Kerobokan Jail months before Lawrence's trial was even winding up.

If the day of the Leslie–Lawrence show was a low point for Renae Lawrence, so too was the first day of her trial. Bustled into court, she had an almost haunted look as she hunched over, covering her face with her hands, head almost on her lap. Cameras got painfully close and she just couldn't bear to sit there like some kind of zoo exhibit.

In the front row of the public gallery sat her father, Bob, and stepmother, Jenny. His face looked almost blank as he watched his beloved child in one of her many dark hours. Another day, as the cameras zoomed close to her face, she'd had enough and told them to back off.

When she had been arrested Lawrence was wearing an earring through her left eyebrow. That was now gone.

Lawrence's trial was generally held on the Friday of each week — the slowest court day. Several times she was the only prisoner there that day, and she had the court holding cell to herself. Sometimes she looked like the loneliest woman in the world. Other days she would be with her new confidant, Martin Stephens. The pair shared food and jokes in the cell, the bond between them evident.

Inside the court there were less jokes. This was serious, life-or-death stuff for Lawrence. Most of the lighter moments came during her easy-going banter with the translator. Dr Wayan Ana is a tiny man whose loud, officious voice is almost a surprise. He is one of those people who almost runs everywhere, a picture of efficiency as he scurries about. He is sought after by police and the court to translate English to Indonesian and vice versa every time a foreigner finds themselves on the wrong side of the law. He was well known to the Bali Nine — he had been there with them from almost the day after their arrests, acting in his capacity as translator during police interrogations. And now he was with them in the court. He would turn up at court each day clutching a diary. He was expressive in translation, articulating and stressing words at the appropriate time.

Dr Ana had quite a rapport with the four mules, for whom he also had a great deal of affection. His months spent with them had provided him with an unexpected bonus — he had learnt enough Aussie slang to fill a dictionary. Like the word 'dunny', which he'd never heard before he met Lawrence. One day during police interrogations Lawrence had interrupted, telling Dr Ana, 'Hey, Wayan, I need to go to the dunny.' He had no idea what she was talking about. 'Dunny, what is dunny?' he asked her innocently. 'Toilet, you know,' she replied.

They taught him slang and he taught them some Indonesian. People say that Dr Ana is one of those people who doesn't have a bad bone in their body and who is never quick to judge. He seemed to be especially fond of Lawrence; in court she would often answer questions in basic Indonesian rather than English, like '*tidak tahu*' for 'don't know' and '*tidak*' for 'no'. She also knew the word for lies — *bohong* — and more lies — *bohong lagi* — phrases she used to describe the evidence of Chan and the others.

One day after a long session, Lawrence complained to Dr Ana about how hot it was in the court. The slow-moving fan wasn't doing much to help the situation. Lawrence said it was '*panas*', the Indonesian word for hot. Dr Ana begged to differ — it was '*dingin*', cold, and the fan was giving him a headache. As they joked around, Dr Ana said that next time he had to translate for Lawrence he was going to bring a cap to wear so his head didn't get so cold from the fan — Indonesians, acclimatised to the heat, are not always fond of fans or air conditioners.

As at all the trials, the four mules testified about the threats of Andrew Chan and Myuran Sukumaran, who, in turn, refused to testify on the grounds that they were involved in the same case. So too did Lawrence's young workmate, Matthew Norman.

For reasons never explained and never really questioned at any length, during both her own trial and during her evidence at Andrew Chan's trial, Lawrence withdrew her earlier police statements in which she had said that she came to Bali in October 2004 with Chan and that Myuran Sukumaran had strapped up the pair with heroin which they then took back to Australia in similar circumstances to this 2005 bust. She had told police that, after the 2004 drug run, Chan had given her $10 000 cash in an envelope, telling her it was 'shut up' money, and instructing her not to bank the cash or tell a soul.

She had also told police of another aborted drug run in December 2004 when, at the instruction of Chan, she had come to Bali with Tan Duc Thanh Nguyen, Matthew Norman and four others, but because of 'financial problems', the run had been cancelled. She told police that from the beginning of her Bali trips, back in the previous October, she did not have the nerve to disobey Chan because from day one he had been threatening her and her family.

During her own trial, Lawrence's withdrawal of the statements was not really questioned by the judges or the prosecutor. She said it was not true that she had come to Bali three times to carry narcotics and she withdrew the statement that she had received the $10 000. But one day earlier, when she testified as a prosecution witness at Chan's trial and withdrew the damaging statements, Judge Arif Supratman was nowhere near as accommodating.

It began with Lawrence telling the court that she did not come to Bali in October 2004 with Andrew Chan.

Q. *Once again … have you ever carried packages before?*
A. No.
Q. *Never?*
A. No.
Q. *Is that true?*
A. Yes.
Q. *Have you been interrogated in the police station?*
A. Yes.

Lawrence was ordered to come forward to the judge's bench, to look at the copy of her signed statement in which she had said the opposite to what she was now saying in the court.

Q. *When Andrew Chan is strapping the packages to your body, did you know the contents of the package?*
A. No.
Q. *So if the package is legal why was it strapped to your body?*
A. Tidak tahu *[don't know]*.
…
Q. *When you came to Bali in October 2004, was that paid for by Andrew Chan as well?*
A. No.

Lawrence told the court that in October 2004 she had come to Bali by herself, and she now denied meeting the people she'd named to police as having been there as well. The air thickened and things became strained as Lawrence looked around for her lawyer, Anggia Browne, who sat in the body of the court, desperately meeting her eyes and pleading for help with the sticky situation she was quickly becoming mired in. Lawrence had undeniably told the police of the previous and aborted drug runs and now she was, in fact, denying this. There was not much Ms Browne could do, as she was not appearing for Lawrence in Chan's trial.

Judge Supratman, known to be stern, saw the exchanged looks and was clearly annoyed. He angrily instructed the translator to tell Lawrence to be polite, to stop looking back and to face forward. It was at this point that Lawrence asked for a toilet break. It was clear to all that she needed to gather her thoughts.

When she came back Judge Supratman again told the interpreter to tell Lawrence not to look back, warning that her punishment could be more severe in the long run. There followed a confusing series of questions and answers about whether Lawrence wanted to affirm her police statements or withdraw them. In the end she withdrew them. No one quite understood the reason for this sudden change of heart. Tactics, perhaps?

Lawrence proceeded to testify that she was scared of Chan and didn't dare disobey him. Once, at his home, she said that Chan had shown her photographs on his computer of him holding guns. This had made her even more frightened. She insisted that she had not known that the packages strapped to her body contained heroin — again, this was at odds with her earlier police statement that she had been involved in a 2004 drug run.

She was asked why, on 17 April 2005, she had not gone to the police. 'Because Andrew said that he had people following us and people that worked for him in both countries,' she told the court. She couldn't take the risk of her family being harmed in any way. 'He said if we didn't do what he wants he'd kill our family and me and send us to the farm.' In the criminal lexicon, 'sending someone to the farm' means getting rid of them — killing them. Lawrence told the judges that she had been stupid, but she'd had no choice.

Lawrence's mother, Bev Waterman, backed up the fact that before her arrest her daughter had appeared to be frightened of her work colleague Chan. Lawrence had returned to live with her mother, stepfather and little brother the previous November. Testifying as a defence character witness, Mrs Waterman told of an occasion when she had heard Lawrence speaking on the phone to Chan. She didn't know what the conversation was about but Lawrence had seemed nervous.

'I asked her who it was that rang and she said it was Andrew. She just didn't seem herself. I did ask her what Andrew wanted and she just sort of said nothing but she just didn't look like she was comfortable telling me that.'

The family's home had been attacked after the arrests — in the middle of the night someone had used grey paint to write the words 'Nine dead cunts' on the front brick wall of the suburban house. Menacingly, a hammer and baseball bat had been left in the garden underneath the writing. The family was understandably frightened.

Parents everywhere must have empathised with Mrs Waterman when, in tears, she pleaded with the judges that her daughter was only young and was a good kid. Any parent who has tried to teach their child about right and wrong knew what she meant when she told the court, 'We spend most of our time trying to put an old head on young shoulders but we can't do it. Renae is very sorry, I know, for what she has done. She has told me many times that. I did ask her why she had done it, and I asked her why she didn't come to me about it, and she asked me a question. She asked me what would I do if I was in her position and my family was threatened. And I have to be honest, I couldn't answer her, because I think I would probably do the same thing to protect them. I am her mother and I love her and I think that she deserves another chance.' What mother wouldn't? The burden of being the Bali Nine's parents was painfully illustrated by one woman's words.

* * *

After all the months in jail, the depression and the loneliness of being Renae Lawrence was later articulated when she delivered her personal plea for mercy to the judges. She was facing life in a foreign prison away from the family and friends she respected and adored. She had tried so hard to protect her family from Chan's threats but she now felt it was to no avail. 'I have in fact failed to protect them, as the emotional trauma I am putting them through is probably almost too much for them to bear.' And the financial burden she had imposed upon them and the anguish of knowing they could only visit her a couple of times a year was 'almost too much for me to bear'.

By the time prosecutors came to make their sentence request or demand in Lawrence's case, they had already sought life sentences for the other three mules. Everybody expected that it would be no different for Lawrence. They were wrong. As prosecutor Putu Indriati said the words 'Twenty years', a gasp went around the courtroom. No one could believe it. Lawrence could barely believe it herself — she had said earlier that she was fully expecting that the authorities would want her locked up for life.

She sat, looking almost stunned, emotionless. Ms Indriati said that Lawrence had been extraordinarily cooperative with police and that the information she provided during interrogations had helped reveal to police the other members of this insidious drug syndicate. However, she said, Lawrence's claims of the Chan death threats should be ignored completely — they were untrustworthy and were not backed up or supported by evidence. The judges should not consider them.

It seemed strange: Lawrence was being rewarded handsomely for her cooperation, but then, she was more involved in the whole thing, having been to Bali twice before, and would necessarily have more information to impart than some of the others. The lighter sentence request didn't seem entirely fair and was quickly picked up on by other defence lawyers, who made this point to the court. It was no secret that the prosecution demands for all the Nine were given the once-over by the Attorney General's office in Jakarta and that these cases were potentially politically sensitive, especially given the furore of the Corby case and the hanging of an Australian man, Tuong Van Nguyen, in neighbouring Singapore.

It seems that an order came down from on high that Lawrence was to be treated more leniently to provide an example of just what it means to be helpful. The same thing had happened in the 2002 Bali bombing trials — rather than death, the two repentant roll-overs got life.

As Lawrence sat in stunned silenced that day, translator Dr Ana showed enough emotion for them both. 'Thanks God, thanks God, thanks God,' he said. It was not an act: he truly was thankful.

XXXII

In Court: Martin Stephens

Some of the words scribbled onto the wall are witty. Some are funny or crude. Most are a fascinating insight into the minds of prisoners. These are the musings prisoners write on the walls of jail cells they live in or where they wait to find out their fate.

Like the holding cell at the Denpasar District Court. Here the graffiti is without any doubt the most interesting thing about the drab, dirty and stuffy place where members of the Bali Nine waited each day for their court hearings. Some days there were lots of people, twenty or thirty, all lined up together on the benches. On other days there were less, and sometimes the only prisoners were Australians.

All the prisoners due to front court that day are locked in, men and women together. The sole toilet is awful and has grime caked around it. One day during Schapelle Corby's trial, before proceedings began, her disgusted mother, Rosleigh Rose, turned up early, donned a set of rubber gloves and got to it with the disinfectant. Cursing about the state of the place, she wanted to spare her daughter having to use a room in such a state.

Then there's the smell, which on any given day is bad, but when twenty to thirty prisoners have spent the day there it's nothing short of putrid. When they head back to the jail they leave behind food scraps and rubbish, cigarette butts and papers. Sometimes cats scurry around, hoping to find a feed amongst the scraps before the cleaner comes in. People with their freedom would rather stay away from places like this.

Given the number of Australians who have spent hours inside this holding cell, you'd think a couple of them might have been unable to resist the urge to sign their autograph on the wall for posterity, or to write some witty comment — but around the time that the Bali Nine trials were taking place, there was no sign of any.

The only mention of the nine Aussies was this inscription: 'Martin E. Stevens' with an arrow pointing down to the word *benchong*, which means 'gay'. It wasn't written by Stephens, because he spells his surname differently, but there was no doubt that it referred to him. Whether a fellow prisoner was having a bit of fun with him, or he had an enemy in the jail who had decided to have a go at him, is a mystery. It could have been one or the other, really, although Stephens is not gay.

Some of the cell graffiti makes for amusing reading. It's mostly in Indonesian, with the occasional phrase in English, and much of it refers to the historic and widespread corruption in the justice system and the concept of justice being for sale to the highest bidder — a perception and practice that the Indonesian Government has strived to wipe out for ever. Translated, the messages say things like 'If you have money you can be free', 'the judge wants money', 'the prosecutor is a bastard' or 'the prosecutor wants money'. The most poignant says, 'I will never be here again'.

Martin Stephens and the other eight certainly wished they had never been there in the first place. During his time spent in the holding cell, Stephens was generous to a T. His mum, Michele, who had moved to Bali to live for the period of the trials, would regularly make him containers full of sandwiches — tuna, cheese and tomato cut into little triangles — which he would offer round to all the prisoners there. The Stephens were of modest means, and making up so many sandwiches so Martin could share them around was very generous under any circumstances.

In the outside world, kindness to fellow human beings is an admired trait, but when you have to live behind high walls with razor wire, sometimes what goes around comes around. The Balinese call it karma. Offering a sandwich to a hungry prisoner can sometimes be repaid tenfold back in the jail when you need an ally or someone to help out.

It was while he was walking away from the steps of this holding cell, after talking to Martin Stephens, that lawyer Wirawan Adnan revealed the blunt message he had conveyed to his scared client: either they kill you or the court kills you. Mr Adnan, a senior Jakarta lawyer who is known for representing the 2002 Bali bombers — including the smiling Amrozi — was laying out the alternatives to Stephens: stay silent, don't give evidence against the others and face the very real prospect of a death sentence; or give evidence despite the threats and take your chances. It was a pretty scary proposition, but Mr Adnan wanted Stephens to be in no doubt that if he was not completely cooperative in court, there was a very real possibility that he would be facing the firing squad.

Stephens had already told police what he knew and who had threatened him. He now had to repeat that in court, in the presence of those whom he claimed had threatened and menaced him, and of whom he was frightened.

To the press Mr Adnan used a snappy analogy about his client: Martin Stephens was a human suitcase. He was not an organiser, an enforcer or even a financier. He was an expendable minion, just the means to transport the drugs home to Australia. Would the court believe it?

Like the other mules — Renae Lawrence, Michael Czugaj and Scott Rush — Stephens claimed that, prior to his arrest, he had no idea of the real reason for his trip. Only his imagination could run wild, he told the court. 'When I came over to Bali I honestly did not know what I was here for.' He delivered a similar line at all the trials at which he testified: if he tried to find out what was going on, he was ordered by Chan not to ask questions.

Stephens pulled no punches in his own trial when he was asked his opinion of his colleague at Eurest. Chan, he said, was an evil person with no heart. Strong, fighting words, but Stephens was passionate in his views of the man he saw as being responsible for landing him behind bars in a foreign country.

Mr Adnan's spiel about the court killing Stephens or the gang killing him appeared to have fired up his client, and Stephens was not holding back. On the other side of the coin, he was effusive in describing his affection for his fellow mule Renae Lawrence. They had initially hated each other but now she was like his sister and best friend — theirs was a bond which would never break.

Perhaps the most amusing moment of Stephens's trial came when the well-dressed and well-to-do Mr Adnan rolled around the courtroom floor, pretending to be a drug mule having heroin strapped to his body. Always a good sport, he didn't show a moment's hesitation in taking on the role-play himself when the judges had wanted a demonstration of exactly how the drugs were strapped on and of who did what. Initially there was some discussion backwards and forwards, with Stephens pointing out that this very thing had been done during a reenactment in the police station and had been filmed by police. Why couldn't they just get the video and play that? It would show who did what.

In the end the video wasn't produced, and there was nothing to do except get a couple of actors for the job. Mr Adnan played Stephens while Stephens played Chan. Resplendent in his black robes, a jovial Mr Adnan happily put one leg then the other on the chair while Stephens carried out a rudimentary display. Then it was down on the floor to show how the gear was strapped to his back and waist.

For this exercise there were no props. But during the trials the heroin, in the plastic bags, was often on display either on the judges' or prosecutors' benches, much to the displeasure of some judges who found the smell overbearing, asking to have it moved. One day a witness in one of the trials went into a coughing fit at the smell and had to go outside for a break. It seemed odd that heroin worth hundreds of thousands of dollars was just left idly to sit on a bench, often spilling out and depositing dust particles. It was, however, a solemn reminder of why these people were here. The drug was usually carried to court each day by a prosecutor, bundled up in old A4 paper boxes. As the weeks dragged on, the boxes got tattier and tattier as mules were asked to identify the heroin and the strappings, and bosses were asked if they owned it. The mules identified it; the bosses said they had never seen it before in their lives.

When Stephens was interrogated by police on 21 April — four days after his arrest — he told officers he had come to Bali for a holiday. In question number fourteen he was asked what he had done during his time on the holiday isle. 'My activities while I was in Bali are swimming, playing jet ski, snorkelling, riding banana boat, shopping in Kuta and going to Mbargo nightclub on Jalan Legian Kuta,' he said. In another interrogation, on 30 April, he said he and Lawrence had been jet-skiing, banana-boat riding, snorkelling and watching DVDs, and they went once to the Mbargo Bar.

Then, when he testified months later at Chan's trial, he was asked what he had done during the five days spent at the Adhi Dharma Hotel. His response: 'Just swum in the pool and stay in the room and didn't go anywhere unless we were told to. We swam in the pool and that's the only place — the pool, the room — that's it unless we were instructed otherwise.'

He went on to say that he had even celebrated his twenty-ninth birthday, on 13 April, in the hotel room because he and Lawerence were forbidden from going anywhere. 'So if I was here for a holiday, don't you think I would go out and party? But I didn't, we weren't allowed.'

Nobody asked about the discrepancy between the police statement and the courtroom evidence, or whether he was hardening up and honing the evidence to convince the judges about the issue of threats and of not really knowing what he was doing in Bali. Although it must be said that in the police statement he was asked simply what his activities in Bali had been, while in court the question related to what he had done at the Adhi Dharma. Stephens and Lawrence had spent the first seven days at the Kuta Lagoon Hotel and on 13 April had moved to the Adhi Dharma, where, on 17 April, the heroin was strapped to their bodies.

Stephens said at his own trial that about two weeks before coming to Bali he had been threatened at Chan's Sydney home, and it was for this reason that he was too afraid to disobey Chan's orders that he travel to Bali. Chan had threatened to kill him and his family, said Stephens; from this night on the threats were constant. 'Every day I went to work he told me what I did that night, who I was with, which made me believe that he had someone watching me.'

Stephens said he had met Chan each day at the sign-in book at work. He was asked if he tried to overcome the threats in

Australia, and replied, 'Well, I tried but everything I did he was on top of it. I never gave up.' Stephens said he had been offered no reward for his role and 'wasn't even promised that my family will be okay once we get back to Australia. I didn't even know what was going to happen.'

Asked what had been his purpose in coming to Bali, Stephens replied simply, 'Just do what I was told.'

Six days earlier, when Stephens had been called to testify against Chan, the tone of his evidence had been even harder. At the meeting at Chan's house, he said, Chan had told him 'not to ask questions and do what you are told and everything will be all right.' He also said that, in threatening him, Chan had shown him photographs of his dad, mum and girlfriend 'doing everyday things, leaving the house, coming home, going for a swim'. Stephens said that in the weeks before leaving for Bali he had even seen people following him. 'That's why I couldn't go to the police or trust anyone, I was constantly being watched two weeks prior to leaving.'

No one in court asked for more detail of the incidents when Stephens believed he had been followed, like the locations or when they took place, or what happened. In court terms it was left relatively untested.

At Chan's trial Stephens said he didn't know the contents of the packages strapped to him until they were tested at the police station after his arrest. 'They said it was heroin, to my surprise.' And the other question which was not really asked was a request for more details of the meeting at Chan's house two weeks before the arrest. Exactly what had transpired there? Stephens had said he was threatened, but what did he think the threats were over? He'd said he was too afraid not to go to Bali — but he didn't know what he was going there for. No one tackled the point. If Stephens and the others were to be believed, Chan was a very clever master of mental torture; people dared not disobey him.

After Stephens finished his evidence at Chan's trial, Chan rejected it all. 'All your statements are rejected by Andrew, do you want to stay with your statement?' Judge Arif Supratman asked the witness.

Stephens was unequivocal. 'I have stayed with my statement from day one and intend to stay with it now.'

Judge Supratman's next question was a good one: 'So, if you stay with your statement, are you afraid for your family?'

'The only reason I am talking is because the AFP has assured us that my family is under police protection and from day one we never talked until the AFP told us in Polda that our police [were] watching our family and everything is safe, so we did. If they didn't do that I would be like them, not talking at all.'

Judge Supratman seemed satisfied and impressed, telling Stephens he was welcome to visit Bali any time, but please, don't do drug transactions. He said the same thing to other witnesses as well.

Martin Stephens enjoys a close and loving relationship with his mother, who supported him every day of his trial. Their bond, and the fact that each time he saw her at the court holding cell they exchanged kisses through the bars, and in court embraced and kissed, prompted some local photographers to good-naturedly call out 'Martin, your mummy's here' each day when she approached the cell, sandwiches in hand.

Michele Stephens gave evidence as a defence witness in her son's trial, telling the judges that when she first heard that her younger son had been arrested in Bali, she thought there must have been some kind of awful mistake. She thought he had gone to Darwin with Matthew Norman to make a furniture delivery, and besides, he didn't even have a passport. But the Stephens were soon to learn that there was no mistake and that their lives were being turned upside down.

The first thing Martin Stephens said to Michele and his father, Bill, when they saw him at the police station was, 'Thank God you are safe'. They had already heard from the Australian Consulate that Stephens was upset and scared for the safety of his family because he had been threatened. Mrs Stephens said that, after this, the family was put on a police instant response program with their local police station, which meant that if the police received a call from the family's phone number they would respond immediately.

At the end of her evidence, Mrs Stephens was asked if she wanted to make a statement. She gave the passionate response of a loving and caring mother who was watching the little boy she had given birth to now facing the fight of his life. Mothers everywhere could sympathise with her, and no doubt prayed that they would never, ever have to walk a moment in her shoes.

'Martin has always been a truthful child,' said Michele, 'tells the truth, doesn't lie. We are a very close family. If Martin had been threatened with his own life he would have told Andrew Chan or whoever threatened him to go away, he wasn't interested, but when he was told that myself and his father would be killed if he did not cooperate, that was different. He loves us, so he tried to protect us, and if I had any doubt that Martin was not telling me the truth, I would not have sacrificed a lot of stuff in Australia and come to live over here to give him my full support, if we did not believe in him 100 per cent.'

After her evidence, Martin Stephens said simply: 'I love my mum. Thanks, Mum.'

As with the others, prosecutors demanded that Stephens be jailed for life. Stephens himself said later that, while he deserved jail time, he didn't deserve to spend the rest of his days there. Soon enough he would find out how long it would be before he could take up Judge Supratman's offer to 'come to Bali any time'.

XXXIII

In Court: Scott Rush

Scott Rush was getting rattled. First he said it must have been the translator's fault. Then he said perhaps he had just agreed with the falsehoods in the statement to speed things up. The prosecutor reminded him to be honest with the court.

Rush had good reason to be squirming in his seat as the prosecution and judges honed in on the reasons why he had told police soon after his arrest that he was promised $5000 to become a drug mule, but now he was telling the court it wasn't true at all and he wanted it withdrawn. He wasn't fooling himself, nor was he fooling anyone else.

Rush had just told his own trial, in his evidence, that when he entered the taxi on 17 April and headed to the airport, he did not know the contents of the packages strapped to his body, he had not asked and he had no suspicion. Nor was he worried that he would get caught by the airport X-ray machines. Asked if he would receive any wage or fee for carrying the packages to Australia, he said no. Was he promised any money? Again he said no.

The judge wanted to make sure that Rush knew of his obligation to tell the truth in his courtroom. 'Yes, sir', came the reply. So, then, was he forced when he gave a statement to police? Rush agreed that he had made a statement but denied that he had been under any pressure. So what about that statement made on 21 April, in which Rush told the police that both he and Michael Czugaj had been promised $5000 by Tan Duc Thanh Nguyen if they successfully carried the packages to Australia? 'No, no, I wish to reject,' Rush said.

However, the matter was not going to be left at that. The questions were coming thick and fast. What about the fact that not only had Rush told police in his statement that he was promised $5000, he had even gone on to tell them what he intended to do with the cash — give some to his parents and use the rest to buy a second-hand vehicle to sell retread tyres? Rush disagreed that he had ever said that.

The eagle-eyed prosecutor noted that on the day of his police interview, at which Rush's English-speaking lawyer had also been present, the official translator had been Dr Wayan Ana, the very same Dr Wayan Ana now sitting next to Rush in court and translating for him. The prosecutor pointed out that Rush had made the comment in two different police interviews and that on 27 April the translator was Dr Ana.

'Is it the translator who gave the answer or what?' he asked, sounding almost perplexed.

Rush: 'I am pretty sure it would have been something like that, yes.'

So mistranslation was to blame, apparently, but it wasn't a very convincing answer. The original police statement had been too detailed for a translator to have made up. The prosecutor wasn't buying it, and reminded Rush that being honest in the court would help him when the judges came to make their decision about him.

Q. So can you explain about the money promised to you in the amount of $10 000? So did you carry the package because of your intention or because Tan [Nguyen] promised the money to you?

A. The packages were strapped to me and the only reason I didn't resist is because I was forced to — it's not a valid question.

Q. So in the statement I was your interpreter at that time. About the fee that you would be given $10 000 by Nguyen if you were successful — is that true or not?

A. It's not true.

Q. At that time you were assisted by your lawyer?

A. Maybe that's because they asked if I wanted to keep all the papers the same from before and I would have said yes to quicken the process.

Q. So in this statement at that time you said yes?

A. I said yes to everything but there may have been things that were false in there.

The point was made and the questioning moved on. Not too many people were convinced by the suggestion that either the translator got it wrong or Rush signed a statement even though it wasn't true. It was a way of debunking the defence case that Rush had come to Bali on a free holiday and had no idea beforehand that he would be called upon to become a drug mule or face death. It followed that if he had been offered $5000 and had already decided how to spend it, he must have had some idea what he was doing in Bali.

Rush's mate, Michael Czugaj, had told police a similar story about being offered $5000. When he testified in Rush's trial he followed suit and withdrew the statement, saying that he too had been misinterpreted. Interestingly, he was never asked about that at his own trial.

Rush said in his own case and all the others in which he testified that Andrew Chan had threatened him and his family with death. In addition, Chan had told him that he had a gun, but Rush said that Chan had never shown him the gun.

Later in his evidence, Rush was asked what regrets he had. His answer centred around his regret at having trusted Nguyen, who, he claimed, had 'trapped' him with the offer of the free Bali holiday. Prosecutors later urged the judges to disregard all this, including Rush's explanation for the $5000 issue, and said that his crime was deserving of life in jail.

Scott Rush's parents, Lee and Christine, were a constant support to him and to the other mules. They lived in Bali for the entirety of the trials and were in the front couple of rows most days when Rush or the other mules were in court. They could easily have passed for members of the media, given the amount of notes they took during proceedings, especially Christine. Sometimes, in the early days, Lee tape-recorded the evidence, and they both took photographs. Notebook in hand, Christine would sit next to the Australian Consulate representative who would in turn be next to a translator. The translator would tell the Consulate staffer what was happening; the staffer would take notes and Christine then took notes from the staffer's material. Some days Lee, his Akubra hat never far from his head when he was not in court, could be seen outside the courtroom, holding a tape recorder up to the loudspeaker.

It was not clear why the Rushes took so many notes; this behaviour was in contrast to that of other parents. However, if the families of some of the other mules were not in Bali, the Rushes would look out for their children as well, bringing food and drinks to their cell, visiting and chatting with them and generally providing support and a friendly face, posting letters and running other errands. Their attendance at other trials, however, was less frequent.

It was obvious that a bond of sorts had developed between some of the mules' parents. Tensions were smoothed over and a newfound purpose meant that some of the parents formed an alliance, at least on the surface.

Throughout the trials, both Lee and Christine Rush appeared stoic, their emotions and pain not often on public display. They were very private people. It was on the day that Scott Rush made his personal mercy plea to the judges that Christine could not stop the tears which welled up in her eyes from spilling over.

'I convey to my beloved mother and father,' said her son, 'as due to their love to me they are willing to leave their work and home to accompany me from the beginning up until now. And I do love you. Because of my behaviour you feel the misery and I promise not to make you disappointed while I am in jail, far from our beloved country.'

Lee Rush testified in his son's defence case. He told how, upon discovering that his son was going to Bali, he had called his lawyer, who had then contacted the Australian Federal Police. He had done so out of 'a father's instinct that Scott was in trouble', he said, but he was not asked why he had harboured such an instinct nor why he thought his son might have been heading for strife. Lee said he had been assured that Scott would be stopped from flying to Bali, and added that it was very strange that his son had gone overseas without telling his parents — at the time he was living at home with them. And he testified that for two months after Scott's arrest, they had visited him three days a week at the police jail. But Mr Rush said he had not asked his son why he carried the narcotics.

'No, I did not ask that question, I was leaving that up to the responsibility of the lawyer that was engaged to look after Scott. We were there to give love and caring for Scott. Not to try and solve the case ... Scott never told us the reason why and we didn't want to interrogate him, that was the job of the lawyer.'

Lee Rush also revealed that, four to five weeks before his son was arrested in Bali, two Molotov cocktails had been hurled onto the front lawn of their home but he had not reported the matter to police. Asked why, Lee said he felt 'I could handle this myself'. So potentially dangerous firebombs had been thrown at the family's home and yet Lee Rush had not called in police, but when his son, who was by that stage nineteen years old, left on an unannounced Bali holiday, Lee Rush had felt enough of a father's instinct to go to police, via his barrister.

Asked if his son had used drugs, Lee said no. And, curiously, when asked if Scott had ever committed any criminal acts for which he had been punished or jailed, his father also answered no. But almost twelve days after Lee Rush's Bali court evidence, the Federal Court in Australia published its judgment in the case brought by Scott Rush and the others against the AFP — and in that judgment it was stated that the lawyer and family friend whom Mr Rush had first called to seek help to have his son stopped from going to Bali had acted for Scott 'on a number of minor criminal prosecutions, concerned, in the main, with dishonesty offences'. The judgment also noted that Scott Rush had 'prior convictions' and was on bail for offences at the time of his arrest in Bali. And, as time went on, details of Scott's criminal history began to surface.

During his own testimony, Scott himself was never asked if he had criminal convictions or whether he had ever used drugs; Michael Czugaj was asked the same question. Rush's lawyer, Robert Khuana, asked Czugaj whether Rush had ever used heroin. He said no.

Through their experiences in Bali, some of the Nine found God; others renewed fractured relationships with their parents and families. Scott Rush said that his arrest had brought him much closer to his parents and family, something which gave him great joy and which had comforted him.

'We are normally not a close family, now we have definitely got more close. It is beautiful you know, I like it,' he says one day during an interview at the court holding cell. He is in an unusually expansive mood, much more talkative than on previous occasions. He also reveals that his arrest had made him 'get in touch more with myself'. Before that he had felt disconnected, living a party life, although he won't go so far as to say it he had been a 'wild' teenager — more normal, he thinks, but he adds that he learned from his party life.

Several weeks later, during another interview, Rush is equally open, happy to linger and chat. On this day he defends his claims that he was threatened and that he had no idea about the true reason for his trip to Bali. 'Of course it's the truth,' he says when asked if he was being honest. What about the judges, does he think they believed him? 'I hope so, because I never had anything to do with that heroin or anything, you know, especially to this degree, so that's why I would have been an easy target, me and Michael.'

During this interview Rush at times appears older than his twenty years. But then at other times he seems so much younger. Sometimes he sounds like he is an actor, reciting lines; then he will be earnest, talking about his ambitions for the future. Mostly he hopes he has one.

Jail is a place for people to renew themselves, he offers. And he wants others to learn from his own bitter experience. 'I am not out to make a worse world, I am out to make a better world,' he says.

Rush regards everyone in jail as a potential friend. Is it easy to make friends in jail, he is asked. Yes, but it's even easier to lose them, he explains. He's met a lot of good people there, and their friendship, he opines, probably means more to him than it does to them.

He tries to socialise with Indonesian prisoners so he can learn the language, and he has started teaching some of the

Indonesian prisoners how to play football. Some have never even seen a football before but, as coach, he thinks he's doing a good job with them and they're getting better; soon they'll be ready for a game.

Rush is learning to cope much better now. And it shows — he looks less drawn, less afraid and healthier. It's easier to cope, he says, if you look at the big picture, not the small one. And, yes, as a Christian he's expressed forgiveness of the drug bosses. He doesn't believe what they did is right, but that doesn't matter — he has forgiveness in his heart.

He would soon learn whether the judges would be so forgiving.

XXXIV

In Court: Myuran Sukumaran

The written testimonials painted a picture of a very different person to the one portrayed during the trial. To the Indonesian police he was known simply as 'the black man'; the Australian Federal Police had never even heard of him. He was likened to the second aircraft engine that helps keep a plane in the air. There was Andrew Chan and there was his sidekick, Myuran Sukumaran, running the Bali Nine drug operation. The mules claimed they were scared of them both.

With his shaved head, a mean-looking scar running down the back of his neck and his sullen disposition, Myuran Sukumaran always looked menacing. He was, after all, trained in karate. But whenever he opened his mouth in court — which was not all that often — it was almost a shock. He had, at least for public display, a gentle and softly spoken, almost lilting, voice. It was at odds with the way witnesses described him. But it wasn't at odds with the character references quite readily provided for the judge's consideration. They told of a kind and caring Christian family man, a regular blood donor, Salvation

Army and Red Cross volunteer and UNICEF child sponsor. It was almost as though the letter writers were talking about someone else, not the man whom prosecutors and Bali Nine members said was an enforcer, someone to be feared.

It must be said that many times throughout the trial it had been difficult for observers to 'read' Sukumaran. Some people you can read like a book — not him. He kept to himself, never spoke or interacted with the media in the court holding cell, and tried as much as possible to keep out of the limelight. His biggest problem was that he didn't have quite the right physical appearance to keep a low profile — his looks made him stand out amongst the Indonesians and the Bali Nine accused.

According to family friends, Sukumaran is quite the opposite to his media portrayal. They see him differently, and that's often the case when it comes to criminal defendants. But back in 1998, when he left Homebush Boys High School, it was with a glowing Year Twelve reference under his arm. There was no sign then that in a mere seven years' time he would be in a foreign land facing a possible death penalty for masterminding a drug ring. It was for these charges that his lawyers invoked the glowing reference, handing it to the judges as part of a bundle of character testimonials to be used in mitigation.

Sukumaran was known at school as Myu, and according to then principal Brian Greene and Year Twelve advisor Traci Lewis's reference, he was extremely honest, reliable, responsible, punctual and well prepared, with high standards, and he was a good example for junior students. He had taken part in national mathematics and science competitions, was a gold-medal winner in karate tournaments and played in the school's second-grade rugby team. He gave blood in the annual school appeal and was a volunteer collector for the Salvation Army's Red Shield Appeal.

'Myu has a friendly disposition and is well liked by all,' says the reference. 'He has a willingness to work and participate in academic activities and sporting activities. Myu has a mature personality and will adequately fit into any work place. Myu is a charming young man, always polite and courteous and takes great pride in his appearance.'

Family friend Victor Sinnadurai had known the Sukumaran family for almost ten years, and he told the court in his letter that Sukumaran had the potential to be a valuable member of society and the community. Mr Sinnadurai had met the Sukumaran family through their local church, where he was a director and secretary. Sukumaran, his brother and sister had all been confirmed in the church, and Sukumaran had been a regular at weekly youth meetings until 2001. He had also been on church youth camps.

'Myuran is generally a very humorous person, jovial, witty and friendly,' wrote Sinnadurai. 'He presents himself well and articulates his mannerism with friendship, sincerity, honesty and trustworthiness. He is a kind-hearted and compassionate person. He is ever ready to help those in need, a regular blood donor and a volunteer helper in the Salvation Army. He is a highly motivated young man with determination to complete tasks when allocated to him ... I understand from his family members that in his current situation in Bali he is reading and meditating in the Bible daily and seeking the Lord for deliverance. Having known Myuran personally well, I wish to appeal to Bali's judicial governing body for a sympathetic hearing and a resolution in favour of Myuran's freedom.'

The sentiments from another family friend were in a similar vein — that Sukumaran was a role model to his brother and sister and cousins, he was polite and responsible, and came from a well-educated and highly respected family.

However, locked up in a Bali jail, painted as an enforcer and drug king, it was difficult to see how, these days, Sukumaran could be a role model to anybody. It seemed almost impossible to reconcile the character references with the person authorities were alleging. Sometimes criminals can be chameleons, and Sukumaran's school reference was written seven years ago — a lot can happen to change a person in seven years. Just what had happened to change Sukumaran from the young man his school teachers remembered to the young man sitting in the Denpasar District Court is a mystery — and he wasn't intending to shed any light on matters. He didn't believe he needed to, anyway, since he had claimed from day one that he had nothing whatsoever to do with any of this business.

In police interviews Sukumaran had denied any role in the smuggling attempt and that was his courtroom stance as well. Time after time when he was called to testify at the trials of the other eight he made the same objection: he was an accused in the same case and he did not want to testify. His stance both puzzled and annoyed judges in the various trials, who began to sound like broken records: *If you cooperate and testify now it can help you achieve leniency if you are convicted in your own case.* It didn't matter — Sukumaran was not budging. In one trial he even went so far as to claim he had not signed the police statement, even though his signature was there in black and white. It was not boding well for him.

One police officer testified that Sukumaran had carried a suitcase containing 350 grams of heroin to the Melasti Beach Bungalows shortly before his arrest; police said tests showed that it was identical to the heroin on the four mules. In court Sukumaran denied carrying any suitcases to the room, insisting that all his gear had still been at the Hard Rock Hotel.

Giving evidence for himself, Sukumaran was no more forthcoming. Yes, he knew Andrew Chan — the pair had gone to school together — but he was in Bali for a holiday and nothing more sinister than that. His testimony included a lot of 'don't knows', 'don't remembers' and 'can't remembers', so many that judges admonished him, telling him to stop saying 'I don't know'. It culminated in one clearly annoyed judge inquiring whether he suffered from any memory-loss ailments.

Q. Have you ever suffered from amnesia?
A. Sorry?
Q. Amnesia. Loss of memory.
A. Ah, amnesia. I have once, it's so long ago I can't remember. It was more than eight months ago.
Q. So you forget things?

Sukumaran mumbled something about being under a lot of stress. The court laughed. It was his case that the police, quite simply, had the wrong man.

Not so, prosecutors said when they told the court in their sentence demand that Sukumaran was indeed guilty and deserved not one shred of leniency. He had been evasive during the trial, creating obstacles and giving confusing evidence; his penalty should be death by firing squad. As always, Sukumaran's face gave absolutely nothing away. Whatever he felt and thought when he heard those awful words 'death penalty' would be a secret locked inside himself. He barely flinched, a widening of his eyes the only sign that he had heard. If a cold hand had gripped his heart or wrenched his stomach, he wasn't showing it. And when it came time, he didn't take the opportunity to make a personal plea for mercy — he left all the talking to his lawyers.

Given the position he had taken since his arrest, it should have been no surprise that Sukumaran wouldn't want to plead for his life. His lawyer, Mochamad Rifan, painted his client as a scapegoat for the mules, who had tried to absolve themselves of any blame by shovelling all the responsibility onto people like Sukumaran. Mr Rifan warned the judges against accepting the four mules' stories about Sukumaran having helped strap the drugs to their bodies, and about being threatened, unless there was more concrete evidence and corroborating information than just their own testimony. They, he pointed out, had a vested interest in giving such evidence.

Clearly angered, outside the court Mr Rifan — a normally genial man with good English — declined to answer media questions in English as he normally did, saying that he would answer only in Indonesian. He generally gives little away, but having just heard the prosecutors say that his client should be shot for his crimes, he made surprisingly critical remarks about the Australian Federal Police and their letter alerting their Indonesian counterparts to the activities of the Bali Nine. It was most unlike Mr Rifan to say anything so strong or, in fact, to say anything like that at all. His client may have been hiding his emotions that morning, but Mr Rifan was not.

XXXV

In Court: Andrew Chan

'I've got God in my hands,' Andrew Chan declared from behind the court holding cell bars. 'What? Did you say you've got blood on your hands?' someone asked. Chan didn't appear to see the irony, but it was a fair enough question given the way he had been portrayed in court by the four mules. However, he was referring to God and the spirituality that had been giving him solace during his darkest hours.

People sometimes find God in the most bizarre places and under the most extreme circumstances. In Chan's case he said religion hadn't just found him, he'd always been a believer and churchgoer, but now he was happy for the world to know about his faith and the strength it was giving him.

This is what he told the judges on the day he was called upon to make a personal defence plea to the court: 'To the judges and prosecutors, today is my defence that I have to defend myself and what I would like to do is address a few words. Firstly, what I would like to say is that no matter what outcome comes out of all this, I am thankful to God myself and thankful that you are listening to this. My life has been changed dramatically since my arrest last year. I could honestly say it is [by] God's strength alone I am standing here today and saying these words to you. My faith has grown towards God and I am thankful for everything. What I wanted to say is that I never tried to organise or even tried to do anything to break the law in any country. I am twenty-two years old and I am a young man. All I ask Your Honour is that you will give me an opportunity to restart my new, fulfilled life. I am not demanding for you to release me tomorrow but, please, I would like the opportunity to come here one day, not just by myself, but with my family. I am sorry for what trouble I have caused the Indonesian system and, of course, yourselves but I never intended to hurt anybody, but I guess the factor is it hurt my family very deeply to see me inside a prison.

'Your Honour, the outcome I wish, of course, and my family, is that you find that you would release me, for I had nothing to participate in this. I didn't say anything in court because if I did I'd be lying. The truth is I know nothing. I am thankful in whatever decision you decide to give me and I respect the Indonesian system, no matter what circumstances, but to go on and tell you about how much faith I have learnt about Jesus Christ, the words I have wanted to say I have presented to you today. So thank you so much Your Majesty and prosecutors, and I pray that you find in your hearts you will give me a second opportunity to redeem myself as a citizen of society and no longer a convict.

'I'd just like to point out that a lot of lies have been said against me, but the true reality is I am not what people put out, what people put me out to be. I have never threatened anybody in my life. I work six to seven days a week and I always try to be a helpful family member of my household. The reason why I always smile is because I feel the Lord's presence anywhere I go and it gives me the courage. I feel it in this very courtroom today and also in myself so thank you for listening.'

It was an odd plea for mercy. On one hand Chan was saying that he would be happy with whatever decision the judges reached and he wasn't asking to be released immediately, but on the other he insisted he knew nothing and had never threatened anybody. Why, people wondered, wouldn't he be screaming to be released immediately if he had nothing to do with this whole sordid business? And what was the reason for the religious references peppered throughout? It's no secret that religion and strong family bonds are attributes that are deeply valued in Indonesian society. Chan was not the only Bali Nine member to home in on these themes in his mercy plea, perhaps hoping to strike a chord with the judges, for whom religion is an integral part of daily life (the judges in the Denpasar Court are mainly Hindu or Muslim, with a few Christians). Others told the court that since being in jail they had either found God or renewed their faith, and begged to be released to restart their new, Christian lives.

A week before this plea, during a strange question-and-answer session in the court holding cell, Chan had told the media of his faith in God, of reading the Bible, praying and attending church services inside jail. It was a bizarre performance, prompting some to question whether he was 'on' something that day. Up to that point he'd shown nothing but disdain for the press, retreating to the cell corner and ignoring questions. But this day he was enjoying the game. He didn't really want to answer anything but he wanted to play the media along, acting the clown and smiling like a Cheshire cat.

It was clear he was loving the attention. He could easily have walked away from the cameras but he didn't. *Are you worried?* 'No, not really.' *Do you have animosity toward those who paint you as being a threatening enforcer?* Shrug of the shoulders. *Is it true?* 'No.' *Are you worried you might get a heavier sentence and that people call you the Godfather?* 'No, not really. I have God in my hands.' *Are you a changed person since you went to jail?* 'I'll let you decide that.' *Have you been praying to God?* 'Oh yeah, you could say something like that.' *Are you completely not guilty of these charges?* 'I will leave the court to decide that.' *What regrets do you have?* 'None, to be honest.' *You must regret being in jail?* 'Not really.' *There is evidence your girlfriend, Grace, is involved in this?* 'Everyone's saying everyone's involved, aren't they.' Then, taking a huge bite from his roll, he told the reporters theatrically 'End of interview' and turned his back, pretending to walk offstage. But then he returned to the bars again, knowing full well that the questions would keep coming.

This was definitely a different Chan to the one the press had seen before. People wondered what was going on — whether he had taken some kind of drug before coming to court — or had he just been a master of disguise all that time?

Chan is far wittier than his usual persona would indicate. When Scott Rush offered him one of his McDonald's cheeseburgers, Chan got stuck into it for the cameras, asking if McDonald's perhaps wanted to sponsor him.

One day Chan turned up at court clutching a book called *Iceman*. The analogy seemed apt — Chan had always appeared to be an iceman: cool exterior, calm under pressure, under control. From day one of his arrest he hadn't tried to hide his face, boldly telling the press that police suggestions he was the 'Godfather' were 'full of shit'. 'Do you think I am the Godfather of things? Do I look like a Godfather?' he snapped. 'Whatever happened to Schapelle Corby happened to me.' His courtroom appearances were no different, his rigid refusal to give evidence in the trials of any of the co-accused, and his insolence, both angering and amusing the judges.

When he was called to testify at Renae Lawerence's trial, he claimed he hardly knew Lawrence and that he wasn't going to give evidence. But in his original police statement, made and signed after his arrest, Chan told officers that he met Lawrence in 2003 at work. In court that day he was a picture of cool contempt and defiance, engaging in a comical exchange with Lawrence's lead lawyer, Yan Apul.

Q. *So do you understand why you were arrested?*
A. No.
Q. *Have you been investigated in the police station?*
A. *What, here? Yeah.*
Q. *So do you think the police statement is a mock-up or not true?*
A. *I don't know.*
Q. *Did you know if there is a case named Bali Nine about narcotics?*
A. *I dunno.*
Q. *So did you know if Renae was arrested and detained because of a narcotics case?*
A. *I dunno.*
Q. *Did you report to the government of Australia that you were detained and arrested in the airport illegally?*
A. *I don't remember.*
Q. *Didn't the government of Australia feel objection to the [illegal] dentention of his citizen in Indonesia?*
A. *I dunno.*
Q. *Do you want to revoke your statement you gave in the police station?*
A. *No, I don't want to make a statement.*
Q. *Can you explain why you don't want to give a statement?*
A. *Um, I'm in the same case, so no, that's why.*
Q. *Can you explain what the case is that you mean?*
A. *I don't know.*

It was too much for Judge Putu Widnya, who burst into laughter at the ridiculous nature of the answers. But while the judges and prosecutors guffawed away, they all knew it was really no laughing matter. Chan must have known, too, because he had already heard the warning that refusing to cooperate could mean harsh treatment down the track. If it bothered him, though, the Iceman didn't let it show, half smirking at his own hilarity that day.

Iceman by Ron Rearick is the true story of a Mafia enforcer who had a penchant for violence and turned to God inside jail, going on to co-direct Born to Choose Ministries and become an assistant pastor in Washington. Another day Chan was reading *Free* by Rita Nightingale, the true story of a young Englishwoman wrongly convicted and sentenced to twenty years' jail in Thailand after heroin was found in her luggage. She served three years before receiving a royal pardon. During her awful years in prison she found God, and after her release she became involved in Christian fellowship work.

On the day of Chan's personal plea, in which he attested to his faith, he sat quietly in the holding cell reading a book called *The Heavenly Man*, the true story of Brother Yun, a Chinese Christian who was jailed due to religious persecution. The book tells of the miracles of God during this wretched period of his life.

So there was a pattern — Chan the avid reader seemed to be scouring everything he could find about the persecuted and wrongly convicted, and religious conversions inside jail.

However, according to evidence given at his trial, Chan was not undergoing a conversion behind bars. From the time he was a small boy he had always been a practising Christian. This was outlined in character evidence given by his older brother, 27-year-old Michael, and by his longtime friend and youth pastor, Mark Timothy Soper, during the closing stages of his trial.

Michael Chan told of a 'good kid' who listened to him and listened to their parents. Andrew lived at home with the family, one of four children, and had a range of friends from many different cultures.

Michael said that both their parents were retired and sick and needed their children, including Andrew, to support them. It was their hope that Andrew would be found not guilty and allowed to return to his family.

His younger sibling, Michael told the court, was not the same person as the one depicted in the trial. Michael said his brother often attended church back home. This point was affirmed by the next witness, Mr Soper, a friend of Andrew Chan's for eighteen years. The families had been next-door neighbours, and Mr Soper's father was the minister at the church attended by Chan. 'Sometimes he goes to our church, sometimes he goes to another church, but often,' Mr Soper told the court. He described his friend as 'very family-oriented and very kind to other people', someone who always helps others. Mr Soper said he had never seen Chan using drugs, adding, 'he doesn't like that'.

The Chan who appeared in court was certainly different to the one depicted in the police mug shot of him which graced the cover of the weighty police dossier, or brief of evidence, against him. Shirtless, with a shaved head, the trace of a goatee, wearing gold earrings in both ears and a gold crucifix on a chain around his neck, he looked like some kind of tough enforcer or standover man. The tattoos on his chest and arms stood out boldly. One was some kind of Maori image, another included the word 'Grace', the name of his girlfriend. Nine months later in court, though, Chan was much softer looking. Dressed in black pants and a white long-sleeved shirt, wearing spectacles, his hair — which he'd let grow — all gelled up, and clutching a book, he could easily have passed for a university student or public servant. There was nothing remarkable about him; no reason, really, to give him a second glance. But the softened image didn't fool the judges — they had the mug shot in front of them every day of his trial.

On the day Chan was called to give evidence in his own defence — and unlike the day he had Judge Putu Widnya in Lawrence's trial in laughter — there were no laughing judges in sight; not even a smile from the bench. Instead, Judge Arif Supratman could barely control his ire, instructing the female translator to deliver a stern warning: 'Tell him to tell the truth, don't lie to the judges, lawyers and prosecutor in this trial. Indonesian judges are not stupid people but we are the people who know the law. Tell him.'

Chan, seemingly unperturbed by the admonishment, was quick with his answer. 'Yeah, I know they are civilised people and I'm telling the truth.' He was reminded again to tell the truth when asked who owned the packages of heroin. 'I don't know. I don't even know who owns it ... I never saw it until they showed me at [the police station], they started throwing it at me saying, "This is yours" and I've never seen it.'

Earlier the entire Bali Nine contingent had been called as witnesses in Chan's trial. Some, like Myuran Sukumaran, flatly denied taking part in the unfolding drama. Backwards and forwards it went like a game of ping pong, Sukumaran saying he didn't want to testify because he was a suspect in the same case, Judge Supratman warning him that if someone had told him to make an objection it was wrong. But Sukumaran wasn't going to budge. It was the tactic employed by most of the Nine, except those caught with the drugs on them, at all of the trials. The only time they agreed to give evidence was in their own defence. And, given some of their answers, observers were left scratching their heads as to the motivation behind such blatant stonewalling, especially in a court system where politeness, cooperation and respect are rewarded and appreciated.

* * *

Tidak tahu means 'don't know' and *tidak ingat* means 'don't remember'. Translators assisting some of the Nine were forced to use the phrases over and over again like broken records.

Take Chan at the beginning of his testimony. Asked if he had ever stayed in the Hard Rock Hotel, he replied, 'From what I believe, yes.' But he couldn't remember how long he had stayed there.

Before Chan started his evidence, the other members of the Nine had already had their say. The four mules all testified about Chan and Sukumaran strapping the heroin onto their bodies and threatening them. Then, while Chan took centre stage, some of the others sat behind him. *Had he ever met the people sitting behind him while he was in Bali?* 'No, I don't remember.' *Let's try that again, just try to remember.* 'I have never met 'em in Australia, no.' Puzzled looks were exchanged behind his back. He worked with Lawrence, Stephens and Norman. Try again: did he know Renae Lawrence? He didn't know her, he said he'd only seen her around at work but never talked to her, telling the judges that Eurest was a big company. It was the same for Stephens, he said. He even went so far as to say that he didn't know Myuran Sukumaran. Only six days earlier Sukumaran had told his own trial, in his defence evidence, that he had gone to school with Chan. Chan said he had never met Sukumaran in the Hard Rock Hotel. It was a lie, whichever way one looks at it: the surveillance police had photographed the pair together on the hotel steps waiting for a taxi and the photograph was part of the dossier of evidence.

There was one answer that really took the cake. In response to the question 'Do you know why you sit here [in court]?' Chan said, 'Um, no, not really.' Yes, he said, he had been questioned by police after his arrest, but he had no clue if the statement had ever been typed up. Not only had it been typed but Chan had signed it. And here it was in the brief of evidence. Chan was beckoned to come forward and check for himself. He was starting to sound ridiculous.

> Q. *As far as you know, all of the witnesses here are liars?*
> A. *From what I believe, yes, from what I've heard, yes.*
> Q. *How do you know that they are liars, you don't even know them? How?*
> A. *Well, no, they are saying that they know me but I don't know them.*

It was at this point that a fuming Judge Supratman, his dark eyes boring into Chan, jumped in to tell Chan that the robed men in front of him were not stupid. With a display like that he certainly couldn't have done himself any favours.

When it came time for prosecutor Olopan Nainggolan to deliver his sentence demand or request and to sum up the case for the judges, he pulled no punches. He described Chan as being the 'driving force' of the Bali Nine operation. A large and jovial man, Mr Nainggolan was happy to later give an analogy — if the Bali Nine were an aircraft, Chan would be the engine. He painted Chan as one of the chief organisers, a financier, a recruiter who dished out the discipline to some of the mules, picked up the heroin twice from the supplier, Cherry Likit Bannakorn, then strapped it to the bodies of the mules. When he got to the part of his demand where prosecutors outlined the mitigating and non-mitigating factors, the list of mitigating factors which could bring Chan some leniency was painfully thin — *tidak ada*. It means 'nothing'.

Mr Nainggolan said that Chan had failed to cooperate with authorities and had given confusing and convoluted evidence. His crime had damaged the image of Bali and was contrary to Indonesia's tough stance and anti-drugs regime. No one was surprised when Mr Nainggolan said Chan should be sentenced to death. And as the prosecutor said the words *bukuman mati* (death penalty) Chan didn't need his translator to tell him what it meant. He already knew.

The flustered translator asked a smirking Chan anyway if he knew what it meant. 'Yes, death penalty, no problem.' The Iceman was cool, calm and collected.

XXXVI

In Court: The Melasti Three

They looked like the three minstrels — black pants and white shirts — sitting side by side, day after day, not saying much. They saw no evil and heard no evil. They contended that they were quite simply in the wrong place at the wrong time.

The Melasti group — so-called because they were arrested at the Melasti Beach Bungalows — were, at least in court, not the most charismatic bunch. For the most part their voices were barely audible; they often mumbled whenever they were called upon to speak. It had been the same during police interrogations: they had chosen not to make any concessions or admissions, and refused to testify against any of the others.

Of the group — Matthew Norman, Si Yi Chen and Tan Duc Thanh Nguyen — Norman looked the saddest. He appeared almost morbid — his eyes held a certain dullness, a faraway look. His body language was the same. Norman is the youngest of the Bali Nine, only eighteen when they were caught, and his tender years were on display when he fronted court. Perhaps it was the shape of his mouth, but a smile barely ever crossed his lips in public. That was the way it remained throughout the trio's joint trial.

So at the end, when Norman stood up to address the judges personally, his plea was the surprise of the group. He chose to tell the judges something of himself and the reasons why he disliked drugs so much, and of his newfound faith. Being in jail had not been easy for him; it was hard being away from his family.

'I don't do drugs, either do my friends,' he told the judges. 'I have seen first-hand what drug effects do to a family. My friend's mum was a drug addict and it really hurt my friend. One day his mum overdosed and almost died and seeing how hurt my friend was made me — I made a promise to myself that I would not take drugs or be associated with anybody involved or using drugs.

'Since my arrest I have learnt many things. One of those things I am proud to say I learnt about is the Bible. I was a believer in Jesus Christ but not a dedicated Christian, and now I honestly am. I read the Bible daily and it helps me get through the day ... In all honesty I was in the wrong place at the wrong time and I ask that you will see towards that decision. I ask you today to give me the opportunity to restart my new Christian life which I have found being in jail. I ask with all my heart you will let me have that opportunity to help other people in life.'

For the first time Norman had opened up and let people see some of what was in his heart. The other two, Tan Duc Thanh Nguyen and Si Yi Chen, did this as well. Both had helped support their families back home, and now things were very difficult. Chen, too, said that he had been in the wrong place at the wrong time and that this was all a big mistake. And he appealed to the judges' sense of family — he was an only child, and if he was forced to spend the rest of his life in jail there would be no one to look after his parents. He assured the judges that he had nothing to do with a plan to export drugs from Bali to Australia. If he had, he said, he would certainly have told the authorities.

Nguyen's plea was in a similar vein. He didn't come from a rich family and his mother had been and in and out of hospital for years; it was Nguyen himself, as the oldest and the only son, who helped support the family financially and paid for the school fees and education expenses of his four younger sisters. Nguyen said he was stunned to learn that other Bali Nine members had fingered him as a financier of this operation. 'How could I possibly be the financier when I could barely look after myself after supporting my sisters?' he asked the court. Nguyen begged the judges to believe that the only key role he had ever played in his life was to his family. It was ridiculous to suggest that he was a bigwig in a drug-smuggling ring.

At the end of the three personal defence pleas, Judge Istiningsih Rahayu took the step of asking all three if they felt any regret. Yes, they all had. Did they feel guilt? No. They felt only regret that they had been in the wrong place at the wrong time. Later, outside the court, Judge Istiningsih explained that the question had been one final bid to uncover whether any of the trio admitted to any criminal actions. Judge Istiningsih had her answer.

The same question had been asked after the three had given evidence earlier in the trial. On this occasion their answers had been largely monosyllabic, and there were lots of instances where they couldn't remember much at all, saying it was all such a long time ago. Nguyen proffered that he had been under pressure at the police station when he gave his statement. What kind of pressure was it? Just verbal. But he couldn't remember whether he had read the statement before he signed it. He said he had no relationship with the people arrested at the airport.

Chen's evidence began in a whisper. He, too, couldn't remember much because it was so long ago. He said he had stayed alone at the White Rose Hotel. *Was he sure he had been alone?* Yes, he was. *But didn't you stay with one of them? Matthew, where did he stay?* 'Can't remember, it's too long ago. Next question.' *So where did Matthew stay?* 'Can't remember.' Surely these kinds of answers — when it was known that he had stayed in room 1022 of the White Rose Hotel in Kuta with Norman — were not helping his cause.

Chen went on to deny meeting any members of the Bali Nine in Australia. He had met them in clubs in Bali, he said. He also told the judges that he had been under pressure during questioning at the police station — 'They were talking really loud and shouting and pushing,' he said.

The next witness was Norman. He agreed he had been at the Adhi Dharma Hotel but he said he hadn't seen Andrew Chan or any of the four mules there. And, contrary to the evidence of Renae Lawrence and Martin Stephens, he said he did not bring a black bag into their room and leave it there at the request of Chan. Asked why he had been arrested, Norman's answer was short: 'They found powder of some sort.'

Compared to the evidence against the other six, the case against the Melasti group was far more circumstantial. They had been arrested in a hotel with a suitcase containing 350 grams of heroin that had been linked, through forensic testing, to the 8.2 kilograms found on the mules. Nguyen was alleged to have helped recruit the Brisbane boys, and Norman was accused of carrying the bag of heroin to the hotel room before the parcels were strapped onto Lawrence and Stephens. Plus there was evidence that Chen and Norman were to be the next couriers, and that they were waiting for a second shipment of heroin to arrive before it was strapped to their own bodies.

The Melasti group's legal tactic, from day one at the police station, had been to say as little as possible; that continued in court. One day, after the prosecution demanded life sentences for all three, their lawyer, MH Rifan — who also represented Andrew Chan and Myuran Sukumaran — was asked if he thought perhaps, in hindsight, the strategy of silence had been an error. He did not.

When Michael Norman gave character evidence for his son, he was asked at the end about his hopes for his son's case. He was earnest in saying that Matthew should be set free and allowed to go home. As the last day of their trial ended, that seemed a desolate hope.

XXXVII

Judgment Day

Judge Suryowati is trying to hide her tears behind a fan. Talking about the death sentence she handed out to Myuran Sukumaran two days earlier makes it worse. She had not wanted to deliver such a crushing penalty and had even tried to talk her two fellow judges out of it. But it was useless: in her heart she always knew that — given the young man's crime — under Indonesian law there really was no other option. She tried anyway. Then when judgment day came all she could see in front of her was the 'gentle' face of Sukumaran and, behind him, his little brother.

Next to Judge Suryowati, fellow Judge I Gusti Lanang Dauh's voice reached a crescendo as he neared the end of the judgment. Stand up. Deliver the sentence — '*Hukuman mati*,' Dauh boomed. Death. The 49-year-old mother of two dropped her gaze and squeezed her eyes; she didn't want anyone to see her crying inside the courtroom. But the minute she got back to her desk, she let it all out. They were the tears of a judge who had just watched a young man throw away his life — a young man not much older than her own two daughters. Now she is still crying.

Judgment day had not been easy for anyone, the judges included. Arif Supratman, whose four children are the same ages as members of the Bali Nine, had prayed constantly before the decision. The only people in the courtroom taking any pleasure in the verdict were the cheer squad for death that had assembled nearby, almost droning out the judges' historic order. *Hidup hakim* and *bagus hakim*, the anti-drugs group yelled, approving of the sentence to end the lives of Andrew Chan and Myuran Sukumaran, the smuggling racket's leaders.

Judge Dauh's voice had risen almost to a shout as he told stunned onlookers that the drugs involved could have yielded 8200 victims. 'All the people in this world know the danger of narcotic abuse,' he said. 'If the heroin was exported by the accused and circulated in the community, if each person used one gram there would be 8200 human beings who would become victims.'

Judge Supratman directed similar comments at Chan: 'The act of the accused and his friends, now famous as the Bali Nine, has made a black mark on Bali as a top tourist destination. The sentence for the accused must be equal to his actions.' He went on: Chan had shown no regret whatsoever; he gave complicated and conflicting evidence; his actions were contrary to government policy aimed at stamping out drugs. So the mitigating factors which might help lessen the sentence — *tidak ada*.

Nothing. None. Zero. It was the same for Sukumaran: *tidak ada*.

Later Judge Supratman said that a drug dealer's crime is of the same magnitude as that of a terrorist. It's just that terrorist's bombs, like those in the Bali nightclubs in 2002, killed 200 people in one night — the impact is sudden. The evil effects of drugs take longer to manifest themselves but are just as deadly, and, in many ways, more deadly, as they affect generations to come. Judge Supratman is not alone in that view — that's why Indonesia and nations across Southeast Asia are unapologetically tough and unrelenting in drugs cases.

Judge Supratman has no feelings either way for Chan. He's a judge; his job is not about sympathy — it's about applying the law. But, personally, for the life of him he can't work out why young people — educated, smart, with jobs and families who love them, like the members of the Bali Nine — would ever want to get tied up with drugs.

At the verdicts for Sukumaran and Chan there was none of the bedlam that had erupted months earlier with the conviction of Schapelle Corby. Sukumaran didn't reveal what he was thinking, just as Chan had sat, emotionless, to receive the same fate a couple of hours earlier. Sukumaran's rapidly blinking eyes were the only sign of his nerves. Earlier he had arrived at court with an angry glare, shouldering media crews out of his way, looking like he was ready to lash out with all his might; Chan had to stop him from punching a photographer. It was the most emotion Sukumaran had shown since the whole sage bagan. But in court he sat like an ocean of calm. Their parents absent, Chan and Sukumaran were supported by their brothers.

In a nearby court two of the mules, Michael Czugaj and Martin Stephens, were being told their futures: they would spend the rest of their lives in jail. Czugaj held hands with his parents, Stephan and Vicki; Martin Stephens exhaled and looked to the floor. What was the use of having a trial in the first place, he wondered later.

It was the same sentence as that handed out by judges twenty-four hours earlier to their co-accused, Scott Rush and Renae Lawrence. The Melasti three — Matthew Norman, Tan Duc Thanh and Si Yi Chen — were still to be told of their life sentences. But none of that mattered at this moment: the Bali court had just handed down its first death sentence for drug smuggling and Andrew Chan had become the first Australian in history sentenced to death in Indonesia. Sukumaran was the second.

The families of the Bali Nine — many of them expecting sub–fifteen year punishments — were horrified at the severity of all the sentences. And they made it known. Led by Lee and Christine Rush, the Australian Federal Police again became the target.

'One thing that we have learnt is that we cannot rely on being an Australian citizen and receiving good treatment from our government,' Mrs Rush said outside the court. 'Our federal police can do, go wherever they want, do anything, anytime without supervision from the Australian Attorney-General or from the Justice Minister.' This time, however, the AFP hit back, with Commissioner Mick Keelty saying that his officers had simply done their job.

As the Rush family was attacking the AFP, their son's criminal record and details of his drug addiction was being made public in Australia. Scott's charges included drug possession, and fraud and theft — the tools of trade for addicts worldwide. There were also revelations that a warrant was out for his arrest after he failed to show on three charges that were due to be heard during the week he was in Bali.

This information had been a closely guarded secret to that point; many journalists were carrying a copy of the warrant and deliberating with their bosses on when to run it. Rush's boy-next-door image fell apart after the revelation, and his parents' attack on the AFP fell on deaf ears. Despite the heartfelt sympathy for his parents, talkback radio and newspaper letter columns filled with support for the AFP and its fight to stop drugs reaching our borders.

It wasn't just Rush who boasted a criminal record, either — a warrant had been issued for Czugaj, who was in police custody in Bali when he was due to appear in a suburban Brisbane Magistrates' Court on driving-related charges. And it wasn't his first appearance in court — he'd had convictions the previous year for wilful damage and public nuisance. The third Brisbane boy, Tan Duc Thanh Nguyen, had also been convicted of drink driving, and Lawrence and Norman had been facing charges in New South Wales before their arrests in Bali. But the ringleaders, Sukumaran and Chan, had a clean slate, with no history of trouble with the law.

None of that mattered now, though: the judges had delivered their verdicts, dismissing any of the claims put forward by the mules that they were threatened. This was an organised network, they were all adults, and they could have sought the assistance of police. None of them had, and now they would pay heavily.

It's interesting to ponder what might have happened if Australian courts had dealt more harshly with the likes of Scott Rush. Indonesia's treatment of drug criminals is clear from the moment holiday-makers set foot inside the country, and it's an attempt by decision-makers to stamp out a flourishing drug trade that is killing many of their young. In Australia, too, the scourge of drug addiction continues to kill young people, destroy families and cost the Australian taxpayer dearly. In the eyes of some, no doubt, our courts need to focus more on punishment, or perhaps more on rehabilitation, but the possibility remains that if intervention had occurred earlier, and Scott Rush had been sent to jail for some of his earlier crimes or ordered into rehabilitation, he might not now be facing life in an Indonesian jail.

Rush's story is a sad one: a young, good-looking lad from a good family in a good suburb, attending a good school, but still going off the rails. And it's nearly impossible not to feel overwhelming sympathy for his parents, described by one friend as the salt of the earth, whose lives have been thrown into chaos at a time when they should be enjoying the fruits of their hard work and welcoming grandchildren into their fold. Likewise with Renae Lawrence, whose parents and step-parents love her dearly and cannot countenance the fact that she will spend the rest of her life in an Indonesian jail. And Matthew Norman, who has a twin seemingly a million miles away in New South Wales. Or Tan Duc Thanh Nguyen, whose parents have shifted house and cut off contact with so many people to hide their desperate sadness. Or Si Yi Chen's parents, whose only child now will live out his days in jail in another country. Or Martin Stephens, whose mother has spent months on end in Bali, to be beside her son.

Or Andrew Chan and Myuran Sukumaran, who, sometime down the track, could be tied to a post on the orders of the Bali court, a hood hiding their heads and dressed in an apron marked with a red cross over their hearts, before they are shot dead. It will be night-time when the police come to get them, but a decoy of cars will be sent out to foil attempts by anyone to follow. A twelve-member firing squad, drawn from the elite paramilitary police called the Mobile Brigade, or Brimob, will be there, ready to take aim and fire. Sometimes it works the first time, other times it doesn't, but to ease the conscience of those holding the rifles, only one or two of them will have live rounds, and the squad's commander always has the right to take a final shot to the head with his pistol to make sure death comes quickly. Chan or Sukumaran's family won't be invited, although they will be given a few days' notice so that they can say their final goodbyes. Under Indonesian law, executions cannot be witnessed by anyone other than the firing squad, its commander, a prosecutor, a doctor and a religious person.

Alternatively, after appeals to Denpasar's High Court or the Supreme Court in Jakarta, Chan and Sukumaran's lives may be spared. If so, they may even come home, along with the other seven, if a prisoner exchange deal is brokered between the Indonesian and Australian governments. Prime Minister John Howard was close to tears a few hours after the death penalty had been ordered, pleading with other young Australians to take heed. Defending the AFP's action in alerting Indonesian police in the first place, Howard promised to lobby the Indonesian government to commute the death sentences, just as he had done months earlier over Singapore's decision to execute Tuong Van Nguyen. His pleas for mercy went unheeded then, and while experts believe a prisoner exchange program with Indonesia is likely, the Indonesian court verdicts flouted the pressure applied by least two Australian ministers to ensure that the death penalty was not sought against any of the Bali Nine in the first place. And it is unlikely any prisoner exchange program can help Sukumaran and Chan if their sentences are not overturned on appeal — the death penalty had not been not articulated in any of the programs to date.

For Myuran Sukumaran and Andrew Chan — and the other seven young Australians and their families — the fight has just begun. They are taking one day at a time. In the immediate future, organiser and mule will need to develop a relationship that allows them to survive side by side in jail. That might not be easy, and had certainly been made harder after some lawyers spoke out against Renae Lawrence's recommended sentence, which meant she ended up getting life like her co-accused. Sobbing and angry, she now wonders why she ever cooperated in the first place. Others can't understand why the court didn't believe they were threatened.

Back in his cell, the swagger has all but disappeared from Andrew Chan, the first person ever sentenced by a Bali court to death for drugs charges. The smirk is still there, but everyone knows it's a front to hide the panic and angst that he and his family are now trying to grapple with. Not just for Chan, but for all nine Australians, the journey they set out on less than a year ago to this holiday island, a paradise on earth, has become a journey to hell. And for some of them, especially Chan and Sukumaran, it will be a one-way trip.